W9-AHH-644

LITERATURE OF
LATIN AMERICA

LITERATURE OF
LATIN AMERICA

Rafael Ocasio

Literature as Windows to World Culture

GREENWOOD PRESS
Westport, Connecticut • London

Library of Congress Cataloging-in-Publication Data

Ocasio, Rafael.
  Literature of Latin America / Rafael Ocasio.
     p. cm. — (Literature as windows to world cultures, ISSN 1543–9968)
  Includes bibliographical references.
  ISBN 0–313–32001–2
  1. Latin American literature—History and criticism. I. Title. II. Series.
  PQ7081.O33   2004
  860.9'98—dc22   2004007987

British Library Cataloguing in Publication Data is available.

Copyright © 2004 by Rafael Ocasio

All rights reserved. No portion of this book may be
reproduced, by any process or technique, without the
express written consent of the publisher.

Library of Congress Catalog Card Number: 2004007987
ISBN: 0–313–32001–2
ISSN: 1543–9968

First published in 2004

Greenwood Press, 88 Post Road West, Westport, CT 06881
An imprint of Greenwood Publishing Group, Inc.
www.greenwood.com

Printed in the United States of America

The paper used in this book complies with the
Permanent Paper Standard issued by the National
Information Standards Organization (Z39.48–1984).

10   9   8   7   6   5   4   3   2   1

To my mother, Julia Matilde Medina Marrero,
for giving me the gift of reading

Contents

Acknowledgments

I should like to thank my sister, Edna Ocasio Medina, for her help in researching bio-critical materials and for her insightful comments on the project.

The following individuals made valuable suggestions for this project or answered questionnaires about the most frequently discussed Latin American writers in their literature classes at the high school level: Lynn Andersen (Chattahoochee High School, Alpharetta, GA), Carlos Betancourt (Eldorado High School, Las Vegas, NV), Peggy Bilbro (Randolph School, Huntsville, AL), Michele S. de Cruz-Saenz (Strath Haven High School, Wallingford, PA), David Ludlow (Northwest Cabarrus High School, Concord, NC), Sylvia Martínez (Campbell High School, Cobb County, GA), Diane Ortiz (Bonanza High School, Las Vegas, NV), Olivia Roller (Decatur High School, Decatur, GA), Patricia Tilton (Frenship ISD, Wolfforth, TX), and Sandra Vera (Lamar High School, Houston, TX).

I am particularly indebted to the staff of the Agnes Scott College's Interlibrary Loan division for their continual assistance: Stacy Schmitt and Debbie Adams.

Finally, I appreciate Agnes Scott College Professor Emerita Eloise Herbert's careful editing of this book.

Introduction

The title of this book may suggest a Herculean task, but the intention is to present a survey of the highly diverse ethnic and socioeconomic political constituencies present in Latin American societies today. Therefore, the selection of Latin American writers, from among an impressive number of candidates, has been limited to those individuals who have displayed a strong interest in local cultural traditions. These writers have an international reputation and are associated with important literary or political movements in Latin America.

This book has two purposes: first, it offers the reader a historical and critical overview of the development of key movements in Latin American fiction from writers of the early twentieth century to contemporary authors of international fame. Second, it presents writers who are also exponents of particular elements of Latin American cultures and civilizations. They represent peoples from a number of countries and regions (e.g., the Caribbean basin, Central America, the South American "Southern Cone," and Mexico, including Mexican towns on the U.S. border). All writings analyzed were originally in Spanish but are widely available in English translations.

In presenting an analysis of important movements in Latin American literature, I focus on the struggles of Latin American writers to document their personal perspectives about their own experiences with Latin American cultures. Because the writers' interest in native cultures often has autobiographical bases, I offer brief biographies that explain their personal circumstances, including their approaches to a given subject. Above all, the authors chosen reflect cultural patterns or social and political movements that have had an influence in the formation of national identities. Public reaction to traditions and customs originating in social, ethnic, or religious groups has not always been positive. Literary documentation of the struggles of these marginal groups to maintain their ways of life has been an important contribution by some of the writers discussed here.

ORGANIZATION

For each writer, separate entries focus on the role of popular culture in works of fiction (short stories and novels). I also give such information about other, nonfiction texts, such as the **chronicles** and the *testimonios.* An introduction to each chapter sets the historical time frame for the literary period and suggests other significant writers not analyzed within the text. These concise introductions also present a summary analysis of representative Latin American cultural traditions. Because some of these customs may not be well known, a historical analysis helps the reader make connections between these movements. I have also included comments on ways of life not usually thought to be part of cultural patterns, for example, military life and life in extreme poverty. The reader will find in the introduction an explanation of my choice of a "culture," as well as my literary analysis of representative writers.

Each entry has two distinct parts. The first offers an analysis of the author's life and its relation to the cultural issue explored in that chapter. It also discusses the influence of that individual on the development of literary movements of national and international importance. The second half of the entry is a critical analysis of a particular facet of Latin American culture. This section draws mainly from literary sources that provide an in-depth study of culture as represented in Latin American literature. I stress the interpretation of character, plot, and setting as these aspects are related to Latin American culture and propose new avenues of analysis for components once considered to be mere reflections of "local color."

Although this book was written as a reference guide or textbook, I have tried to avoid jargon. It has an interdisciplinary purpose with references to literary, political, economic, and social movements of importance in Latin America. The use of critical vocabulary is limited to a minimum of key words related to Latin American culture or literary movements. I explain technical words, which appear in bold face and with an explanation, eliminating a need for cumbersome footnotes or glossaries. Those terms represent important concepts in the development of Latin American literature, so they often refer to more than one movement.

A time table of historical events traces relevant incidents in Latin America from the Conquest to modern times. These events, both political and social, reflect significant changes in national institutions, and often in literary production. Other items listed are literary happenings in Latin America.

A note on the bibliography: all novels, short-story collections, or books analyzed will appear in the main text using their Spanish titles and original dates of publication, followed by English titles and publication dates. The bibliography lists only the English translations. There are infrequent references in Spanish to important works not translated into English. I have suggested translations for those titles in the text only. In addition to the listing of the works analyzed, the bibliography suggests other works by each author, along with critical works in book form and in English, if available.

SELECTION

Because this is a reference book for American high school students with a limited knowledge of Spanish, I have restricted the critical analysis to literary texts available in English translations. The works selected are representative of the individual author's style, and they have content focused on issues of national cultures. Although intended for students taking Latin American literature courses, the book also provides complementary reading for world culture courses as well as human geography, political science, history, and anthropology courses. College students in introductory courses in Latin American civilizations also may find the book useful.

Literary selections chosen for analysis address the development of diverse Latin American cultural traditions. Latin American countries have struggled to express national identities since the time of the Spaniards' arrival in the Americas after 1492. I present the history of Latin America beginning with the first European recordings of the conquistadors' experiences with native customs. I provide case studies that show the many ways in which local traditions of ethnic groups, mainly of native indigenous and blacks, play important roles in literary texts. Mindful that the landscape can exert an influence over human behavior, I also examine depictions of Latin American nature and its function in the development of plot and character.

Chapter 1, "Writing about the Americas: From the Colonial Period to the Nineteenth Century," is an introduction that explains the interest of writers of Latin American fiction in documenting Native American traditions. (*Native American* is used in this book to refer to any of the aboriginal peoples of the Western Hemisphere.) Writings about the Americas by the first explorers and conquistadors are known today as *chronicles.* They offer complex documentation of indigenous cultures. These important documents are written in the first person from the perspective of a reporter speaking about specific local social, political, or economic traditions or customs. Columbus, the first of these chroniclers, provided ample written records of his first encounters with various native groups of the Caribbean islands on October 12, 1492. These chroniclers were, however, military men, to whom the conquest of the Americas was a justifiable event from political and religious points of view. Despite these biases, a close analysis of the military chronicles reveals that the conquistadors may have attempted to overcome indigenous opposition by understanding cultural differences. Of course, that knowledge was limited, restricted to the knowledge necessary to subdue the indigenous peoples' opposition to Spanish culture, including political and economic control.

Two groups that offered dissenting perspectives from that of the conquistadors were priests sent by the Church and supported by the Catholic kings, and the natives, who also served as chroniclers of their own history. The presence in the Americas of priests at the earliest stages of the conquest went beyond their original task of conversion. They established the Roman Catholic Church as a body of importance among other Latin American social structures. A considerable number of priests openly opposed the enormous control by the founding conquistadors, however. They began an international campaign demanding respect for the natives' human rights and recorded a number of indigenous religious beliefs. The contributions of the Catholic Church to local religious practices are still a matter of controversy.

The first writings by native chroniclers provide another perspective on the complex process of the Conquest. In their role as chroniclers of events that they had either witnessed or researched by means of historical documents or through oral testimony, they challenged the views that the Spanish chroniclers presented. They also wrote interesting interpretations of the developing national cultures.

Africans were another significant ethnic component in the development of contemporary Latin American cultures. Peoples from various African nations came as slaves to the Americas in the earliest period of the conquest of the Caribbean countries. Their influence on the Caribbean islands and along the South American Atlantic coast, where black traditions have created distinctive cultures, is evident today. Unlike the indigenous in mainland Latin America, the slaves in the Caribbean were effectively silenced; local authorities allowed few first-person accounts. This book examines one rare example of such an account, that of a Cuban man, a former runaway slave.

I conclude chapter 1 with two discussions of the earliest writings produced by Latin Americans, analyzing the baroque and nineteenth-century periods. The baroque, which coincided with Spain's Golden Age during the sixteenth and the seventeenth centuries, marks the beginning of an emerging literature from Latin America that was read in Spain. This fact is important because it reveals the fast maturity of Latin American writers. The literature produced during the baroque period and the nineteenth century also offer significant glimpses of Latin American cultures, particularly of character types specific to local traditions. Nineteenth-century Latin American literature produced after the first wars for independence in 1810 coincided with the European literary movement known as Romanticism. In Latin America, this period took on a profound nationalist character, as the emerging Latin American countries sought to define their individual values. The exploration of local traditions and characters became an important literary component.

Chapter 2, "Latin America's Twentieth-Century Literature: Historical Movements and Landscapes," explores main themes and movements from the earliest part of the twentieth century that represent precursors of Latin America's complex literary production. The influence of the Mexican Revolution on an emerging national literature was significant because it was only after this political event that Latin American fiction became strongly related to a historical movement. The changes that followed this first armed conflict with a socialist background in the Western Hemisphere went to the core of social structures, particularly in rural communities. For the first time in Latin American history, *campesinos,* or peasants, became characters of importance, their social and political struggles emerging as notable literary motifs.

The changes went beyond a strong call for economic justice for underclass social groups. The political activism of the intellectuals, or of writers associated with social projects, was evidence of an increasing interest in using literature as a vehicle for achieving changes. These authors were involved in nationalistic campaigns that promoted the documentation and exploration of native cultures as part of the search for national values and identity. Their literary production made extensive use of regional customs, including native characters who became protagonists of their own stories. As in the case of the Mexican bandits, these characters would have international recognition as readers in Latin America and in other areas found out about revolutionary events through these colorful protagonists.

Latin Americans took two approaches in their quest for documentation of traits representative of a national identity. The first involved a process of reexamination of precolonial and colonial histories with careful study of characters associated with these movements. Such native characters were viewed in a sort of psychological profile, a reflection of broad national values. In the second tendency, the characters' setting, the social background from which they developed, had an important role in revealing their behavior, reason of being, or motivation. The expansive Latin American landscape, therefore, took on an important role in literature, no longer serving as mere background as it had during most of the nineteenth century.

The literary trend known as **criollismo** explored native traits associated with characters within specific Latin American geographic boundaries. Derived from the widely used term **criollo,** often used to describe a Latin American–born individual, **criollismo** intended to display native characters who had become symbols of human ingenuity in overcoming the many natural obstacles in the landscape. The relationship between the character and nature was the focus of the criollismo movement. In the past, this relationship often appeared characterized in rather negative terms because of the powerful, overwhelming natural elements present in Latin American nature. The criollista writers had an ideological purpose that went beyond the reproduction of folklore; they intended to transform motifs of Latin American reality into literary symbols and to produce a psychological study of representative Latin American characters.

The *novela de la tierra* is the product of an important movement that focused on native traditions as subject matter and on characters associated with Latin American local customs. It was inspired by realist trends to provide a trustworthy documentation of the background elements that determined their characters' behaviors. *Novela de la tierra* makes the *tierra*, the land, a central component of novels that examine the effects of the wild Latin American nature on characters associated with specific social and governmental systems. This is the case of *Don Segundo Sombra* (1926) and *Doña Bárbara* (1929), novels widely read throughout Latin America, even today.

Two trends associated with the novela de la tierra are *indigenismo* and *negrismo,* which center on specific ethnic backgrounds of the indigenous and the black populations. Different from the literary approaches of the *novela de la tierra,* these literary directions attempted to develop experimental narrative techniques. In them the writers documented the abuses of power and the mistreatment experienced by Latin America's marginal groups. Another important role of these writers was their participation in political movements that fostered political activism on behalf of these populations. Social activism was also at the core of the *negrista* movement, particularly in the works of Cuban Nicolás Guillén (1902–1989).

Chapter 3, "The Coming of Age of Modern Latin American Literature: The Boom," studies the emergence of the *Boom,* which may be Latin America's most experimental literary movement. It is represented here in the writings of Colombian Gabriel García Márquez, of Mexican Carlos Fuentes, and of Peruvian Mario Vargas Llosa. The movement began during the sixties, when a number of works of fiction of exceptional quality broke away from restrictive literary techniques, rejecting the preference for the realistic approach of previous movements such as the **criollismo.** Works by Boom writers use highly innovative forms in terms of style and narrative technique, as well as in the development of unusual characters. The Boom may be considered the beginning of a modern Latin American literature with strong international appeal. A tribute to the Boom authors' importance is the fact that forty years later, they continue to write best-sellers and are often cited as literary mentors by up-and-coming international writers.

The production of the Boom writers is large, and it explores diverse subject matters and literary themes. In common these writers display a strong interest in breaking away from narrative devices associated with highly traditional Latin American literature, mainly the predictable plots of previous generations. This chapter examines the literary experimentation of Boom writers by a close study of their use of the **vanguard.** This movement, strongly present in European and American literatures produced during the period of the First and the Second World Wars, was not only their inspiration but also their rebellious approach to a trend of international importance.

The Latin American Boom writers experimented with the literature of the surrealists. One important addition to the fiction of Latin American surrealist writers was their handling of native cultures. Under the influence of surrealism, they offered a new vision of Latin American societies. Depiction of complex Latin American political and economic structures, explored by **criollista** writers, became for this newer generation an ideological goal of high importance. It was more than just a realistic reproduction of folklore or a photographic approach to social ills. Contemporary Latin American writers had a more cosmopolitan view of their native societies, including the exploration of cultural icons specific to native backgrounds. Their characters, inspired by real social and political figures, would become known internationally as representatives of Latin American cultures.

Unlike earlier, realist writers, Boom writers sought to explore Latin American reality by means of experimental narrative forms. This break with traditional aesthetics introduced several radical elements, such as the development of an unusual story often experienced by a less-than-credible protagonist or produced by a narrator who may or may not be trustworthy. These changes were made possible partially because of writers' exploration of European vanguardism. They are the **fantastic** and the **magical realism** movements, today closely related to Latin American literature, the preferred approach for experimental writers.

Latin American Boom writers depicted national historical events by means of narrative devices associated with the fantastic. In a departure from realistic, concrete, logical literary techniques, their approach was both experimental and symbolic. Such changes made Latin American literature intellectually more challenging; it departed from previous realist literature, which had presented symbols that they considered too concrete, too simple, or too obvious in meaning. The appeal of magical realism, a movement that today characterizes Latin American literature, lies in the strong connection drawn among cultural, social, and religious-bound components. Central to the plots in works of magical realism is the overwhelming presence of unusual events, often of fantastic nature. They are portrayals of Latin American society, an important element of a metaphysical and psychological approach to the exploration of Latin American identity and, by extension, of the human psyche.

Chapter 4, "Women Writers: New Perspectives on Latin America," gathers a number of women writers who have emerged as distinguished representatives of the latest literary trends, including their association with **feminism.** They continued the exploration of Latin American sociocultural and political themes, but their protagonists are women characters. Unlike male Boom writers, women writers have examined Latin American societies from the point of view of female characters; they document important historical events that exerted an influence on women's cultures or those in which women had an important role. A central theme of the work of women writers is their analysis of the national character with emphasis on the peculiarities of sociopolitical and economic structures and their restrictions on women.

Latin American writers' exploration of history has also provided an opportunity for the development of female characters, something that had been ignored in formal national historiography and had not found a literary voice in traditional aesthetics. These characters are important not only because of their literary significance, but also because they join their male counterparts as representative of social types present in modern Latin American societies. Besides their literary value, they also present a valuable lesson in the ways in which women in Latin America have historically overcome social and economic restrictions.

Another important contribution of Latin American women writers is their opinions about issues pertaining to so-called women's literature. They often reveal their opinions in critical statements about their own writing and in discussions of specific problems encountered by women writers in Latin America. Their comments reflect the ongoing critical conversations in Latin America about the role and purpose of literature by women writers. As expected, their opinions on this subject, including their opposition to machismo in Latin American societies, are varied and often contradictory.

Latin American writers have also participated as activists in a variety of political trends. Their involvement in radical social movements goes beyond their strong commitment to feminist causes. This chapter traces their involvement in significant events of resistance to the rise of military governments in Latin America, beginning in the eighties. Writers often took bold positions against dictatorial governments, criticizing them in spite of harsh official repression. The literature inspired by this dark period in Latin American history followed the literary aesthetics and purposes of the ***testimonio,*** a technique that seeks to document political incidents in a first-person narrative. A special contribution is their documentation about how women also suffered illegal incarceration and torture under the dictatorship of military governments. Some of these writers, like thousands of other activists, were forced into exile.

Chapter 5, "Writing about Cultural, Ethnic, and Religious Identities," examines the struggle among popular and indigenous communities to maintain their history and ways of life. I stress the fact that today indigenous communities throughout Latin America continue to experience open marginalization from national social and political institutions. They are often pressed to abandon their ancient customs as the sole condition for their incorporation into mainstream societies. Adherence to native languages, religious beliefs, and social patterns has become a tool for expressing political discontent.

Campesinos, or farm workers, another group with close links to regional cultures, have experienced similar racist attitudes. Of mixed ethnic background, the campesinos, unlike native groups, have incorporated into their rural culture a number of the elements of "learned" culture. They have failed to gain social and political recognition, however. As their experience indicates, insensitive governments see the campesino as a disposable manual laborer, to be exploited by absentee landowners and oppressive governments. Their heritage is usually ignored or considered too "rough" to be included in a definition of national identity.

This chapter focuses on the strong presence of indigenous and campesino groups of El Salvador, Guatemala, and Nicaragua. The choice of this Central American region is one influenced by both geography and ideology. The peoples of these countries have played an important role in the development of traits associated today with Central America. Although they represent a considerable percent of their countries' populations, they have been kept marginal to mainstream social institutions. Struggles for recognition of their human rights have been chaotic, as reflected in their involvement in strikes and guerrilla groups. In chapter 5, I trace the voice of indigenous cultures and campesinos in political movements that seek human rights protection from oppressive national governments and reparation for crimes against humanity committed in their communities.

Chapter 5 ends with an analysis of the ways in which religious thinking, especially liberation theology, proposes liberation from social, economic, and political boundaries for the underprivileged campesino. This effort was controversial because the campesinos began demanding political justice through violence, using armed force in an attempt to accomplish their goals. As in the case of indigenous communities, the political platform contained a strong religious message, a lesson to the world to learn from the struggle of their native communities.

This book aims to open a multidisciplinary discussion of Latin America's global influence. Mindful that the history of Latin America is complex and diverse, I have chosen a variety of texts that are representative of social and aesthetic movements. I am hopeful that the reader will appreciate the vibrant national identities from these analyses, which include social and political components that are not usually included in the study of cultural and literary traditions. The reader may find lessons in this literary review of Latin American history, recognizing that writers in that part of the world address issues related not only to their own countries of origin, but to our own multicultural, American society, and to cultures around the globe.

Chapter 1

Writing about the Americas: From the Colonial Period to the Nineteenth Century

CHRONICLES: THE RECORDING OF LATIN AMERICAN INDIGENOUS CULTURES

Interest among writers of contemporary Latin American fiction in documenting Native American cultures and traditions can be traced to the writings by Christopher Columbus and other early Spanish explorers. Beginning with Columbus's written record of his first encounters with various native groups of the Caribbean islands on October 12, 1492, the work of these explorers offers complex ethnographic documentation of indigenous cultures. It also provides up-close details of military expeditions, including their approaches to overcoming indigenous opposition by understanding cultural differences. This rich cultural documentation supports the multifaceted efforts to effect a rapid conquest of the Americas, a vast and ethnically diverse territory. As Spain became the main military power behind the colonization of the New World, updated reports on the many native peoples encountered facilitated colonizing projects. Ultimately, the research on indigenous cultures played an important role first in the process of military domination and later in the native peoples' submission to European social standards of living.

The explorers' plentiful testimonies about their discoveries and military campaigns are known collectively as **chronicles.** Their importance today is multiple. The texts are outstanding firsthand sources of information, covering mainly anthropological, sociological, and geological subject matters. The information recorded is useful in the understanding of the complexity of the colonizing projects, particularly when the indigenous population offered military opposition. The writers, known as **chroniclers,** were witnesses to the events they described and their accounts, according to their testimony, were truthful statements of the historical events narrated.

The chroniclers comprised a diverse group of individuals, trained in various fields of the humanities. Among them were navigators, explorers, soldiers, priests, and scientists. In common they provided the first glimpses of this newly encountered territory—the so-called Indies—so foreign, and therefore exotic, to the emerging European nations of the early fifteenth century. They were writing for an increasingly powerful colonialist Spain, hungry for positive reports on many aspects of the trips of discovery and conquest. The Spanish court was especially eager for news of the pacification of the indigenous groups. "Pacification" was a code word for the natives' submission to the Spanish rulers. Once conquered, the American territories would provide money, an eagerly awaited prize because Spain was heavily involved in costly military expeditions in several European countries.

The objectivity of the chroniclers is debatable, because they all had ulterior motives in drafting their eyewitness experiences. Some were seeking fame; they attempted to gain historical recognition of their own contributions in the colonizing process. Others sought money that they claimed was due to them in payment for their military services. The vast amounts of treasure (especially on the American continent) provoked irate demands for the rewriting of the history of specific periods in the conquest of certain territories, such as Mexico and Peru. These multiple versions of the same events provide today's historians diverse perspectives and angles in approaching the massive enterprise of the conquest and colonization of the Americas.

For the purpose of this book, the chronicles that have survived stand out as the earliest descriptions of native Latin American cultures. In them, students of Latin American studies find a multifaceted view of the American territory, including the many native groups, their languages, their religions, and their social customs, which are among the most noticeable differences. They are also important because of their depiction of individuals of key indigenous groups. Detailed physical descriptions of them are plentiful, a testimony to the Spaniards' interest in the natives. Both the exuberant American landscape and the wild and exotic natives would soon capture the Spanish and European literary imagination.

The chroniclers made no attempt to hide biases against native religious customs, so alien to the Spanish Catholics. In fact, most chroniclers appear to have made a conscious effort to point out specific examples of what were considered barbaric religious traditions, including in graphic terms some of the indigenous groups' practices of human sacrifices and ritual cannibalism. The accusations of bloodthirsty behavior, which included brutal war tactics, contrasted with the chroniclers' admiration for some of the natives' social structures and, in the case of the advanced civilizations, for their highly developed cities. This tension, a sort of controlled admiration for the enemy, is present even in the most severe of the chroniclers. Despite the natives' unwillingness to give up easily to Spanish control and, consequently, to end the bloody confrontations, the chroniclers succumbed to the richness of the American indigenous cultures.

Christopher Columbus

The first European record of an American indigenous cultural group was that of Christopher Columbus (1451–1506). Columbus had an extensive knowledge of navigation, acquired in years of intense research of ancient documents that pointed to uncharted territory westward across the Atlantic Ocean. He was also a seasoned sailor and had had his share of conversations with more experienced sailors, who filled his head with stories of a mysterious western territory. In August 1492, as he ventured into his first trip of exploration under the patronage of the Spanish Catholic kings, he was sailing with a purpose in mind: finding a faster, westbound route to India, highly desirable for wealthy commercial trade. His landfall in the Bahamas and the Caribbean confirmed his research of undiscovered islands off the coast of India. Believing that he had reached the outer boundaries of India, accordingly, he named these islands the "Indies" and the inhabitants, "Indians."

Columbus's writings about the Caribbean indigenous peoples are entries or diary letters addressed to the Catholic monarchs, Queen Isabella and King Ferdinand, absolute rulers of the first unified European state. These letters provide the powerful Spanish king and queen with detailed descriptions of his findings, mainly his impressions of the Caribbean islands' lush environment and his portraits of the natives. His descriptions of the New World are highly positive, perhaps because of his personal interest in encouraging the Spanish rulers to embark on future explorations. They are positive, too, because he was under the impression that he was writing from India, and therefore his outlook is that of an expectant winner.

Columbus's letters are the first descriptions of the American inhabitants and of their surroundings. For example, in the following passage, Columbus's detailed description of the natives' physique reveals his interest in ethnographic documentation:

All that I saw were young men, none of them more than 30 years old, very well built, of very handsome bodies and very fine faces; the hair coarse, almost like the hair of a horse's tail, and short, the hair they wore over their eyebrows, except for a hank behind that they wear long and never cut. Some of them paint themselves black (and they are of the color of the Canary Islanders, neither black nor white), and others paint themselves white, and some red, and others with what they find. And some paint their faces, others the body, some the eyes only, others only the nose. (65)

This passage stands out today as the earliest literary characterization of the American inhabitants. Viewed as exotic beings worthy of display, the first natives who arrived with Columbus in Spain at the end of the first trip in 1493 were paraded conspicuously during the religious celebrations of Palm Sunday in Seville. The natives' introduction during such an important religious day seems to suggest the Church's role in their European acculturation.

Columbus's descriptions of the Caribbean natives show his assumption that certain personality traits are reflected in their beautiful physique. This explains Columbus's direct statement to the monarchs that the natives' pleasant disposition was an indication of their willingness to serve the Spaniards: "They ought to be good servants and of good skill, for I see that they repeat very quickly whatever was said to them" (65). Thus, Columbus's view of the Caribbean indigenous people, presented as tame and therefore prone to service, facilitated the royal decision to make them slaves. Upon his return from his second trip in 1496, Columbus took some five hundred natives back to Spain. They were sold in Seville's slave market. In the Americas, the government-approved program of slavery, known as *encomienda,* or the "entrusting sharing" of the natives, became one of the most debated crimes against humanity, denounced by pro-indigenous groups in Spain and elsewhere in Europe. The system, ratified as civil laws in 1512, provided specific disposition for the treatment of the indigenous workers. Unfortunately, the *encomenderos,* as the masters were known, openly ignored the laws and proceeded to abuse the native populations.

Columbus's letters also contain glowing accounts of the islands' lush environment. For instance, writing from the island of Cuba on October 28, 1492, he wrote,

never beheld so fair a thing: trees all along the river, beautiful and green, and different from ours, with flowers and fruits each according to their kind, many birds and little birds which sing very sweetly. There were great numbers of palms, of a different kind from those of Guinea and from ours, of middling height, and the trunk without any bark, and the leaves very big, with which they cover the houses; the land very flat. (82)

The cultural relevance of this text, as in the case of the descriptions of the natives, is significant. Columbus made sure that the Spanish king and queen recognized the commercial potential of these islands: "and there may be many things that I don't know, for I do not wish to delay but to discover and go to many islands to find gold" (70), he wrote on October 15, three days after his official landfall on his presumed island of the Indies. His desire to ascertain signs of gold may explain his schematic descriptions of these surroundings, which are presented in generic categories as rivers, trees, and birds. He was certainly in an obvious rush to explore the islands for gold and not in the business of writing detailed botanical descriptions.

It is important to stress, however, that Columbus's descriptions appear within the medieval literary trend of the *locus amoenus.* This concept assumes that in a perfect and untainted natural setting, the human spirit is most likely to experience perfect love and to achieve higher spiritual emotions. The Caribbean islands and later the American continent, with their exotic inhabitants and overwhelmingly powerful nature, would take two basic modes of representation. On one hand, nature is a reflection of the most engrained human virtues, also reflected in the beautiful physical constitution of the natives. On the other hand, as the explorers proceeded to conquer native cultures for their enrichment, the natives, aided by an equally powerful nature, fought back, despite the Spaniards' technical superiority. For the European reader following these gruesome accounts, the wars became a reflection of the most hidden human emotions, an exploration of the dark side of the human psyche.

Juan Díaz

Some early explorers found themselves attracted to the wild nature and inhabitants of the Americas. This is the case of Juan Díaz, who traveled to the Yucatan Peninsula in 1518 as a member of a military expedition headed by Juan Grijalva. Cultural data make Díaz's chronicle a document of ethnosocial interest that goes beyond his report as a military professional. For instance, Díaz displayed interest in recording native languages. Such words as, for instance, *maíz* (corn), *taquín* (gold), *managi* (a local fruit), *jurel* (fish), and *canoe* would soon become part of the Spanish spoken in the New World (De Fuentes 6, 7, 9, 10). Many of these native words are today part of the regional variants of Spanish, independent from other Peninsular linguistic forms.

Díaz's positive examples of indigenous cultures abounded in spite of the natives' military opposition to the Spaniards. In one statement he pointed specifically to a village's constructions and effective layout:

> This village or town had its streets cobblestoned in a concave form, raised on the sides with a hollow down the center, and along that hollow the pavement was of large stones. The whole length of the street had many houses belonging to the townspeople, made of stone foundations with mud walls and thatched roofs. The people of this place seem, from their buildings and houses, to be very skillful people, and if it were not for several building that seemed to be new, one might assume they were buildings made by Spaniards. (De Fuentes 6–7)

This description is colored, however, with an underlying tone of superiority that marks the natives as primitive beings in their social behavior. The most obvious example of these people's inferiority is their religious practices. This is a contradictory statement. Although Díaz appeared to cast a negative light on indigenous religious practices, which he labeled as "idolatrous," he shed light on a highly developed symbolic belief system. A surprisingly positive outlook appeared in Díaz's admiration of a tower where the religious ceremonies took place: "This tower was eighteen steps high, with a solid base, and measured one hundred and eighty feet around. At the top was a small tower of the height of two men, and inside were bones and ash, and certain figures that are the idols they worship, and from the nature of these it is presumed the people are idolatrous" (De Fuentes 6).

Andrés Tapia

The primitive religious practices stand out as a common denominator for most chroniclers, who found themselves compelled to criticize them with varying intensity of judgment. It is also evident that as more advanced native groups came into contact with the explorers, the religious cultures became themes of considerable importance to the chroniclers. Examples are plentiful. One writer was Andrés Tapia, a captain in Hernán Cortés's expedition to Tenochtitlán, the fabulously wealthy Aztec capital. Writing from Cozumel in 1519, Tapia's description of the island's inhabitants' religious practices was basic, with a noticeable lack of attention to details. His explanation for the natives' claims that an idol spoke during ceremonies that included sacrifices was openly condescending: "The idol was made of baked clay and was hollow, set with lime against a wall with a secret entrance behind it, where it looked as though a man could enter and invest himself in the idol" (De Fuentes 20).

Tapia's approach to depiction of the Aztec religious belief system was, however, noticeably different. As Cortés's army entered Tenochtitlán in 1519, Tapia took notice of complex religious traditions, which included human sacrifices, as he had done in earlier encounters with other native groups. The Aztecs were highly advanced in their religious practices, housed in temples that rivaled the European architectural concept of sacred grounds or churches. In fact, it can be argued that the Aztecs' massive sacred architecture is one of the few native cultural manifestations that find no equivalent within the Spanish social structure: "The courtyard of the idols was so large that there would be space enough for the houses of four hundred Spanish people" (De Fuentes 41). The facilities were tended by some five thousand men. Tapia effectively painted them as evil with repeated descriptions of brutal human sacrifices, including the abundance of blood as part of ritual offerings: "The images were of idols, and in their mouths and over parts of their bodies were quantities of blood two or three fingers thick" (De Fuentes 43).

The bloody sites included the display of some 136,000 human skulls as part of the architecture of one of the temples (if the reader is to trust the accuracy of such a count). The effect presented a challenge for the Spanish priests who attempted immediate conversions. The process increased in violence as indigenous groups attempted to resist the Spanish imposition of their Catholic faith. In the early stage of the religious indoctrination of the Aztecs, Tapia states, the Spaniards claimed that their Christian God, although invisible, was invincible. Tapia's account of the Spaniards' challenge to prove the superiority of the Christian God fell within the limits of the fantastic.

This was the case of Tapia's testimony about a miracle, his explanation for the earliest appeasement of the Aztecs following curtailment of the worship of their gods. The story is short and concise, set within the historical line of action as a main reason for the Aztecs' initial acceptance of the Catholic hierarchy of saints and other divine intercessors. After they had cleared away the blood, other sacrificial gifts, and Aztec religious symbols, a former religious tower became a consecrated church containing two altars. The locale, as Tapia presented it, must have been conspicuously humble. The only decorations of the altars dedicated to the Virgin Mary and to Saint Christopher were wooden carvings. Such crude religious iconography must have appalled the Aztecs, accustomed to artistic statues, richly decorated and with plenty of gold offerings.

As the Spaniards separated the Aztecs from their idols, a drought fell on the land, bringing havoc to the cornfields. The Aztecs believed that it was a punishment from their rain gods and proceeded to claim permission from the Spanish military authorities to reinstate their traditional religions. In answer to their pleas, the Spaniards organized a Christian religious procession and a mass took place, followed immediately by heavy rains. Tapia's editorial comment was that the "Indians marveled greatly" (De Fuentes 44). The Spaniards were willing to embark on fantastic adventures, aided by religious icons. Tapia did not doubt that the rains came upon the dying cornfields because of divine intervention by the right God. The implication that divine approval was on the side of the Spaniards was found in many chronicles. Such ethno- and religiocentric focus today clouds the veracity of history developed through the chronicles, and it has promoted new interpretations of the Conquest process.

Anonymous Chronicler

There were, however, chroniclers who recorded details of indigenous cultures apparently without any motive other than sheer desire for ethnographic documentation. One unknown chronicler, a member of the Cortés campaign in Mexico, is such a case. His chronicle appeared printed in the second half of the sixteenth century as part of a compilation of Italian writings about exploratory trips by the Spanish and the Portuguese (De Fuentes 165). It is a testimony of European thirst for in-depth information about American indigenous cultures. His chronicle is multifaceted and covers a considerable number of socioeconomic details of life in the territory of New Spain, today Mexico. Through his detailed accounts, the reader gains a more positive depiction of native Mexican societies. For instance, there is a positive picture of the highly developed urban organization of the cities: "many of their cities were more orderly than ours, with very handsome streets and squares, where they had their market places" (De Fuentes 168).

Writing after the defeat of the Aztecs, the anonymous chronicler's panoramic description of New Spain is set within the literary conventions of the *locus amoenus:* a fertile territory, geographically diverse, still unexplored by the Spaniards. This is certainly a paradise, with large rivers, freshwater springs, forests, plains, and mountains (De Fuentes 167). Still awaiting exploration (a process that the chronicler predicts will take at least a hundred years), the country had proven to have plentiful mines of gold, silver, copper, tin, and iron (De Fuentes 167). Further proof of the country's benevolent nature is its fertile soil, which in some instances produces two or three crops a year (De Fuentes 167).

In this chronicle, as in others, natives had successfully inhabited this generous earth to their advantage. The writer was speaking of the Aztecs, who, despite their cruel socioreligious behavior, had produced a rather advanced civilization. Like other chroniclers, this writer dwelled on the Aztecs' barbaric religion, but he was writing from a historical perspective and did not claim to have witnessed such ceremonies. Glowing descriptions of the city of Tenochtitlán are plentiful, especially those of the fabulous temples and residences of the nobility. The chronicle also includes frank statements about the superiority of these constructions to comparable architectural examples in Spain. This is a bold statement because the chronicler described the city after the fall and partial destruction of Tenochtitlán and in the midst of the Spaniards' founding of today's Mexico City. Despite the Spanish fortifications, which the chronicler described as a "Spanish castle, city or citadel" (De Fuentes 181), the chronicler continued to praise its superiority: "No city in Spain has its houses over such a large area, nor does it have better or bigger ones" (De Fuentes 180). This proud attitude can be viewed as the beginning of a long tradition of a cultural rivalry between Latin America and Spain. It also points to the earliest manifestation of a **mestizo** identity, a merging of Native American and European cultural values. Today mestizo traditions have come to symbolize the fusion of two radically different cultural traditions that make up the prolific manifestations of Latin American culture.

The chroniclers as self-appointed historians played an important role in disseminating data on American cultural traditions. The technological superiority of the Spaniards and their brutal physical aggression in warfare were clearly effective tools of domination. In the following section, there is discussion of the chroniclers' key role in conveying factual information about rebellious indigenous groups. Their collective writings may be taken as a profile of the indigenous mind, providing information that was useful in establishing sociopolitical domination after the Conquest.

MILITARY CHRONICLES

Columbus's landing in the Caribbean islands began an intense campaign of trips of explorations that led to the discovery of a larger and wealthier continental territory. Known as the **Conquest,** this exploration was a complex process that combined military expertise with the religious conversion of the native inhabitants and a search for scientific knowledge. The Conquest started with Christopher Columbus's well-equipped second trip, in 1493, as he headed back to the "Indies," still with the intention of finding a faster route to Asia. His zealous efforts to dominate indigenous opposition led initially to use of military force. Because of these brutal practices against the indigenous populations, most Latin Americans consider the conquest of the Americas as the darkest period of Latin American history. At the root of this negative view is a compendium of the crimes that Columbus and later conquistadors committed against the natives, commonly referred to as the **Black Legend.**

It was Spaniards who documented the crimes against the indigenous populations. The perspective of the writers differed in regard to the tactics used for submission of native groups. This section analyzes the military chronicles as firsthand documentation and as historical accounts pertaining to the conquest period. Although the core of these texts was detailed description of military campaigns, they contain ample comments on the indigenous cultures as the conquistadors and soldiers first encountered them.

The conquistadors wrote the history of the exploration of the Americas when Spain had reached a peak in its acquisition of humanist knowledge. The expeditions that set out after Columbus's first trip aimed not only to explore the uncharted territory of the Indies, but also to add to the scarce data on the unknown territory. The process was, however, a military venture. Today, to the readers of these trips of exploration, the conquistadors appear to be mere adventurers and seekers of wealth whose tactics of warfare depleted the indigenous population at a horrifying rate, but the conquistadors' legacies are at the core of Latin American culture today. Knowledge of their individual approaches to pacification and of their civil legacies in the founding and administration of the first Latin American cities is a useful tool in understanding certain national trends ranging from religious traditions to military practices. The strength of the military and guerrilla groups in certain countries also speaks to the impact and ramifications of violence in contemporary Latin American society.

In the recording of key events in the exploration and colonization of the Americas, the name of Italian-born Amerigo Vespucci is prominent. Vespucci (1451–1512), a cartographer trained in physics, geometry, and cosmography, began a series of exploratory trips in 1497. He ventured into the northern territories of South America in 1499 and later into the Brazilian coast and the south, nearly reaching the Río de la Plata in 1501. He also explored Central America, reaching the Gulf of Darién, today Panama, in 1505. Because of his detailed writings on his findings and the maps drawn of his trips, the increasingly explored landmass became known as America in 1507. For some historians, this decision is unfair to Columbus, but it reflects the general view of the latter as a cruel and despotic man and as an initiator of crimes against American indigenous groups.

Explorations of the Americas continued at a surprisingly fast rate. Then came the colonizing period, which included not only pacification of the indigenous population but also the founding of cities. The colonization period started in La Española (today Haiti and the Dominican Republic), toward the end of Columbus's first trip in 1492. During his last two trips (1498–1500 and 1502–1504), Columbus set up commercial enterprises, such as mines for river gold and agricultural and cattle projects, on this island. The colonization of the largest Caribbean islands, Puerto Rico (1508), Jamaica (1509), and Cuba (1511), produced for Spain and Europe the first contact with American agricultural products such as tobacco. The conquest of these Caribbean islands led to later pacification of the continent. Heavy military punishment against indigenous peoples, commonly practiced in the Caribbean, was a weapon used on a grander scale in the conquest of the continental territories. The rapid destruction of the Caribbean indigenous populations (nearly eradicated within about fifty years) provoked the beginning of an international campaign against Spanish mistreatment and violation of the human rights of the American natives.

By today's military standards, a single nation's rapid conquest of such a large territory is remarkable. Columbus's third and fourth trips took him to the northern coasts of South and Central America. One of the most important of the early explorers who accompanied him was Vicente Yáñez Pinzón (a navigator of Columbus's first trip), who in 1500 reached Venezuela and Brazil and then navigated the mouth of the Amazon River. Organized travels to Central America took place in 1509 with Alonso de Ojeda, who explored the coast of Veragua (today Costa Rica). Vasco Núñez de Balboa's discovery of the Pacific Ocean in 1513 promoted further commercial interest in the establishment of permanent cities on mainland South America, for instance, of Colombia's Santa Marta (1526) and Cartagena de las Indias (1530).

Of particular interest to a North American reader are their incursions into what is today U.S. territory, following reports of natural wonders and cities of immense wealth. Such is the case of Juan Ponce de León, conqueror and first governor of the island of Puerto Rico, who, while seeking a "fountain of youth," discovered Florida in 1512. In quests for fabled cities, Francisco de Coronado (1510–1554) marched north from the western coast of Mexico and in 1540 explored southeastern Arizona, to arrive at the Grand Canyon and the Colorado River.

Tales of a vast, fabulously rich and unexplored land inspired further exploratory trips. Reports by the explorers and the conquistadors about their exotic findings soon became well known throughout Spain. Their texts provided additional characterizations of the Latin American natives, including detailed descriptions of the behaviors and customs that were so radically different from European standards. Numerous reports offer detailed accounts of the explorers' findings, covering a wide range of topics. There were accounts of the vast American geography and its native animals and plants, as well as the religious practices and defensive mechanisms of native peoples, the organization of their cities, and details of their social customs. These accounts also led to legends of incredible wonders of wealth to be found in the mythical American geography.

Hernán Cortés

The most prominent of the earliest explorers was Hernán Cortés. Born in 1485 to an impoverished but noble family, he embarked at age nineteen on a voyage to the Indies, like many young men coming to age at the beginning of the Conquest. He arrived in La Española, where he was part of an army that suppressed indigenous uprisings and founded cities across the island. This was the beginning of his military training; he learned important skills, such as the tracing of runaway enemies in a rugged and exuberant topography. In 1511, he was on the island of Juana (today Cuba), where in reward for his fierce warrior spirit in controlling the natives, he became mayor of the city of Santiago. Located on the extreme western point of the island, Santiago was part of a major plan for pacification of the island, which was the largest of the Spanish Caribbean territories.

Thirsty for more adventures, Cortés explored the coast of the Yucatan Peninsula in 1518, along with Juan de Grijalba. This trip increased Cortés's desire to seek a greater fortune and political power. In 1519, after much lobbying, he gained permission to start the exploration of mainland Mexico.

Cortés's process for the military subjugation of the nations on his way to the fabulous Aztec city of Tenochtitlán took place at a rather easy pace.

Although he encountered opposition and engaged in warfare with minor tribes, Cortés successfully rallied local native support against Moctezuma, supreme emperor and ruler of an extensive empire. Cortés's grand entrance into Tenochtitlán and its fall in 1521 are extensively documented in his letters to Charles V, king of Spain. Although the conquest of Tenochtitlán represented the end of the **Mexica** empire (today known as the Aztecs), the purpose of Cortés's letters was to open gates to other unconquered, wealthy native cities, and he expected to lead or direct these expeditions.

Cortés's autobiographical accounts of his military endeavors are known today as "letter-reports." They provided King Charles V with detailed narratives of Cortés's strategies in suppressing rebellious groups of natives. Serious accusations of his fiscal mismanagement of the campaigns, including his underreporting of the riches found (for which the king was to receive considerable payments) and of abusive treatment of the natives prompted Cortés to write these letter-reports of his activities. In fact, Cortés wrote some of these letters as an outlaw because, at the beginning of his military expedition against the Aztecs, he had chosen to ignore official orders from the governor of Cuba (in charge of the internal organization of Cortés's campaign) to abort the expedition and return to Cuba for further instructions. At the end of his life, although officially recognized as conqueror of Mexico and neighboring Honduras, Cortés had failed in his ambition to receive appointment as governor of Mexico.

Cortés's letters (five written between 1519 and 1526) were printed and distributed throughout Europe after 1522, and they appeared translated into Latin, Italian, Flemish, and German. The historical focus of the events was his military strategy, which led to the defeat of the Aztecs. Cortés's focus on himself as the center of his narrative allowed little space to introduce other characters involved in his military expeditions. His triumphant trip to Spain in 1528, part of his scheme to retain control of Mexico, illustrates this point. Like Christopher Columbus before him, Cortés came to the Spanish court as a powerful and immensely wealthy landowner. Backed by natives (some of them nobles), he offered to the king exquisitely crafted gold jewelry, exotic birds, tigers, and other rare American animals. This image of the "strongman," of a figure that monopolizes governing procedures, is a key to understanding today's Latin American strongmen in politics.

Cortés's letters transcended his project of self-promotion, however. They stand out today among the earliest descriptions of Mexican indigenous groups. Like other explorers in Mexico before him, Cortés succumbed to the enchantment of the American landscape, a diverse topography that harbored empires of mythical proportions. Cortés used the word "marvelous" in efforts to describe Tenochtitlán, for example. He claimed that a description was an impossible task, saying it "would demand much time and many and skilled writers" (85). Initially he called this wonderful city equal and even superior to a Spanish city; he wrote that despite its lack of "a knowledge of the true God or communication with enlightened nations, one may well marvel at the orderliness and good government which is everywhere maintained" (94). In his letters, Cortés often observed this dichotomy: advanced knowledge that allowed for the development of a great city, in contrast to the "barbarous" nature of the Aztecs, mainly expressed in their practice of human sacrifices.

Cortés's many positive descriptions of elegant Tenochtitlán became well known. Although he was writing eyewitness reports as a history of events, Cortés's letters were also a response to the Spanish thirst for reading about extraordinary adventures fought and won despite tremendous challenges. Because Cortés was the commander of these expeditions, his portraits of the natives, not surprisingly, were generally negative. He wrote freely of the Aztecs' thirst for blood, reflected in their guerrilla warfare tactics and many human sacrifices.

Bernal Díaz del Castillo

Cortés's accounts of his military enterprise in Mexico aroused dissenters; some opposed his methods of pacification, and others claimed that he either exaggerated or erred in the documentation of key events. This is the intention of Bernal Díaz del Castillo (1495?–1584), who in his *Historia verdadera de la conquista de la Nueva España* (*True History of the Conquest of Mexico,* 1568) refuted Cortés's accounts by revealing many instances of Cortés's ignoring the role of key individuals (both Spanish and native) involved in the fall of Tenochtitlán. As an eyewitness to the events, Díaz del Castillo offered a more objective historical account of the events, including a well-rounded picture of the Mexican natives and their diverse cultures. His accounts also had detractors, however, because Díaz del Castillo wrote his book during the 1560s, some four decades after the arrival of Cortés in Mexico in 1519.

Bernal Díaz del Castillo was much involved in the early expeditions to Mexico. In 1517, he took part in the exploration of the Yucatan Peninsula under the leadership of Francisco Hernández de Córdoba. Díaz del Castillo was among the first Spaniards to show intimate knowledge of indigenous cultures. He even claimed to understand some of the native languages.

Díaz del Castillo's *True History* contains detailed descriptions of the characters involved in Cortés's expedition to Tenochtitlán. He provided documentation of the individuals whom Cortés considered marginal to his own military deeds. For instance, there is the case of Jerónimo de Aguilar, a shipwrecked Spaniard found in Cozumel who, because of his knowledge of indigenous languages and culture, served as Cortés's translator. His story of life as a slave of a native chief for eight years, narrated with difficulty to

Cortés because Aguilar claimed to have lost advanced skills in speaking Spanish, must have fascinated Díaz del Castillo. Aguilar, whom Díaz del Castillo characterized as indigenous, displayed his acculturation into patterns of native social behavior.

Díaz del Castillo's most valuable literary contribution is perhaps his close scrutiny of the two most important indigenous characters in Cortés's military achievement, Malintzin and Moctezuma. Malintzin, baptized as Marina, was a native woman given to Cortés as a slave by a local *cacique,* a chief. She was of noble origin, sold into slavery by her own parents as part of a convoluted political scheme, so she had in-depth knowledge of indigenous diplomatic matters. She became Cortés's interpreter and his consultant on social matters dealing with indigenous cultures. Marina is today a rather controversial figure because Mexicans consider her a traitor to her people. She was, nonetheless, among the first indigenous characters depicted in the historical chronicles, adding to the exotic image of the "Indians."

The most notable indigenous figure for both Cortés and Díaz del Castillo was Moctezuma, the Aztec emperor. The "Great Moctezuma," as Díaz del Castillo praised him frequently, was the ruler of Tenochtitlán, a city of such grandeur that Díaz del Castillo called it an "enchantment" and wondered whether it was real or an illusion (190). Moctezuma ruled this fantastic realm, which Díaz del Castillo placed within the literary trend of the books of chivalry, a popular genre of the time. As in the books of chivalry, Díaz del Castillo's lengthy passages about Tenochtitlán's wonders (the palaces, temples, parks, and markets) surpassed the limits of reality known in Europe. The wealth of Tenochtitlán appears in many passages that surpass, in detail and in number, those of Cortés. It had a lasting impact on Díaz del Castillo, for even in old age he insisted that there was no other city like it. For Moctezuma, the last ruler of that perfect city, Díaz del Castillo expressed high praise. In his passage on Moctezuma's death at the hands of the Aztecs, he called the ruler a "father." All of the men in Cortés's army, including Cortés himself, cried and lamented openly his unjust death.

Two other texts about expeditions of exploration and conquest stand out for their novel presentation of incredible events that the authors experienced in the Americas. The first example is that of a shipwrecked Spaniard-turned-native, a subject matter of particular impact on the literary imagination. Alvar Núñez Cabeza de Vaca (–1559?), a survivor of an ill-fated expedition to Florida in 1528, narrated in *Castaways* (1542) his experiences as a defenseless survivor coming into contact with native groups in today's Florida (the Apalacches) and Texas (the Karankawa), among other places. After amazing adventures, Núñez Cabeza de Vaca and three other survivors arrived eight years later in Culiacán, in northern Mexico. His memoir of this fantastic trip, with plentiful characterization of the indigenous groups, was the core of his testimony. Although without weapons and therefore at the mercy of his enemies, Alvar had more positive views of the natives than had writers of earlier accounts. Like other chroniclers, he was greatly impressed by the American land and by the variety of native animals.

Some eighty years after the publication of *Castaways*, Catalina de Erauso (1585?–1653?), recorded her adventures with some of the remaining rebellious indigenous groups in South America. Better known today as the "Lieutenant Nun," Erauso entered Latin American history as a rather strange historical character in unusual circumstances. She escaped from a Spanish convent where she was a novice and, disguised as a soldier, arrived in Panama in 1603. Her military career took her to the warfronts in Chile and Peru before her secret identity became public. The text described here is her defense of herself as a good and effective soldier and a moral citizen.

Erauso wrote her testimony (between 1626 and 1630, but not published until 1829) within the tradition of the picaresque. She is writing as a *pícaro,* a mischievous character who by means of deceits and tricks survived the vicissitudes of war. Her accounts, like those of Cabeza de Vaca, are significant documentation of the cross-cultural processes experienced in the development of the mestizo, a new Latin American racial identity. Her text is unique, however, in that she is a woman speaking of issues related to war against native groups, and this female point of view is rare indeed.

The military chronicles, with their specific purpose of providing proof of the Spaniards' military supremacy, may appear the least significant source of documentation of Native American cultures. On the contrary, as the Spanish armies encountered more indigenous groups, there was growing need for data on indigenous cultures. Later military operations took shape on the basis of results of previous expeditions.

Priests accompanied the military campaigns, an unusual characteristic in European conquest of the New World. The priests' writings about their role in the evangelization of indigenous groups and, in particular, their recording of native cultures are the focus of the next section.

RELIGIOUS TEXTS

Chroniclers who witnessed the many facets of the Conquest period provided detailed documentation of American cultural patterns. The main purpose of their memoirs was to gain recognition as active participants in the conquest or in the colonization. Most of the chroniclers therefore gave positive reviews about the intervention campaigns against indigenous groups. Expression of an opposing point of view resulted from a clash between the personal interest of the chronicler (usually financial) and the official limits set on the American colonists.

As stated previously, chroniclers recorded in great numbers the native religious practices that they encountered and fought. The Spaniards aimed to stop such pagan cults as idolatry of multiple gods and prominent display of human sacrifices on a large scale. Religious conversion became an integral part of the Conquest. Catholic dogma became synonymous with acceptable behavioral patterns in line with the Spanish approach to Western civilization. Roman Catholic priests (Dominicans and Franciscans) arrived in considerable numbers after Columbus's second voyage in 1493 and created a complex campaign of evangelization. The forced conversion of natives into the Catholic faith, mandated by Pope Alexander VI in 1493, became a central component of the political campaign of the Conquest. In fact, it can be argued that the wars against the American native groups were fought under platforms of religious ideology. Imposition of Christian belief led to conversions and also to radical changes in the indigenous communities' social fabric.

The forced conversion banned a considerable number of native socioreligious customs. Priests documented those cults, targeted as obstacles to religious conversion or evangelization. There are in the accounts, however, noticeable contrasts between points of view of the lay chroniclers and those of the priests. The priest, unlike the soldier, was interested in gaining deeper cultural knowledge of the indigenous groups that he was serving in the role of preacher. Three aspects stand out in the chronicles written by priests: the presentation of natives as characters of their own story; the documentation of native religious practices, in particular, the recording of rituals and oral legends; and the compilation of dictionaries of the native languages.

A number of priests documented the native cults within the context of the Spaniards' brutal wars against native groups, leading to their imprisonment and subsequent slavery of natives. As natives became part of the war booty, they became slaves in a system known as the *encomienda.* In this American-born system, the natives became "entrusted" to the care of an *encomendero,* who, in exchange for the natives' work, was to provide them with religious and civil education and an income. The *encomienda* did not protect the natives, however, when the *encomendero* subjected his workers to the most vile and inhuman treatments and also denied them their rights as granted by the Spanish crown as early as 1512. These laws, known as the Leyes de Burgos, even by today's legal standards intended to protect the natives from abuses. For example, the laws provided specific regulations for the maximum length of continuous work in mines (five months), provided a generous maternity leave, and had specific provisions for the amount of food and for living quarters that the *encomendero* was required to provide for his workers. The laws also provided the right of an education, mainly religious conversion within the Roman Catholic faith.

The violations of human rights and the physical abuses committed against the natives fed the so-called Black Legend. Emerging European powers fiercely challenged the authority of Spain over the American territory and the natives living there. Their accusations of mismanagement and cruelty against native groups fueled Spain's increasingly negative record in the

Americas. The Black Legend served other European countries' ambitions to take part in the distribution of the bountiful American riches.

The first formal protests against the violation of the *encomienda* bylaws came from priests who had come to the Americas as part of well-thought-out programs of evangelization and indoctrination. Their clashes with civil authorities, and in particular with wealthy *encomenderos,* were apparent in their accusations of open and outrageous violations of the *encomienda.* In one case, in 1511, Fray Antonio de Montesinos, a Dominican priest, openly condemned abuses against the natives of the island of La Española. Deaths from mistreatment may be partially responsible for the elimination of indigenous groups on the greater Caribbean islands within a fifty-year period.

Bartolomé de las Casas

Drawing from Fray Montesinos's public denunciations, another socially committed priest, Fray Bartolomé de las Casas (1484–1566), took to the Spanish court cases of violations of the natives' human rights. His documentation of these violations, like those of other chroniclers, were detailed, eyewitness accounts based on his extensive experiences of living on the major Caribbean islands since 1502. There he had witnessed the bloodiest campaigns against rebellious indigenous groups. He was writing from a pacifist point of view as a Dominican priest with ample experience in the evangelization process. His historical accounts of the conquest, *History of the Indies* (1527) and *The Devastation of the Indies* (1552), stand out for their graphic exposé of atrocities committed by the Conquistadors. Las Casas's books sought to defend the natives against oppressive practices such as torture and indiscriminate punishment, which included barbarous death penalties against unruly or runaway slaves.

Besides Las Casas's historical significance as a defender of indigenous groups, his books today are sources for the study of native cultures and are primary data for the earliest images of indigenous groups who become active characters in their struggle against the barbarous colonization process. Writing on behalf of the oppressed, Las Casas established a passionate defense of the natives, portraying them as rational human beings. This concept was highly debated in the Spanish courts, but in 1537 the Church arrived at a halfway stand by accepting that American natives had the ability to understand the Church's dogma. Thus, Las Casas's attacks against the violence he witnessed were supported by the authority of biblical scripture and canonical law. The mismanagement of the *encomienda* became, therefore, a terrible crime that went beyond violations to the civil code.

In his characterization of natives, Las Casas used the medieval literary motif of the **locus amoenus,** a place of beauty where the human spirit achieves its maximum capacity for goodness. The indigenous groups inhabited such a territory of natural perfection and possessed an idyllic social order, where they lacked only the presence of the true Christian God. Their leaders' beautiful physical characteristics reflected their innate positive psychological makeup, producing a portrait of wise and trustworthy individuals. Such is the case of two allied *caciques,* or regional chiefs, Guarionex and Mayobanex, from the island that is now the Dominican Republic; they claimed for their people equal treatment under the Spanish law.

The stories about Guarionex and Mayobanex are examples of these chiefs' highly developed psychological profiles, which include most prominently their committed friendship with and loyalty to their subjects. Written as a medieval **exemplum,** a story with a didactic intention, these natives' experiences are examples of the terrible consequences of the brutal handling of the *encomienda.* The story is simple: Guarionex, a former *cacique,* is subjected to the harsh conditions of a gold mine, where he works along with his surviving subjects. Knowing that a rebellion would mean death to him and his followers, he seeks refuge with the unconquered kingdom of Mayobanex, a former political ally. Chief Mayobanex welcomes his runaway friend, despite his own people's complaints that such asylum will bring only devastation to all. The Spaniards mobilize a large military contingency, and they soon locate Guarionex's hiding place. Threatened "with fire and slaughter to their utter destruction," Mayobanex refuses to turn over Gurionex to the Spanish military forces. Mayobanex's message to the Spanish authorities lists his reasons for not submitting to the Spanish civil authorities. It is a rational attack against the mismanagement of power by the Spanish authorities:

Tell the Christians that Guarionex is a good and honorable man. He has done evil to no one—that is a public, a known fact. For that reason, he is worthy of a heartfelt help in his humiliation and flight, worthy of support and protection. But the Spaniards are evil men, tyrants. They come for one reason, to seize land not theirs. They know only how to spill the blood of people who never provoked them. Therefore, say to them, I do not want their favor, nor to see them, nor hear them. Instead I intend to try, with all the power I have, my people have, to smash and drive out the Christians from this land. I take the side of Guarionex. (Las Casas 83)

Mayobanex fails to keep Guarionex out of the Spaniards' reach, a promise that the reader assumes is symbolic because the great chief knows well the military superiority of the Spanish army. At the end, as expected, the rebellion is contained, but only by means of trickery on the part of the Spanish. The two great native leaders are captured, and their followers are enslaved. Their deaths are not fitting for these noble characters: Guarionex drowned himself on his way to Spain, and Mayobanex died in prison.

Las Casas's testimony encountered opposition, of course. His documentation of the Caribbean, an area that he depicted with particular poignancy, was officially challenged. One refutation is in the works of Gonzalo

Fernández de Oviedo (1478–1557). Fernández de Oviedo's portrayals of the natives were absolutely negative; they appear as a degenerate, subhuman species, not capable of achieving rational behavior. Unlike Las Casas's positive depictions, Fernández de Oviedo's *Sumario de la natural historia de las Indias* (1526) and *Historia general y natural de las Indias* (1526–1546) characterize the natives by means of images that stress animallike qualities and deny any capability of rational behavior. As for the inhumane treatment against unruly indigenous groups, he heatedly defended it as a necessary means for the maintenance of a rising Spanish empire.

The Church's evangelization campaign was undoubtedly a factor of major importance in the socialization of the indigenous groups. The Roman Catholic Church was an influential colonialist power in its support, on religious grounds, of military battles against rebellious native groups and in its participation in the *encomienda* system. The earliest priests in the Americas, such as Las Casas, found themselves at a crossroad as they experienced firsthand the great diversity of the American natives. Their testimonial documentation of their experiences is today an obligatory point of departure in the understanding of modern American religious practices.

Bernardino de Sahagún

The role of priests as teachers of European civilization was formidable in the face of the social restrictions imposed on the indigenous communities. Amid the evangelization campaign, priests compiled the first dictionaries of indigenous languages. Fray Bernardino Sahagún (1499–1590) and Fray Diego González Holguín (1560?–1620?), for example, produced dictionaries that facilitated the communication so necessary for political and religious subordination of the native groups. They also drafted grammar treatises that promoted the recording of a rich indigenous religious oral tradition. These complex transcriptions of native religious stories had a positive reception that may have ensured the survival of a considerable number of cultural traditions.

Sahagún, a Franciscan priest who arrived in Mexico in 1529 as part of a religious contingent, participated in the establishment of a grammar school for children of indigenous nobility. Located in Mexico City, this liberal arts school offered boys a curriculum in Nahuatl, Spanish, and Latin, and it included instruction in logic, philosophy, theology, and the fine arts. In 1540, Sahagún had started to transcribe the Nahuatl phonemes into the Spanish alphabet, a task that allowed him to transcribe local indigenous legends, history, and religious customs. This was the genesis of *General History of the Things of New Spain,* a compilation of twelve books written in Nahuatl and in Spanish, transcribed between 1578 and 1580.

General History compiles an impressive ethnographic documentation of data pertaining to the indigenous groups of central Mexico. His intention went beyond the chronicler's role as historian of events surrounding the Conquest; some of what Sahagún wrote about was from secondhand sources, mainly from old natives who remembered the incidents. He was writing, however, as a priest who stressed the indigenous cultural mind in relation to their reactions to events of the Conquest and colonization.

An example of Sahagún's unique historical approach to the conquest of Tenochtitlán is evident in his accounts of the myths about the arrival of the Spaniards in Mexico. The chapter titled "The War of the Conquest: How Was It Waged Here in Mexico" details a series of eight omens, strange occurrences that preceded Cortés's military invasion against the Aztecs. Beyond the significance of the omens within the Aztec religion (for instance, a comet that appeared in mid-afternoon, bursting into three heads), Sahagún transcribes these events in a narrative style that merges reality with the supernatural, a trend that will be known in the twentieth century as **magical realism.**

Another special contribution of Sahagún's *General History* is the drawings that accompany the text. There are some 1,846 of these, produced by local indigenous artisans trained in late medieval drawing style. The drawings point to miniscule details that enrich the data discussed in the text. They are also significant because of the self-representation of native culture by means of elaborate drawings that, before the arrival of the Spaniards, had been used as written texts. None of those pre-Hispanic texts survive.

Diego Durán

Other notable religious accounts include that of Fray Diego Durán (1537–1588), who described in his *The History of the Indies* the religious practices of indigenous Mexican groups, in particular, those of the Tepanecs. Unlike some previous chroniclers, Durán showed a positive attitude in his depiction of indigenous cultures, perhaps because he had lived in Mexico as a child. He is also known for his *Book of the Gods and Rites and the Ancient Calendar,* written for the Dominican order in 1581. Another historical account, *Historia natural y moral de las Indias* (1590) by Father José de Acosta (1539–1616) presents the native groups of Mexico in a positive light.

The *Popol-Vuh*

The most famous transcriptions of indigenous religious legends are the collection known as the *Popol-Vuh* belonging to Central America's Maya-Quiché. The Quiché, like the Aztecs before them, suffered an aggressive invasion from 1524, which resulted in the loss of significant religious traditions as the centers of worship were destroyed in military interventions of Maya-Quiché cities. Fortunately, an anonymous native transcribed a substantial number of Maya-Quiché myths, subtitled the *Book of Advice*, perhaps around 1544. He wrote in the Quiché language but used the characters of the Latin alphabet. The stories reveal the Mayan religious belief system as they present a highly sophisticated cosmology and theology. This text, lost today, survived in a Spanish translation by Francisco Jiménez, a priest who may have added strong biblical echoes, in particular from the book of Genesis. That rendition of the revised stories into equivalent biblical stories may have been a part of the evangelization campaign.

The *Popul-Vuh* stories nonetheless retain in their story lines and narrative structures a strong relationship with Quiché religious traditions, revealing a complex theological and philosophical system. One example is the carefully arranged divisions of the stories that reproduce the intricate stages of the Mayan-Quiché calendar. The stories, like the calendar, display a sophisticated arrangement of time that gives the plotline notable flexibility and allows for multiple story lines reminiscent of today's narrative techniques. Within a time frame of cycles, the *Popol-Vuh* stories take the reader into a mystical world in which, much as in biblical stories, events provide important lessons, both from the theological point of view and in a pragmatic way of life.

The impact of the *Popol-Vuh* on contemporary Central American literary tradition is notable. It can be argued that its complex narrative structure and obscure symbols have inspired writers to explore experimental literary trends. For instance, Guatemalan novelist and short story writer Miguel Angel Asturias (1899–1974), while studying at the Sorbonne in 1939, did extensive research on the *Popol-Vuh*, leading to its translation into French. Later, Asturias's literary production drew from Mayan-Quiché mythology as he embarked on complex experimentation with surrealism. His novel *Hombres de maíz* (*Men of Maize*, 1949) reflects numerous technical and thematic similarities to *Popol-Vuh* stories. A testimony to his literary success was his receiving the Nobel Prize for Literature in 1967. The impact of the religious practices of other ethnic groups, such as those of imported Africans, as I discuss later, is also important in contemporary Latin American literature, particularly in Caribbean literary production.

NATIVE CHRONICLERS

The study of Latin American ethnography from an eyewitness perspective took on new dimensions in works produced by native scholars. They came from diverse social and cultural backgrounds, but collectively they made strong statements about a colonial system that severely limited the rights of indigenous populations and of other marginalized groups. Viewed from a modern perspective, they were the voice of the masses, claiming for their people social justice and equal opportunities under the law. Unlike the Spanish chroniclers, who in some instances also became committed activists, the native chroniclers boldly went a step further by proposing solutions to the problems they denounced. These solutions were often anchored in calls for a return to ancient indigenous ways of living.

Native chroniclers displayed a keen interest in the documentation of indigenous cultural data. These recordings are their most significant contribution to the anthropology of pre-Colombian civilizations. They are more significant than the observations of the Spanish chroniclers because native chroniclers had fewer linguistic barriers and were not writing as outsiders commenting on and interpreting foreign cultural traditions. In fact, because many of the cultural traditions were accessible only through oral accounts, the native chroniclers understood their unique role as disseminators and preservers of native cultures. Their writings are especially important because many of those traditions, such as religious practices, are extinct today.

Huamán Poma de Ayala

Huamán Poma de Ayala is prominent among the first native chroniclers. Little is known about Poma de Ayala's personal background, other than his claim to noble and full Incan ancestry. His *Primera crónica y buen gobierno (First History and Good Government)* was written from 1567 to 1615, in his old age, as a treatise with advice for the Spanish King Phillip III. The king never received the text, however, and it was lost until its discovery in 1908 in the Royal Library at Copenhagen.

Poma de Ayala's book is a sociopolitical document that openly protests the poverty and the suffering of the indigenous people of Peru. Several factors make this book especially interesting as anthropological testimony. Addressing his king, who did not read Quechua, Poma de Ayala made a political statement about Phillip III's responsibility for acquiring in-depth knowledge of Incan culture. His including in the Spanish text some passages in Quechua (the ancient language of the mighty Incan empire) indicates his esteem for his native language.

The use of Spanish also reveals several interesting facts. It was Poma de Ayala's second language; that was obvious in his often-faulty grammar and irregular use of stylistic devices drawn from Quechua linguistic structures. This record of Peruvian Spanish spoken by a Native American is a case study for linguistic research. In Spanish, Poma de Ayala writes of his sense of an emerging bicultural identity, the so-called **mestizo** or **criollo** culture. Mestizos, the Latin American–born generations of mixed ancestry, maintain elements from both cultures. One result is their bilingual ability to sustain a rich cultural life both in Spanish and in other native languages. This developing Peruvian criollo identity shows a strong influence of Quechua, a language that he fully identified with the ancient Quechua culture. Praise of Incan culture (as reflected in the many indigenous and criollo customs) was at the heart of Poma de Ayala's text.

Poma de Ayala's point of view is that of a committed activist with a profound empathy with the indigenous populations. Drawings depicting violent scenes emphasize his bold presentation of the numerous cases of violation of the human rights of the marginalized natives. These drawings depict graphically the frequent crimes and unjust punishments against native populations. The message was clear: Only by gaining in-depth knowledge of the present condition of the Inca would the imperial monarch be successful in fulfilling his God-given responsibility to deliver "a good government." Poma de Ayala offered a list of serious irregularities in the Spanish management of Peru, including his open denunciation of local governors and of other public officers, of public safety agents, and of representatives of the Roman Catholic Church. His dislike of the Spanish government is notable. His highly negative view of the Spanish mistreatment of the native Peruvian can be considered an early precursor of an independence movement.

His open criticism of the ill-treatment of native populations and his pride in native traditions make Poma de Ayala one of the first exponents of a contemporary Latin American sociopolitical movement known as **Indigenismo.** His stand was direct, challenging the unacceptable Spanish administrative institutions, in contrast to the highly developed former Inca governmental system:

To sum up what I have to say, the Spaniards in Peru should be made to refrain from arrogance and brutality towards the Indians. Just imagine that our people were to arrive in Spain and start confiscating property, sleeping with the women and girls, chastising the men and treating everybody like pigs! What would the Spaniards do then? Even if they tried to endure their lot with resignation, they would still be liable to be arrested, tied to a pillar and flogged. And if they rebelled and attempted to kill their persecutors, they would certainly go to their deaths in the gallows. (141)

Today this political front seeks financial reparations for many indigenous communities victimized by repressive and racist military governments, by guerrilla fighters, or by drug traffickers. The call for social justice on behalf of the destitute indigenous has become known internationally through the voice of Rigoberta Menchú, a Guatemalan indigenous activist and Nobel Peace Prize recipient (1992). In her writings, like Poma de Ayala before her, Menchú explores ancient Mayan customs; she praises them as her people's unique contributions and as their defense against modernity with its vices and excesses. Also like Poma de Ayala, Menchú, in her eyewitness account, strongly expressed in her autobiography, *I, Rigoberta Menchú: An Indian*

Woman in Guatemala (1984), details numerous crimes against Guatemalan natives at the hands of repressive governments.

Inca Garcilaso de la Vega

Another native Peruvian, Garcilaso de la Vega (1539–1616), in his *Comentarios reales* (1608–1609; 1616) embarked on an exploration of native traditions, many of them from small indigenous groups marginalized and excluded from an emerging national identity. His case is also noteworthy because of his personal background, which he proudly traced in his intricately researched anthropological and historical account. De la Vega was a mestizo with a prestigious family history: a direct descendant of Peruvian nobility and a Spanish father who participated with conquistadors Pedro de Alvarado, Francisco Pizarro, and Diego de Almagro in the conquest of Perú. Like Poma de Ayala, de la Vega actively sought to uncover and to preserve the rich Peruvian cultural traditions, including the rich Quechua religious system. He was writing, however, from a multiethnic perspective because he produced his *Comentarios* in Spain after formal literary training. Because of de la Vega's learned dual citizenship critics have challenged his objectivity; however, in his analyses he approached the emerging national Peruvian identity from a mestizo perspective, setting up a process in which the Spanish and the Quechua traditions merged into a hybrid Peruvian national identity.

In *Comentarios,* de la Vega explored in detail the oral history accounts that he had heard as a child and as a young man from important Incan personages, some of them his own relatives. Because the Incans did not develop a writing system (other than the **quipu,** a complex system of strings and knots mainly for accounting purposes), their vast knowledge was transmitted via oral traditions. De la Vega drew from ancient indigenous folk motifs, including stories with a strong religious background. This is the case, for instance, of de la Vega's accounts of an omen prior to the arrival of the Spaniards, who would come to the Incan empire at a time of civil strife.

Like those of the *Popol-Vuh,* the historical accounts in *Royal Commentaries* are complex, showing highly developed plotlines, well-rounded characters, and an experimental style in the representation of events of distant times. De la Vega's scholarly interest went beyond a desire to reproduce anecdotal or anthropological data. He was writing during the Spanish Golden Age, at a time when Spain produced its best-known masterpieces, such as Cervantes's *Don Quixote.* With his *Comentarios,* de la Vega attempted to incorporate the rich Incan traditions into mainstream culture.

Comentarios does display rich anthropological data. De la Vega's broad knowledge of the Incan empire produced rather sophisticated comments on the agricultural, governmental, and social systems. His critical opinion included a clear motive to produce a new history of the Incan empire. He drew his data predominantly from pre-Hispanic oral traditions, from various chronicles, and from other written sources dealing with the conquest of the Incas. He covered an expansive historical period and vast subject matter, but the topics on which he commented most frequently are religious belief and traditions of worship.

Unlike the Spanish-born chroniclers, de la Vega wrote his history from a personal level. He and Poma de Ayala were writing as Native American speakers, conscious of their role as interpreters of the folktales and of other popular knowledge that came to them in an indigenous language. They both created for themselves privileged positions as the voice of their people. De la Vega, a trained man of letters, went a step further than Poma de Ayala. His position on the importance of Peruvian history (including his detailed reproduction of native characters descriptive of an emerging national identity) provided material worthy of literary exploration.

Poma de Ayala and de la Vega injected their interpretations of Peruvian history into their personal and family memoirs, and they were both writers committed to a cause. At the core of their production is a strong call for social justice and acceptance of differences in ethnicity. Of particular importance for today's reader is de la Vega's definition of mestizo, a term that bore a negative connotation. During de la Vega's time, however, it had already acquired a strong ethnopolitical association with forging an American identity: "The children of Spaniards by Indians are called mestizos, meaning that we are a mixture of the two races. The word was applied by the first Spaniards who had children by Indian women, and because it was used by our fathers, as well as on account of its meaning, I call myself by it in public and am proud of it, though in the Indies, if a person is told: 'You're a mestizo,' or 'He's a mestizo,' it is taken as an insult" (607).

Alfonso Carrió de la Vandera

A third example of testimonial documentation by a native chronicle is that of Alfonso Carrió de la Vandera (c. 1715–1783), whose *El lazarillo de ciegos caminantes* (c. 1775–1776?) presents a travelogue of his experiences on a trip from Buenos Aires to Lima. Carrió de la Vandera did not identify himself as a member of an ethnic group. In his time, he denied authorship, claiming it for his servant and guide Calixto Bustamante, "el Concolorcorvo." The travelogue's strong anti-Spanish sentiment may explain the true writer's hesitancy to acknowledge authorship. Self-described as "an Indian pure and proud" (40), Concolorcorvo is also the book's narrator. There was a native travel guide who came along on this arduous and dangerous route. His intimate knowledge of the area is evident in his detailed comments on the various ethnic groups whom the traveling caravan encountered. He wrote in particular of their customs, frequently described and, most important, commented on by Concolorcorvo and his master, Carrió de la Vandera.

Concolorcorvo stated the book's purpose directly as "diversion of the travelers" (40), offering anecdotes and anthropological data of the areas traveled, in the wide territory between the cities of Buenos Aires and Lima. Drawing from its title, we could extend Concolorcorvo's role to that of a "guide for blind people" for a Spain that is still eager to get to know the American territory. Spanish readers were still interested in detailed knowledge of the American territories, including the rich topography, socioeconomic conditions, ethnic characteristics, and local products. The title also seems to suggest, however, that Spaniards, like Carrió de la Vandera, were blind to and ignorant of the American reality. Therefore, *Lazarillo* makes bold sociopolitical observations on the South American territories of today's Argentina and Peru. Like Poma de Ayala and de la Vega, Carrió de la Vandera focuses on the changing cultural structures leading to the development of emerging national cultures.

El Lazarillo stands out for its interest in reflecting American life and its differences from Spanish lifestyles from the viewpoint of ethnicity and class structures. The components of American society were clearly established, with no deviation from that order permitted. In order of power, the first place was that of the white Spaniard (represented throughout the text by various characters, including Carrió de la Vandera), followed by the "half-breed," or **mestizo,** the Indian, and the black. Each level had characteristics and attitudes that the narrator used to explain differences that are obvious between the territories. *The Lazarillo* is, therefore, a document that intends not only to copy a new world, but also to examine it in the light of social concepts.

The rigid stratification of colonial Latin American society was established during the beginnings of the Conquest. The exclusive, closely knit racial divisions were evident, for instance, in Poma de Ayala. The reader of *Primera crónica y buen gobierno* may have been shocked by the rancor that this indigenous chronicle stirred up against the mestizo because of the annihilation of the true native. *El Lazarillo* also reflected this preoccupation with racial purity. The use of anecdotes is a remarkable element in the presentation of the interaction among these social groups, which often appear confrontational. These clashes were often rooted in insurmountable ethnic differences. They reflected numerous problems encountered in the late colonial American socioeconomic structure. For instance, it is evident that certain ethnic groups (mainly the indigenous and the blacks) were restricted to low-paid, despised manual labor.

A close reading of the texts produced by Latin American–born chroniclers is today an indispensable tool for understanding the Latin American identities emerging after the conquest. Their point of view was highly critical, unlike that of their Spanish counterparts. Native chroniclers saw themselves as part of the troubled political scene that they were describing. Because they were part of the oppressed peoples, they saw themselves as effective voices for protest. Their expertise in multiple aspects of the rapidly developing Latin American societies appeared unquestionable.

The three native chroniclers analyzed here display common characteristics in their interest in documenting native Latin American cultures. First, it is evident that their attachment to the land, symbolized in the overwhelmingly powerful Latin American landscape, is part of the psychological profile of the various ethnic groups on the continent. Although geographic accounts abound, nature is presented as home for the natives and not as a foreign or mysterious backdrop, as Spanish chroniclers often portrayed it. The native chroniclers' view of nature was therefore less literary. They did not portray themselves as living in a lost paradise, a common motif among Spanish-born chroniclers.

The second important characteristic among native chroniclers is their insightful approach to Latin American indigenous cultures. They placed themselves as functioning members of an ethnic-bound community, so that their view of that culture was that of an insider, and therefore their expertise was trustworthy. Unlike the Spanish chroniclers, native chroniclers were not mere observers who related events outside a cultural context. Testimony anchored in personal knowledge is the text's strongest device. The writers were not, however, free of racial bias against particular cultural groups. Their testimony responded to political agenda in favor of certain social groups, as did the writings of Spanish chronicles before them. The modern reader must be cautious because personal prejudices may exert strong influence on the narrative line or the critical analysis.

The native chroniclers' proactive indigenous stand becomes their most prominent characteristic in texts that sought judicial and financial retribution. As already stated, the chroniclers openly confronted high authorities, pushing for fair treatment under the Spanish colonial imperial system. Their constant cry for social equality and for respect for the natives' human rights illustrates the point.

The legacy of rich ethnographic data was perhaps the native chroniclers' most significant contribution to the cultural documentation of ancient Latin American civilizations. Their extensive multidisciplinary knowledge produced rich texts that are in the vanguard of modern anthropology and that set them apart from the linguistically restricted accounts of most monolingual Spanish chroniclers. These detailed accounts of ancient customs have become today bases of a rich pro-indigenous movement, covering diverse creative facets in literature, in music, and in other modern arts.

AFRICAN SLAVERY

Commercial enterprises, exploitation of mines (mainly of gold and silver), and development of extensive agricultural projects became Latin America's sources of income after the establishment of the first Spanish cities in the Americas. The first laborers were of indigenous groups, who worked for landholders under the *encomienda* system. As the numbers of indigenous workers started to dwindle, especially in the Caribbean, in Central America, and in coastal South America, their replacements soon came from Africa. Although Africans arrived in most Latin American countries, it is in the Caribbean basin that the strong black influx would develop one of the most distinctive popular American cultures.

The precise date of the arrival of the first slaves from Africa is still a matter of debate. It appears, however, that in 1505, King Ferdinand allowed the entrance of some seventeen Africans, who arrived as slaves into the Dominican Republic. The number of African slaves increased rapidly in the Caribbean. A conservative estimate indicates that 75,000 slaves inhabited this area by the end of the sixteenth century. It was the beginning of a shameful period that would extend until the late nineteenth century. In fact, Spain would be the first and the last European power to allow slavery in its American colonies. The continuous massive importation of Africans would provide the Caribbean with a new "native" population, as the indigenous groups soon disappeared by extermination or their numbers became too insignificant to have impact on the development of a national identity. Thus, African culture became the substratum of most contemporary Caribbean popular traditions.

The earliest African slaves had little protection under the Spanish civil laws. Nor were there sufficient observers, as in the case of the indigenous peoples, to record in-depth data of their ancient oral traditions. Their incorporation into an accepted socioreligious way of life took place within the institution of the *cofradía*. Slaves from the same tribal origins (e.g., Bantu, Congo, Yoruba) gathered in *cofradías*, which were intended for their evangelization. This concept was not an American product. The African *cofradía* had existed in Spain since the mid–fifteenth century as slavery flourished on the Iberian Peninsula. For their part, Africans welcomed the opportunity to gather because they had "secret societies" or specialized religious groups. Some of these groups flourished in the New World. For instance, the **Efik,** located in the Calabar area prior to their enslavement, were organized as **Egbos,** well known for their secret society. In Cuba, the Egbos regrouped as **Abakúa.** Today these active practitioners of ancient religious practices ban from their activities all except the initiated. These cultural traditions (following the patterns of their African forebears) are still transmitted via oral legends, known in Cuba as *pataki.* The Cuban *pataki* records ancient religious practices, including stories with a strong pedagogical content. Today this rich folk narrative often appears in several genres—poetry, narrative, and drama.

Because of their secrecy and because of the landowners' failure to monitor the *cofradía's* activities, Africans succeeded in preserving their cultural and religious traditions. Some manifestations of black popular culture, such as music, won acceptance faster than others. Civil regulations restricted them, however, because musical gatherings had a potential for organized civil disobedience. In particular, the use of the drums in public performances was under tight control, because the authorities understood their dual religious and social roles. The rich African musical heritage has survived today in numerous popular rhythms, such as the Cuban **mambo,** the Puerto Rican *plena,* the Dominican **merengue,** among others.

Among the best-known African-based cultural byproducts in the Americas, religious practices are prominent. The most representative cases are the Haitian **Voodoo,** the Brazilian **Macumba,** and the Cuban **Santería.** The lively presence of these religious activities among predominantly black communities maintains their affinity to pure forms of an African-based theology and a complex belief systems. These religious practices are today part of a vibrant African–Latin American culture and an integral way of life for millions of inhabitants of the Caribbean basin. A testimony of the strength of these religious practices is their rapid importation and spread in the United States in recent years. Santería, for instance, has a strong presence in cities such as Miami, New York, Chicago, and Los Angeles.

The origins of Santería have been the focus of detailed studies in Cuba. Contemporary Cuban customs reflect the great impact of a rich African heritage. Through gatherings of the *cofradías* came preservation of key cultural and belief systems. The first Cuban *cofradía* was founded in 1598, under the auspices of the Virgin of the Remedios. Founders of this *cofradía* intended to provide space solely for the evangelization of the slaves, and they sought to provide religious education by means of the veneration of saints. Thus, each *cofradía* was named after a saint under whose protection the slaves came together in religious communion. The evangelization was merely oral because landowners kept the slaves illiterate. This rather primitive approach to evangelization led to a merge of African and Roman Catholic religious practices. The process, known as **syncretism,** produced native cults, which, unlike other popular cultural products, remained underground and unlawful.

The religious syncretism begins with the **Orisha,** the African counterpart of the Roman Catholic saints. The Orisha, like the saints, are divine entities, supernatural spirits associated with natural forces. The Africans, forced by their masters to abandon devotion to the Orishas, received the Saints as replacements; however, they simply replaced images in their worship. To the uninitiated, this worship would appear acceptable within the Catholic canon. Two other facts accelerated the spread of the African belief systems: the Church's lack of interest in supervising the *cofradía,* and the opportunity to engage in unmonitored activities in slave dwellings on the plantations.

In addition to their importance as religions, these African-based practices took on a political significance as centers of political dissent among slaves and freed blacks. One evidence of their power is the action in 1782 of Galvés, then Spanish governor of Louisiana, to prohibit entrance of slaves from Martinique and La Española (modern Haiti and the Dominican Republic) because of the belief that blacks from those islands practiced voodoo extensively. This prohibition remained in effect until the Louisiana purchase in 1803.

Numerous slave revolts were associated with cults or secret societies. One of these rebellions took place in Haiti in 1757, a prelude to Haitian independence from France in 1804. Mackandal, a runaway slave, a **Houngan** or voodoo high priest, led the uprising. Cuban writer Alejo Carpentier (1904–1980) immortalized Mackandal's movement in *El reino de este mundo* (*The Kingdom of This World,* 1949), a novel that initiated **magical realism,** Latin America's best-known literary movement of the twentieth century.

Despite the significant number of slaves in the Spanish-speaking Caribbean, there was little interest in recording the activities of slaves or of freed blacks. In the Cuban literary scene of the mid–nineteenth century, there are writings descriptive of black culture; they belong to the *costumbrismo* movement. Writing as eyewitnesses, *costumbrista* writers expressed their opinions of the customs that defined proper taste or illustrated acceptable traits of an emerging Cuban identity. Not surprisingly, when dealing with black traditions (mainly music, including dances, lifestyle, food, clothing, and religious practices) *costumbrista* writers' attitude was highly negative. They marginalized black culture to the "inferior" social classes, and, if mentioned at all, it was ridiculed or censored as barbaric. Black religious ceremonies, precursors of modern Santería, were constantly under attack; the writer viewed black practitioners as primitive and barbaric, foreign to acceptable Cuban cultural values.

Another aspect of *costumbrismo* is political, an expression of discontent or disagreement. Cuba is the most noticeable case as a territory still under Spanish control throughout the nineteenth century until the U.S. intervention during the Spanish-American War in 1898. Some Cuban *costumbrista* writers took, for instance, a more lenient attitude toward black customs, which they portrayed as cornerstones of an emerging popular culture. Many of these novelists were also abolitionists, who opposed the wealthy sugarcane industry that had made Cuba a worldwide producer of sugar, dependent on an active slave trade. That lasted until the abolition of slavery in 1886. Three of the best-known examples of such writer-activists are Cirilo Villaverde's (1812–1894) *Cecilia Valdés* (*Cecilia Valdes or Angel's Hill,* 1839); Anselmo Suárez Romero's (1818–1878) *Francisco,* written between 1838 and 1839 (because of political censorship it circulated underground in Cuba until its publication in New York in 1880); and Gertrudis Gómez de Avellaneda's (1814–1873) *Sab* (1841), which promoted positive views of black traditions and condemned the aging slavery system. Because of their antislavery ideology, neither *Sab* nor *Cecilia Valdés* had their first editions in Cuba. *Sab* was published in Spain and *Cecilia Valdés* in New York, where Villaverde had sought refuge in self-imposed political exile.

Gómez de Avellaneda's controversial *Sab* called for the abolition of slavery and for equal treatment for women under the law. The story line was daring for its time: Sab, a slave secretly in love with Carlota, the daughter of his owner, in a letter written hours before his untimely death declares his love for her and his contempt for the slave society that legally restricts their right to marry. His declaration of love goes beyond his social stigma as a slave (literacy of a slave was contrary to the social power structure); it openly touches on Carlota's inability to marry without her father's approval. In Sab's call for social justice, he defiantly equates slavery with the subordinate condition of women in a patriarchal society:

Oh, women! Poor, blind victims! Like slaves, they patiently drag their chains and bow their heads under the yoke of human laws. With no other guide than an untutored and trusting heart, they choose a master for life. The slave can at least change masters, can even hope to buy his freedom some day if he can save enough money, but a woman, when she lifts her careworn hands and mistreated brow to beg for release, hears the monstrous, deathly voice which cries out to her: "In the grave." (144–5)

Although Avellaneda's novel was published in Spain, it was banned in Cuba. Chapters of *Sab*, however, circulated underground in Cuba, feeding an emerging abolitionist movement.

Slavery as an attractive subject matter became an interest of foreign visitors to Cuba. One in particular, Swedish novelist Fredrika Bremer, stands out for her close observations of the treatment of slaves in her memoirs *Homes of the New World*. A well-known feminist, Bremer visited Cuba in 1851. Like Gómez de Avellaneda, she equates the violations of blacks' civil rights with the legal restrictions on women and their subjugation to a father figure or a husband. Bremer's diary is of particular value today because most of the other eyewitness accounts of slavery were the work of men. In her observations of daily life on a plantation, Bremer looked at family-related details usually ignored in most documents of the time.

These authors' abolitionist ideals and positive portrayal of black popular cultures were indeed revolutionary. As in the United States, they were opposing a powerful society economically dependent on slavery. They challenged the social structures that allowed slavery to continue until the late nineteenth century. In fact, their humanitarian literary stance in favor of full rights for slaves and blacks predates similar American works, such as Harriet Beecher Stowe's *Uncle Tom's Cabin*, the first U.S. abolitionist novel, published in 1851.

Today Cuba continues at the forefront of advanced anthropological and sociological research of their rich black popular culture. One work in particular stands out for its unique nature: *Biografía de un cimarrón* (*Biography of a Runaway Slave*, 1966) by ethnographer and novelist Miguel Barnet (1940–). He wrote it after recording interviews with Esteban Montejo, a 103-year-old man who narrated for Barnet his earliest memories as a child growing up as a slave on a Cuban plantation. Montejo's conversations with Barnet reveal the many dangers he survived as a runaway slave and as a participant in the War for Independence against the Spanish regime, which led to the Spanish-American War of 1898. Cuba was a powerful proslavery bastion because the island's economy depended on black workers for a booming sugarcane production. In fact, after the Haitian revolution (1793) resulted in the independence of the first Latin American country (1804), Cuba became the world's largest producer of sugar and a wealthy colony of struggling Spain. In order not to confront the powerful landowners and sugarcane planters, the Spanish had lenient attitudes toward slavery that allowed the entry of slaves into Cuba even after Spanish courts had declared such practices illegal in 1820. Despite pressure from Great Britain and the United States, slaves continued to arrive illegally until the abolition of slavery in Cuba in 1886.

Montejo was born in 1860 on a Cuban sugarcane plantation to African-born parents that he never met because he was immediately sold and transferred to another plantation. His testimony to Barnet (recorded in 1963) about the slave's daily routines includes many rich details of the activities of the various African groups arriving in Cuba illegally. Many of these new arrivals were children because it was understood that more of them would fit into the ships because of their size and more of them would survive the ocean trip and be malleable to endure forced work because of their young age.

Montejo's testimony of life on a sugarcane plantation speaks of the physical struggle in cutting the sugarcane and of the various stages in the refinement of sugar. Montejo vividly remembered that masters constantly exploited slaves and subjected them to hazardous work-related activities. He eventually escaped to become a runaway slave, or *cimarrón*. His activities as an outlaw, barely surviving the physical hardships of life in the forest, included avoiding capture by paid seekers of runaway slaves. Montejo summarized his life as a solitary runaway slave in a poignant statement that expresses his fighting spirit: "I've always liked independence. Sassy talk and idle gossip do no good. I went for years and years without talking to anyone" (57).

Montejo's extensive coverage of African life on a Cuban sugarcane plantation is his most significant contribution to the recording of a vibrant popular black culture. His accounts of the many social and religious aspects of the life of slaves make his testimony unique; such firsthand documentation is rare in the Spanish-speaking Caribbean countries. Although not always portrayed in a positive light, these African traditions are presented as part of an emerging Cuban national identity. In contrast to the biased recording by Cuban *costumbrista* writers, Montejo had a positive outlook toward many black traditions. His testimony was also political; he actively condemned the oppressive system of slavery. Thus, Montejo's purpose in recording his memoirs goes beyond an interest in anthropological documentation. The former runaway slave drew on his own experiences in presenting the fighting spirit of African slaves. The author, Barnet, sees in Montejo's triumph a political statement. Consequently, Barnet calls the reader to explore the roots of contemporary black Cuban history from multidisciplinary, sociopolitical perspectives.

THE BAROQUE PERIOD

Although still a matter of controversy among critics, the documentation of an incipient Latin American identity, reflected in literary production, can be traced to the baroque period. Throughout the seventeenth century, Spain experienced a booming publishing phenomenon in all genres. In this period, Spain produced its first literary figures of international fame, such as novelist Miguel de Cervantes y Saavedra (*Don Quixote,* 1605), playwright Lope de Vega, and poet and playwright Calderón de la Barca. Their literary experimentation and new themes are still a source of inspiration.

The flourishing literary publications that appeared in Spain also had an impact on the increasing number of readers in the Latin American colonies. Although restrictions on literary material imported from the motherland were still in effect, Latin Americans eagerly awaited news about the newest trends. In the Americas, poetry was the preferred literary genre, and the number of poets writing was indeed remarkable. Although most of the American poets followed the conventional baroque themes and subject matters of Spanish poets, others ventured into American-based themes. Such is the case, for instance, of the Mexican Bernardo de Balbuena (1568–1627), whose poem, "Grandeza mexicana" ("Mexican Greatness," c. 1604) sings praises to the wonders of Mexico's capital.

The reasons for the exploration of American material were numerous. For one thing, the American territory continued to exert interest on Spanish readers, who were still following closely the development of this exotic territory. Whether or not poets writing from the Americas had the Spanish literary market as their ultimate readership, their increasing interest in American motifs became a trademark of an incipient movement in Latin American poetry. Furthermore, active communication between the Americas and Spain allowed incorporation of a new social type, the "Indiano," or native of the Indies. "Indianos," such as the celebrated poet Inca Garcilaso de la Vega, had visited and lived in Spain for extended periods. During the baroque period, these Americans became literary figures of certain importance and literary significance.

Juana Inés de la Cruz (1651–1695) was one of the most important American-born poets of the Spanish baroque. Indeed, de la Cruz's prolific literary production (poetry, play, and theological essays) makes her a remarkable exponent of the baroque movement. Born Juana Ramírez de Asbaje in Mexico, she was a child prodigy who displayed unusual musical and mathematical knowledge at an early age. As a teenager, she gained entrance to the viceroy's luxurious quarters in Mexico City, where she had access to the best library collections of the Americas. She gave up her successful post as the court's poet to become a nun, and she took a religious name that was also her literary signature. Despite the Church's careful restrictions on her writing, she became among the best-known intellectuals of her time.

Aside from its literary sophistication, at the level of the best Spanish baroque style, Sor Juana Inés's work has national relevance because of its exploration of American subject matters. In particular, critics have pointed out her songs, inspired by American motifs, as precursors of a rich Latin American poetic tradition based on **bucolic,** or nature-inspired, themes. Of special historical importance is her poetry inspired by the linguistic patterns of black slaves. These poems are antecedents to a formal black literature, known in the earliest decades of twentieth-century Caribbean literature as *poesía negrista,* or black poetry.

Another outstanding poet writing from the Americas was Juan del Valle y Caviedes (1652?–1697). Although he was born in Spain, he arrived in Perú at a young age and spent his life in that country, so important to the Spanish crown because of its large mining industries. Unlike Sor Juana de la Cruz's classic style, the populist tone of Caviedes's satirical poetry had a strong appeal to the masses. His poetry contains a strong social element; he addressed issues controversial in the Lima of his time. For instance, his poems against medical doctors and lawyers (some of whom he mentions by name) are among the first examples in Latin American literature of a sociopolitically committed poetic production, later associated with the preindependence period of the early part of the nineteenth century.

Caviedes also recorded events of interest to the Lima population, such as the construction of important buildings, the building of a protective wall around the city, and the earthquake of 1687. Of particular interest to today's students of linguistics is his use of Quechua words, incorporated into the literary text as mainstream vocabulary. He also recorded details of Peruvian flora and fauna, adding to interest in the Latin American landscape as a literary motif.

A narrative with strong American-related elements is *Infortunios de Alfonso Ramírez* (*The Misadventures of Alfonso Ramírez,* 1690) by the Mexican Jesuit, Carlos de Sigüenza y Góngora (1645–1700), one of the first novels with an American-born protagonist. Written in the literary style of the **picaresque,** or a novel of adventures, the protagonist, Alfonso Ramírez, is a **pícaro,** a drifter and adventurer, who leaves his native Puerto Rico in quest of the riches to be found on the American mainland. As a penniless old man, Ramírez tells his life story to Sigüenza, who then writes and publishes the novel.

For today's reader, *Infortunios* is important on various levels of literary significance. Ramírez is the main character with a fascinating life story, but, unlike previous protagonists such as the conquistadors, he is not a heroic figure. His problem is political; he is a victim of the tight social structures imposed by colonial Spain. This documentation of Ramírez's agitated life, as drafted by Sigüenza, may be considered a prototype of the genre of the political *testimonio*. Testimonial writing came into fashion in Latin American literature in the 1960s.

Blacks are other characters of literary importance, often as representative of the hybrid cultures that developed in Latin America. The black woman who dealt with unorthodox religious cults, equivalent to modern witchcraft, was a subject of Colombian writer Juan Rodríguez Freyle (1566–1640). His *El Carnero,* written in the 1630s but not published until 1859, is a compilation of stories revealing the history of Colombia from its colonial beginnings, with emphasis on marginalized social characters, particularly those living beyond the margins of the law. This is the case of "A Deal with Juana García," a story of an old black woman, and former slave, who provides services to women eager to deceive their husbands in sexual matters.

The story is unusual in several regards. As a social commentator on sexual customs during the colonial period, Rodríguez Freyle documents the women's right to seek revenge against deceitful husbands. It is curious, however, that punishment came only to the black woman, condemned to death by the Inquisition despite her protest that "Each of us women did it, but I alone pay!" (56). Documentation of women's practices of black magic, which in the story appear as concrete examples and not mere hearsay, can be considered antecedents to the literary treatment of unusual and unexplainable events of twentieth-century magical realism. Above all, Rodríguez Freyle documents Colombian characters who react to the social and political conditions of their times. Almost a century later, another Colombian writer, Gabriel García Márquez, would become renowned for his treatment of popular characters associated with his native country's political and social conditions.

THE NINETEENTH CENTURY: THE BIRTH OF LATIN AMERICAN LITERATURE

The political formation of the American nations, beginning with the first wars for independence in 1810, coincided with the European literary movement known as **Romanticism.** In Latin America this period took on a profound nationalist spirit, as the emerging Latin American countries sought to define their individual national values. It was a period of major political change for them, initially represented in the intellectual platforms of distinguished Pan-American personalities, such as liberators Simón Bolívar and José de San Martín. In the literature produced after the independence movements, writers approached their native countries' specific needs by serving in two important roles: they became chroniclers of the sociopolitical events taking place, and they started the first attempts to produce a national literature.

Latin American writers therefore initiated an ambitious project that merged social needs with an intellectual project to produce a "native" literary production. One important by-product of a national literature is the emergence of a local readership. Another is the beginning of a strong presence of writers in the political arena. A considerable number of writers took active part in political events in their native countries. This political involvement of Latin American writers is still a common practice today.

The Romantic era was an exciting one. The new countries, now free from Spanish political and intellectual control, experienced a series of events related to the end of the colonial period. With a new positive outlook, they undertook an impressive number of political, social, and economic reforms. For the first time, Latin Americans were responsible for their own decisions. A feeling of freedom and hope was captured in the Romantic-inspired literature of the period.

In the earliest stages of the development of national literatures, documentation of local traditions led to a degree of nationalism. The movement, known as *costumbrismo,* closely depicted native customs and characters as representatives of national values (either social or political). This was an updated version of a previous movement produced during the late period of colonial Latin American literature. The American *costumbrista* writers of the postcolonial era went further, however; they used Latin American customs either as a literary symbol of importance or as an integral part of the plot. *Costumbrismo* would also be a precursor of the rich realist tradition of the early part of the twentieth century. For the emerging Latin American nations, local customs were distinctive features of emerging national identities, which set them apart not only from Spanish traditions but also from the customs of other, neighboring Latin American countries.

The political transition into independent countries did not occur so smoothly as they had expected, however. Despite local attempts to follow the U.S. model, with its liberal constitution and a centralized federal government, frequent political upheavals produced the first strongmen, or *caudillos.* These dominant political figures would become precursors of the twentieth-century Latin American dictator. Although the dictator as an overpowering center of national political life is certainly not limited to Latin

America, his presence has become a common fixture in its political systems. These dictatorships have often been responsible for such social and economic conditions as the rise to power of military governments and massive emigration, particularly of political refugees seeking asylum in the United States.

Political divisions and national upheaval are the themes of "El matadero" ("The Slaughter House," written 1839, published 1871) by Esteban Echeverría (1805–1851), a best-selling author in his native Argentina whose literary production (short stories and poetry) began a strong Romantic tradition. In addition to his contributions to Argentine literature, Echeverría's trip to Europe as a young man introduced his readers to current European literature, particularly to the poetry of Lord Byron, whose influence is visible in Echeverría's poetry. Echeverría was also famous for his campaign against the dictatorship of Manuel de Rosas (1793–1877), whose government caused Argentina to declare war against Bolivia (1837) and forced a French blockade against the country (1838–1839). Because of his political campaigns Echeverría had to go into exile in Uruguay in 1840, and he died in Montevideo in 1851. His political efforts were not in vain, however; Rosas's government was deposed in 1852.

Today "The Slaughter House" is considered a remarkable precursor of the modern Latin American short story. It is also a remarkable example of a fine literary work that serves as an agent of political activism. This close relationship between literature and political thinking is among the foremost characteristics of contemporary Latin American literature. Literature as a political weapon has also prompted a significant number of Latin American writers to serve in political offices, as presidents of their countries, or as members of legislatures.

"The Slaughter House" is a short story with strong echoes of the political scene that Echeverría was fighting against as a member of a politically committed intellectual community. Written in 1839 but not published until thirty years later, the story offers a symbolic reading of Rosas's bloody dictatorship. The story opens in a slaughterhouse in Buenos Aires during the Lenten season. The country is under the total control of a ruler who remains nameless; he is characterized by epithets such as the "most Catholic Restorer" (61) or "the Restorer" (63). The association between his government and the Catholic Church is another daring political statement. "The Restorer," like the Church, has strong control over the country. He has even issued mandatory dress codes. Failure to observe the regulations leads to punishment. The Church has control over the citizenry, and its control goes beyond spiritual matters, as its restrictions on eating meat imply. The Church's implicit acceptance of Rosas's government is another of Echeverría's political statements.

Echeverría boldly accused Argentine religious and political institutions of corruption and of inefficiency in developing the country into a civilized state resembling that of the European systems he had experienced firsthand. The slaughterhouse becomes a symbol of the current state of the Argentine government, bloody and violent in its methods to sacrifice cattle for human consumption. Amid such an inhuman setting, a murder takes place. An innocent bystander, a political opponent of Rosas's government, is trapped and violently tortured because of his refusal to follow the mandated dress code. He also challenges his persecutors by voicing his rage against the repressive government. In the end, the young man dies, tied up as on a cross, a clear symbol of religious connotations.

Romantic characters in Latin American literature are remarkable for their passionate beliefs, which often go against religious or political institutions. They are representative of an emerging Latin American character, like the young protagonist in "The Slaughter House." He is depicted as the ideal Latin American citizen: one committed to a social or political cause and not afraid to suffer a terrible death in defense of his ideals. This type of Romantic character is portrayed, therefore, in didactic fashion, as a model for the young Latin American countries to follow.

The Argentine **gaucho,** in reality the rough cowboy that colonized the immense and wild pampas, is perhaps the most famous Romantic character in Latin American literature. Hailed as a stern pioneer of the last Latin American frontiers, his figure is an outlaw who remains marginal to both the law and civilization. The gaucho was the Romantic character par excellence, often portrayed as a loner who prefers the wilderness of the pampas rather than the systematized urban life of the emerging cities. He, like the conquistadors before him, was a stern and brave character. The pampas, just like the American Wild West, became synonymous with adventure and the exotic, an untamed territory testing the limits of physical prowess and resourcefulness.

Although the gaucho was indisputably a character that attracted literary coverage, it also raised plenty of controversies. Two works stand out for their creation of the gaucho as a powerful figure: an essay, *Facundo: Civilización y barbarie en las pampas argentinas* (1845) and a narrative poem, *The Gaucho Martín Fierro* (Part I, 1872; Part II, 1879), by the Argentines Domingo Faustino Sarmiento (1811–1888) and José Hernández (1834–1886). These works are also significant as initiators of the first ethnic, or culturally bound literary production, known as *literatura gauchesca* (gaucho literature). They would have an impact on numerous Argentine writers, such as the internationally famous short story writer Jorge Luis Borges. Elsewhere in Latin America, the commercial success of the books contributed to the development of other important literary figures.

Sarmiento stands out today as one of the greatest exponents of the Romantic movement in Latin America because of his open attack against Juan Facundo Quiroga, a local strongman of rural origins. His *Civilización y barbarie: Vida de Juan Facundo Quiroga* explores the struggle of Argentina (and, by extension, of most Latin American countries of the time) between the "barbarism" of nature and the "civilization" of the emerging cities. Sarmiento's case study indicates that the struggle is both symbolic and physical. His ultimate goal was the triumph of the city, characterized as the solution for the country's incorporation into idealized Western-style patterns of living.

Sarmiento presents the wild nature of the Argentine pampas as being responsible for the development of the strongman, Facundo, a gaucho who gained regional political control by means of violent tactics characteristic of the gaucho lifestyle. Sarmiento's in-depth study of the sociological background that allowed Facundo to rise to power serves today as a psychological profile of a Latin American dictator.

José Hernández opposed Sarmiento's negative view of the gaucho. His narrative epic poem *Martín Fierro* (*The Gaucho Martín Fierro*) became an immediate best-seller in Argentina. The first edition was sold to gauchos in their *pulperías,* or general market stores, infamous drinking places of the gauchos. By 1878, there were eleven editions of the poem, with more than 50,000 copies in circulation in Argentina and abroad (Carrino 5). Hernández's balanced portrayal of the gaucho documents their tightly structured social customs, in contrast to Sarmiento's idealized concept of the modern city. Hernández also attacked Sarmiento as the president of Argentina (elected in 1868) who initiated bloody campaigns against native groups in his efforts to establish new cities in the wilderness. To further the controversies, gauchos often were forced to participate in these military interventions. In short, Hernández's poem attempts to offer a more balanced view of the life of the gauchos, who also had been victims of terrible political circumstances that shaped their state of mind and customs.

Strongmen living as outlaws as the heads of bandit groups were also common literary characters throughout the nineteenth century. They were evil characters who appeared to be invincible, like the wild nature around them; in other words, they were barbarians. This theme will continue in the literature of the twentieth century. In particular, the so-called *novela de la tierra,* the novel of the land, would explore the presence of strongmen who, by means of their extraordinary physical strength or political power, maintain control of villages or towns.

Although characters of local origin such as the gaucho, representatives of a way of life unique to Latin America, were a common literary motif, other, rather uncommon personages also became part of the rich *costumbrista* tradition of the nineteenth century. Some of these characters were of an earlier time. The writers' sources of documentation were varied, such as chronicles of the Conquest period, or legends, oral stories that preserved in the popular memory events or characters of long ago. The combination of documented sources and oral traditions became known as a *tradición,* a short narrative, which under the label of "tradition," attempted to explain certain characteristics inherent in Latin American countries. The *tradición* was a

popular genre, widely available to an eager readership in newspaper installments or as part of printed collections of short stories.

The most famous writer in the *tradición* style is the Peruvian Ricardo
Palma (1833–1919). His *Tradiciones peruanas* (*Peruvian Traditions*), written between 1872 and 1883, attempted to document the native Peruvian
heritage (Spanish and indigenous) and to present a historically based analysis of the current state of the nation. From an informal perspective of an
ethnographer, the Peruvian oral stories explained local traditions in their
positive and negative aspects. As director of the National Library, Palma had
access to special documents (for instance, he knew well the work of another
Peruvian, the colonial poet and chronicler Inca Garcilaso de la Vega) and to
unpublished, firsthand historical accounts that trace the creation of Peruvian
identity. Another important contribution was his linguistic interest in
Peruvian Spanish and in popular native sayings, or proverbs.

Palma's interest in the documentation of the origin of colorful local sayings is evident in his story "Fray Gómez's Scorpion." Written as an explanation of a popular saying, "It's as valuable as Fray Gómez's scorpion" (85),
the story is Palma's reinterpretation of a legend that traces the miracles
allegedly performed by a local friar. The scorpion is a jewel of incalculable
value that a humble friar, Fray Gómez, produced to provide money for a
God-fearing businessman. This was a miracle, because Fray Gómez (according to a popular legend) had transformed a live scorpion into the jewel. At
the end of the tale, almost as part of the miracle, the businessman, now a
wealthy and respectable citizen, as agreed, returns the jewel to Fray Gómez,
who in turn restores it to its original form.

The psychological element of this *tradición* diverts the reader's interest
from the question of authenticity of a miracle and directs it to the dramatic
revelation of the character. The reader concentrates not on whether the miracle was possible, but on whether the supposedly well-intentioned businessman
would return the jewel to Fray Gómez as he had agreed. This test of one businessman's honesty and religious piety was a social commentary of importance.

This interest in historical documentation led to development of the historical novel. In Latin America, the historical novel of the nineteenth century explored the lives of less frequently documented historical characters,
usually from native indigenous peoples, whose history had often been
ignored or told only partially. A remarkable example of the historical novel
with a positive attitude toward the "Indians" is *Enriquillo: The Cross and the
Sword* (1882), by the Dominican Manuel de Jesús Galván (1834–1910).
The novel reexamines the historical figure of Enriquillo, the *cacique,* a local
chief in the Dominican Republic who stood up against abuses by conquistadors. First, he became a legend among the dying indigenous groups and
later, a symbol of national independence from foreign domination.
Enriquillo, as a symbol of the national values of the Dominican Republic, is
of particular importance because the natives of that island (as on most of the

Caribbean islands) were exterminated or mixed with the Spanish and the Africans by the end of the sixteenth century.

The Romantic movement also created bucolic scenery of great beauty that appeared later in the sentimental novel. This is the case in *María* (1867), by the Colombian novelist Jorge Isaacs (1837–1895). The beautiful and powerful Latin American landscape (richly depicted by both Spanish and native chroniclers) is the backdrop for the tragic love story of two young protagonists. *María* is the epitome of the classic Romantic story: María dies while waiting for the arrival of her beloved, Efraín, who had been sent to London to study medicine. By today's standards, their love story is stereotypical; María is dependent on a male protagonist for her ultimate happiness. After Efraín's departure, she becomes ill and enters into a fatal decline. Despite the story's clichés, *María* is still the basis of films and soap operas.

The novel presents the Colombian landscape as a mirror image of María's and Efraín's love story. It is a perfect literary setting for a sentimental novel: "The mountain was fresh and tremulous under the caresses of the last night-breezes. The herons were leaving their sleeping places, forming in their flight undulating lines silvered by the sun, like a sash abandoned to the caprices of the wind. The flocks of parrots rose from the reedy growths, on their way to the cornfields; and from the heart of the range, the diostedé hailed the day with his sad and monotonous song" (21). Echoes of the medieval *locus amoenus,* that special place created specifically for love, are strongly evident in Isaacs's novel. Nature also predicts the novel's tragic end. Amid natural phenomena, María and Efraín recognize an omen, a black bird's ominous singing, that comes to interrupt their tender encounters. This basic technique adds tension to the story line because the reader (as are the protagonists) is unclear about the potential meaning of this event.

María also has a literary plan that goes beyond the stilted traditional Romantic novel. The novel stands out today for its incorporation of a number of subplots. One is its portrayal of the life of marginal characters, for instance, that of the African slaves Nay and Sinar. That plotline adds meaning to the main story, but it also describes Colombian rural traditions, particularly those of Colombia's black population. It portrays slaves' popular culture in a positive light, although it is seen as marginal to mainstream traditions. Isaacs sets black music and songs within the framework of Efraín and María's tragic love story:

> Now the moon from us is sinking—
> > Row on, row on.
> Of what's my lonely negress thinking?
> > Weep on, weep on.
> Thy sable night now covers me,
> > Saint John, Saint John;
> Thy night is no more black than she,
> > No more, no more.

I see the distant lightnings shine
    On sea, on shore;
No brighter than those eyes of mine—
    Take oar, take oar. (271)

Latin American writers' use of diverse literary themes and characters during the Romantic period reveals their intention to produce the first works of interest to a national readership. It was a remarkable project, including the incorporation of native cultures and the exploration of the untamed and expansive Latin American geography as integral components of the literary text. Throughout the twentieth century, there would be exploration of "native" character types, particularly those that fall outside the mainstream (for example, native indigenous groups, blacks, and the economically marginal, such as peasants). Some of the protagonists would become synonymous with Latin American literature as representatives of national identities and cultures.

BIBLIOGRAPHY

Alvar Núñez Cabeza de Vaca. *His Accounts, His Life, and the Expedition of Pánfilo de Narváez.* Ed. Rolena Adorno & Patrick Charles Pautz. Lincoln: University of Nebraska Press, 1999. Vls. 1–3.

Asturias, Miguel Angel. *Men of Maize.* Trans. Gerald Martin. New York: Delacorte Press, 1975.

Barnet, Miguel. *Biography of a Runaway Slave.* Trans. W. Nick Hill. Willimantic, CT: Curbstone Press, 1994.

Carrino, Frank G. "Introduction." *The Gaucho Martín Fierro.* Trans. Frank G. Carrino, Alberto J. Carlos, and Norman Mangorini. Albany: State University of New York Press, 1974. 1–10.

Carrió de la Vandera, Alfonso. *El Lazarillo.* Trans. Walter D. Kline. Bloomington: Indiana University Press, 1965.

Columbus, Christopher. *Journals and Other Documents on the Life and Voyages of Christopher Columbus.* Ed. and Trans., Samuel Eliot Morison. Norwalk, CT: Easton Press, 1963.

Cortés, Hernán. *5 Letters of Cortés to the Emperor.* Trans. J. Bayard Morris. New York: W.W. Norton, 1962.

De Fuentes, Patricia. *The Conquistadors: First-person Accounts of the Conquest of Mexico.* Norman: University of Oklahoma Press, 1993.

De la Vega, Garcilaso. *Royal Commentaries of the Incas and General History of Peru.* Trans. Harold V. Livermore. Austin: University of Texas Press, 1966.

De las Casas, Bartolomé. *Indian Freedom: The Case of Bartolome de las Casas.* Ed. & trans. Francis Patrick Sullivan. Kansas City, MO: Sheed & Ward, 1995.

Durán, Diego. *Book of the Gods and Rites and the Ancient Calendar.* Trans. Fernando Horcasitas & Doris Heyden. Norman: University of Oklahoma Press, 1971.

———. *The History of the Indies.* Trans. Doris Heyden. Norman: University of Oklahoma Press, 1994.

Echeverría, Esteban. "The Slaughter House." Trans. Angel Flores. *The Oxford Book of Latin American Short Stories*. Ed. Roberto González Echevarría. New York: Oxford University Press, 1997: 59–72.

Erauso de, Catalina. *Lieutenant Nun. Memoir of a Basque Transvestite in the New World*. Trans. Michele Stepto and Gabriel Stepto. Boston: Beacon Press, 1996.

Galván, Manuel de Jesús. *Enriquillo: The Cross and the Sword*. Trans. Robert Graves. Bloomington: Indiana University Press, 1954.

Gómez Avellaneda, Gertrudis. *Sab*. Trans. Nina M. Scott. Austin: University of Texas Press, 1993.

Isaacs, Jorge. *María*. Trans. Rollo Ogden. New York: Harper & Brothers, 1890.

Menchú, Rigoberta. *I, Rigoberta Menchú: An Indian Woman in Guatemala*. London: Verso, 1984.

Núñez Cabeza de Vaca, Alvar. *Castaways. The Narrative of Alvar Núñez Cabeza de Vaca*. Ed. Enrico Pupo-Walker. Trans. Frances M López-Morillas. Berkeley: University of California Press, 1993.

Palma, Ricardo. "Fray Gómez's Scorpion." Trans. Harriet de Onís. *The Orthodox Book of Latin American Short Stories*. Ed. Roberto González Echevarría. New York: Oxford University Press, 1997: 85–89.

Poma de Ayala, Huamán Felipe. *Letter to a King: A Picture-History of the Inca Civilization*. Ed. and trans. Christopher Dilke. London: George Allen & Unwin, 1978.

Rodríguez Freyle, Juan. "A Deal with Juana García." Trans. Margaret Sayers Peden. *The Orthodox Book of Latin American Short Stories*. Ed. Roberto González Echevarría. New York: Oxford University Press, 1997: 50–56.

Sahagún, Bernardino de. *The War of the Conquest: How It Was Waged Here in Mexico*. Trans. Arthur J. O. Anderson and Charles E. Dibble. Salt Lake City: University of Utah Press, 1978.

Sigüenza y Góngora, Carlos. *The Misadventures of Alfonso Ramírez*. Trans. Edwin H. Pleasants. Mexico City: Imprenta Mexicana, 1962.

Villaverde, Cirilo. *Cecilia Valdes or Angel's Hill*. Trans. Sydney G. Gest. New York: Vantage Press, 1962.

SUGGESTED READINGS ON THE DISCOVERY AND CONQUEST PERIODS

Adorno, Rolena. Guamán Poma: *Writing and Resistance in Colonial Peru*. Austin: University of Texas Press, 2000.

Bohlander, Richard E., ed. *World Explorers and Discoverers*. New York: Macmillan, 1992.

Howard, David. *Conquistador in Chains: Cabeza de Vaca and the Indians of the Americas*. Tuscaloosa: University of Alabama, 1997.

Jara, René, and Nicholas Spadaccini. *1492–1992: Re/discovering Colonial Writing*. Minneapolis, MN: Prisma Institute, 1989.

Jones, Mary Ellen. *Christopher Columbus and His Legacy: Opposing Points of View*. San Diego, CA: Greenhaven Press, 1992.

Keen, Benjamin. *Essays in the Intellectual History of Colonial Latin America.* Boulder, CO: Westview Press, 1998.

León-Portilla, Miguel. *Bernardino de Sahagún, First Anthropologist.* Trans. Mauricio J. Mixco. Norman: University of Oklahoma Press, 2002.

Lewis, Bart L. *The Miraculous Lie: Lope de Aguirre and the Search for El Dorado in Latin American Historical Novel.* Landham, MD: Lexington Books, 2003.

Marks, Richard Lee. *Cortés: The Great Adventurer and the Fate of Aztec Mexico.* New York: Knopf, 1993.

Sale, Kirkpatrick. *The Conquest of Paradise: Christopher Columbus and the Columbian Quest.* New York: Knopf, 1990.

Thomas, Hugh. *Conquest: Montezuma, Cortés, and the Fall of Mexico.* New York: Simon & Schuster, 1993.

Williams, Jery, and Robert Earl Lewis. *Early Images of the Americas: Transfer and Invention.* Tucson: University of Arizona Press, 1993.

Wood, Michael. *Conquistadors.* Berkeley: University of California Press, 2000.

Chapter 2
Latin America's Twentieth-Century Literature: Historical Movements and Landscapes

THE MEXICAN REVOLUTION (1910–1920)

Although novels and short stories of the nineteenth century occasionally depicted key historical events, it was only after the Mexican Revolution of 1910 that Latin American fiction became strongly related to a historical movement. The Mexican Revolution, the first such armed conflict with a socialist background in the Western Hemisphere, had a strong impact on Mexican society. It produced profound changes in social structures, including the internal organization of religious institutions such as the Roman Catholic Church. One radical sociopolitical change was the empowerment of peasants, who comprised a sizeable percentage of the national population and who became active agents of a revolutionary movement. To combat their abject poverty, they sought to gain equal rights to own land, a distinctive first step in a struggle that continues today. The possession of land brought a more nearly equal representation of a diverse ethnic population in governmental affairs. This legal victory may be the Mexican Revolution's greatest contribution to Latin America's struggle for social justice.

In its fight against antiquated social structures, the Mexican Revolution caused Mexico to become one of Latin America's emerging, modern countries of the early twentieth century. It also attempted to address Mexico's tumultuous relationship with foreign powers, particularly the United States. Military intervention by the United States in the mid–nineteenth century had exerted a strong economic influence over Mexico, leaving the United States in partial control of Mexican imports and exports.

The history of U.S. aggression against Mexico began in 1845 with the American proposal to purchase what is now California, parts of New Mexico, and land south of Texas, along the Río Grande. Negotiations failed, and in 1846 the U.S. Congress declared war on Mexico. After a war devastating for the Mexicans, including the American occupation of Mexico City in 1847, Mexico ceded a large amount of land to the United States. The Treaty of Guadalupe Hidalgo in 1855 granted the United States roughly 55 percent of Mexican territory, including much of its arable land, today's California, Arizona, New Mexico, and areas of Utah, Nevada, and Colorado. Besides the terrible economic effects of such a loss of national territory, Mexico's legal system was unable to unite the diverse political factions that rose in reaction to this national disaster. The political tensions and the extended rule of Porfirio Díaz, Latin America's first dictator of the twentieth century, led the country into a series of civil wars and eventually after 1910 into what would become the Mexican Revolution.

The inability to bring the country together under a unified federal structure and the frequent military aggression by guerrilla movements led to serious economic consequences that plagued Mexico. By 1861, Mexico's international debt was so enormous that President-elect Benito Juárez announced a two-year cancellation of its payments. One result for Juárez, a lawyer of indigenous ancestry, was internal divisions in his party's attempts to uphold a liberal constitution ratified in 1857. His decision to stop payment of the international debt eventually prompted military aggression by Spain, England, and France.

This new invasion of Mexico created economic havoc and led to the strengthening of the national military forces, as well as the emergence of military heroes. This is the case of General Porfirio Díaz, who in 1862 successfully fought the French troops in Puebla. The battle, known today as Cinco de Mayo, has become synonymous with Mexican nationalism in the face of international aggression. Finally, however, Mexico was forced to accept foreign domination by a French-appointed ruler, Maximilian, who became emperor of Mexico, with Napoleon III's political support, beginning in 1864. Although foreign-imposed rulers, Maximilian and his wife, Carlota, succeeded in bringing European social customs to Mexico. Even today their lives in Chapultepec Palace are the subject of Romantic stories. Maximilian was ousted and executed in 1867.

Of importance to a student of contemporary Latin American history is the development of national military heroes, strongmen who would be instrumental in shaping modern Mexico. President-elect Benito Juárez, for example, a man of Native American background, became the founding father of the new Mexico and created its image as a modern country.

Despite his personal popular support, Juárez's government was openly opposed. General Porfirio Díaz challenged Juárez's fourth term as president, which he won not by a clear majority of votes but by confirmation by the congress. Díaz, also a candidate for the presidency, rejected the Congress's arbitrary appointment of Juárez as president, and he took Mexico City by military force on November 21, 1876. His rule in Mexico's presidential office lasted until 1911. Díaz's extensive period of political domination, an effective dictatorship, is known today as **Porfiriato.** It is the beginning of a series of Latin American dictatorships, characterized by highly effective control over the existing political parties, predominance of military force to ensure public compliance, and dominance over social bodies such as the Church.

The beginning of the Mexican Revolution illustrates Mexico's internal political struggles against reelection of the aging Díaz. One opponent, Francisco Madero, openly challenged the validity of the elections, charging Díaz with electoral fraud. Exiled to San Antonio, Texas, on November 20, 1910, Madero declared a revolution against Díaz and proclaimed himself president of Mexico. Díaz resigned the following year, and Madero was elected president.

It was not, however, a smooth political transition; Madero's government failed to unite diverse revolutionary trends that sought radical social changes. Finally, his own military forces challenged Madero. In 1913, General Victoriano Huerta declared an end to Madero's government, and Madero was assassinated. In the following years, there were bloody civil confrontations between various factions headed by Emiliano Zapata and Francisco (Pancho) Villa. In 1914, seeking an end to the confrontations, Huerta resigned, and Venustiano Carranza took control of the government.

Carranza's rise to power was not, however, by popular election. He gained control of the country by keeping the forces of Zapata and Pancho Villa at bay. Villa had become a local hero, representative of the true spirit of the Mexican Revolution. One example of his military strength was that his guerrilla army survived pursuit by a U.S. army when Villa had boldly attacked American cities on the Mexican-U.S. border. Today Villa's deeds, particularly his attachment to the underdog, are remembered in popular folk stories and songs both in Mexico and among Mexican-American groups in the United States.

The end of the armed Mexican Revolution came after a series of political assassinations. Although a constitution had been approved in 1916, military powers continued to control the government. In 1919, Carranza's forces assassinated Zapata, who had attained increasing popular acceptance because of a more aggressive plan for social reforms. After Carranza's assassination in 1920, Alvaro Obregón, a general, was elected president. After the assassination of Pancho Villa in 1923, Obregón was successful in incorporating the various, disparate revolutionary ideologies into an official government. This revolutionary government, which by 1929 became known as the Institutional Revolutionary Party, would control the office of the president until 2000 and the election of Vicente Fox.

The numerous events involved in the complex political movement known today as the Mexican Revolution were reproduced in detail in Mexican literature. Of particular importance is the historical short novel *El Zarco* (*The Bandit,* 1901) by Ignacio Manuel Altamirano, who traced events following the War of Reform (1858–1860).

Manuel Altamirano (Mexico, 1834–1894)

Altamirano was a full-blooded native Indian who learned Spanish at age fourteen. Despite his rural upbringing, he became a lawyer of note and a well-known political activist in support of Juárez's platforms. He was an eyewitness of and participant in the earliest revolts in 1854, a result of popular dissatisfaction after the Mexican-American War of 1846. His experience as a soldier includes participation in the battle against the French during their occupation of Mexico (1862–1867). These experiences gave him firsthand data about Mexico's unstable political condition. He came into close contact with characters involved in those battles. An intellectual committed to social change, he was the founder and editor of newspapers. In 1889, he served as a Mexican consul in Spain.

El Zarco focuses on the guerrilla events that preceded the Mexican Revolution of 1910. Altamirano's approach is realistic. He also displays a strong interest in documenting Mexican folklore and social customs. *El Zarco,* a novelette, dwells on the chaotic political conditions of Mexico as Juárez sought political and economic solutions. Altamirano's interest in documenting key historical incidents was also part of an in-depth examination of emerging national values and a tribute to President Juárez's social and political reforms. *El Zarco* was published posthumously seven years after Altamirano's death.

El Zarco takes place in 1861 in Yautepec, a small village in the province of Morelos, located in the Southern region known as *tierra caliente,* a fertile area well known for production of citrus fruit. As the story opens, the country is experiencing devastation in the War of Reform; the federal government is unable to defend its citizens against brutal attacks by *bandidos.* These bandits, in heavily armed guerrilla bands, attack defenseless villages, murder travelers, kidnap rich estate owners for ransom, and create political havoc despite efforts by the federal government to organize an effective country.

The novel begins with a description of Yautepec's carefully planned but ineffective defense system against attacks by local bandits encamped nearby. The story's protagonists are women, who were left alone to defend their households. Doña Antonia, a widow, is planning her escape to Mexico City, along with her beautiful daughter, Manuela. Afraid of an impending attack and fearful for her only daughter, now old enough to marry, Doña Antonia wishes to travel to Mexico City to stay with an older brother. The problem is how to make the dangerous trip, because the bandits are known for their bold attacks against travelers, even those accompanied by private defenders. Pilar, Doña Antonia's godchild, keeps the women company, while they await an opportunity to leave.

Within the male-dominated social structure of the time, Manuela ought to have married already. Nicolás, a reputable local blacksmith has courted her, but she disdains him. Manuela is fiercely opposed to maintaining any relationship with an "Indian," an unworthy suitor for a wealthy, white girl such as herself. In one scene, Manuela and Pilar make flower garlands; Manuela refuses to use orange blossoms, the traditional flowers of wedding bouquets. Pilar, who is plaiting her garland with orange blossoms, blushes at the mention of Nicolás, who comes to interrupt the scene.

Nicolás brings bad news. A band of bandits, led by a bloodthirsty young chieftain, known as El Zarco, has taken refuge outside their town. They are reported to be responsible for the massacre of a wealthy English family traveling to Acapulco. The bandits have brutally assassinated them for their possessions, rumored to be a small fortune in jewels. At the news that the bandits are closing in on Yautepec, Doña Antonia decides to proceed immediately with her plans to leave town. Strangely, Manuela opposes the idea, despite the fact that she has earlier expressed her boredom and anger at being subjected to a house arrest of sorts.

The reader knows of the hidden reason behind Manuela's unwillingness to leave town at such short notice. She has secretly met with El Zarco, who meets her romantic expectations; he is a dashing young white man, blue-eyed, like his nickname, Zarco, which means blue. In Manuela's estimation, only he is worthy of her love, not Nicolás, whom she considers of low class despite the young man's booming business and his strong reputation as a pillar of the community.

A naïve young woman, Manuela refuses to believe the reports about Zarco's bloody assaults on unsuspecting victims, even though he has given her jewelry as keepsakes, which she subsequently hides. Some of the pieces, she notices, are covered with dried blood. Nonetheless, she secretly wears the jewelry and dreams about the day she will escape with Zarco to become his wife.

Zarco keeps his promise to take Manuela to his hideout. On the first day, Manuela faces the grim reality of a makeshift guerrilla camp. Instead of the glamorous life she has dreamed of as Zarco's wife, she finds herself surrounded by heartless ruffians. They constantly remind her of her dependency on Zarco for survival. She also realizes that Zarco will not keep his promise to marry her or to be faithful. In the camp, she also witnesses the brutal torture of a Frenchman, who has been kidnapped for his money. Manuela feels desolate and repentant but sees no way to escape from her new life of crime.

In the meantime, Doña Antonia is seeking help from the authorities in finding her daughter. Her claims find no sympathy from the commander of the federal forces camped close to Yautepec. When the commander refuses to act, Nicolás confronts him. This questioning of his authority by a humble, local civilian leads him to imprison Nicolás. The outraged town opposes this unfair decision, particularly because it is the bandits, not Nicolás, who should be imprisoned. Pilar visits the prison to protest the injustice, and Nicolás is freed. After his release, he becomes interested in Pilar.

Nicolás does not change his mind about freeing Manuela, however. A rescue party sets out to find her, made up of a private guerrilla army organized by a local man whose family had been killed by bandits. In the end, they catch Zarco and his men, who were preparing to ambush Pilar and Nicolás's wedding party, as well as Manuela. Zarco is hanged as Manuela watches. Although she has come to hate her life as the mistress of a bandit, she dies unrepentant, resentful of Pilar's luck in marrying Nicolás. At the sight of Zarco's horrific death, Manuela falls dead, blood running from her mouth.

El Zarco is an important literary and political text. Altamirano's characters reflect the Mexican social classes of the time. He was writing from a populist perspective, a man of humble ethnic origins who, like his protagonist Nicolás, worked hard and overcame racial barriers to become a political activist and a community leader. This strong representation of social change gives Altamirano's novel a strong pedagogical character.

As a politician, Altamirano promoted literacy programs for the lower classes, peasants, and indigenous populations. Some, like him, were marginalized from mainstream Mexican society. It is possible that some of Nicolás's characteristics may be autobiographical. This positive portrayal of a marginalized character was innovative because most of the literature of the nineteenth century either presented natives in a negative light or simply never presented them at all.

El Zarco was intended as a political explanation of the events that led to the War of Reform. It is Altamirano's testimony against the brutal guerrilla tactics of warfare that he had experienced firsthand as a soldier. His novel also presents his proposed methods for Mexico's social and economic emergence as a Latin American power of the early twentieth century.

His literary models were European, particularly his preference for the Romantic trend of historical novels. *El Zarco,* for instance, carefully depicts historic moments that explain impending changes in Mexican social and national values. With his focus on the Mexican civil wars, Altamirano attempted to capture the profound changes in traditional social values to promote incorporation of marginalized groups as effective agents of change. This is the case of the collection of inhabitants of Tepeyac, who, at the end of the novel, oppose the weak federal forces and aid in the capture of the feared bandit Zarco.

Also within the Romantic tradition is Altamirano's successful incorporation of Mexican folklore as worthy literary material. This was a departure from his predecessors, who clung to classical literary models. Altamirano's protagonists are unusual for his time because they present popular characters from the lower classes, including the bloodthirsty bandits. Despite his role as an evil antagonist, Zarco has the most interesting descriptions: "The horseman was dressed after the fashion of the *plateados,* a style later adopted by the *charros,* or cattlemen. His jacket of dark cloth was worked with silver and his trousers, slit at the seam, were fastened with a double row of silver buttons linked with chains of the same metal. His dark felt sombrero with wide, upturned brim, had a silver chinstrap extending across the crown, studded with gold stars. Round the flattened crown itself was a double band of silver, and on each side hung two silver tassels" (42–43). The reader today recognizes the *charro,* or Mexican cowboy, in this description.

Altamirano's political position included incorporation of lower social classes into discussions of the political destiny. It can also be argued that because Altamirano's intended readers were peasants, he included characters that would appeal to that growing social group. The novel's rich depictions of Mexican customs of the *tierra caliente* region of the province of Morelos have two purposes. First, they promote Mexican culture and positive national values. The author may have addressed folklore and local color to peasant groups, many of whom recently had learned to read and write in mass national campaigns against illiteracy. Second, the novel functions as a tribute to the countless protagonists who remain nameless in the official history of their fight against opponents of prerevolutionary social reforms.

The Mexican Revolution became an important subject in Mexican literature. It led to a sub-genre known as the literature of the Mexican Revolution. This production also had strong influence throughout Latin America. It brought attention to new literary trends and a renewed interest in sociocultural documentation of Latin American culture. The literature of the Mexican Revolution also documented the complex events that were taking place in Mexico. Perhaps for the first time, international readers met Mexican characters, in particular the peasants and native groups representative of an emerging Mexican national identity. They also had a closer glimpse of events in the complicated movements of the Mexican Revolution.

Mariano Azuela (Mexico, 1873–1952)

Azuela is considered the initiator of the historical genre known as the literature of the Mexican Revolution. Like Altamirano, Azuela wrote about incidents that he had witnessed. He had been Francisco (Pancho) Villa's army surgeon in guerrilla warfare from 1910 to 1920. He was also a committed activist; his writings vividly depict the revolution as a struggle against an unjust status quo. In 1941, he received a prestigious national award for his broad literary production. He was buried with other heroes of the revolution in an official ceremony in Mexico City. Azuela's literary works with strong historical content are well known outside Mexico and are often read as data complementary to the history of the Mexican Revolution.

Azuela's novels, *Los de abajo* (*The Underdogs*, 1916) and *Las moscas* (*The Flies*, 1918) focus on particular incidents of the many battles of the Mexican Revolution. As a political movement, the Mexican Revolution was a complex and lengthy process with diverse facets and personalities. Azuela's keen eye promoted a direct, methodical approach to the recording of historical events and faithful depiction of local characters in a novel technique associated with **realism.** In an emerging literary trend, Latin American realist writers adopted a basic intention: a verifiable reproduction of notable events or of characters of importance in the development of emerging nations. The main intention of all these writers was political; the literary work became an opportunity to explore and perhaps suggest solutions to pressing national problems.

Azuela's simple and direct literary style supports his attempts to offer a trustworthy documentation of historical events and of characters associated with the revolutionary movement. Azuela's observations of the slow progress of the revolutionary cause moved him also to become a reporter. Although in both media Azuela openly expressed his positive view of the revolution, he was not afraid to criticize the mismanagement of revolutionary forces, particularly the splitting up of the leadership into opposing groups controlled by strongmen.

Azuela continued the nineteenth-century trend of *costumbrismo*. His careful characterization of local personages and his depiction of revolutionary heroes and their opponents reproduce everyday customs and incidents of historical relevance. His *costumbrismo* is, however, radically different from that of his literary predecessors. Azuela's literature exhibits a strong political aim to explore the Mexican revolution as a historic occurrence of worldwide importance. He also recognized the literary potential of the events and characters associated with the Mexican revolution. He intended his literature to become known beyond Mexico, especially in the United States, where he lived in Texas.

Azuela's novel *The Underdogs* became internationally known shortly after its publication, and it has become perhaps the most analyzed novel of the Mexican Revolution. Azuela had inside political knowledge of the internal struggles of the government of President Francisco Madero. During Madero's administration, Azuela had served in a rural political post. After Madero's assassination in 1914 and Victoriano Carranza's seizure of the government, Azuela took the side of Pancho Villa's forces. Under the Villa leadership, Azuela served as a doctor and political consultant. The rich data that Azuela carefully recorded during this period, mainly from 1913 to 1915, became the historical background of *The Underdogs*. The novel was first published as a series of articles by the newspaper *El Paso del Norte*, in El Paso, Texas.

The Underdogs can be viewed as representative of the political saga that produced modern Mexico. The Mexican Revolution was a monumental movement of considerable upheavals that created a chaotic social panorama. As a military movement of national proportions, the Mexican Revolution involved a considerable number of unlikely heroes, including peasants, indigenous peoples, and women. Their suffering and successes found voice in Azuela's *The Underdogs*.

The narrative focus of *The Underdogs* is on Demetrio Macías. He is a humble peasant who had openly opposed Don Mónico, the oppressive local landowner. Unfair rural practices, supported by laws that prohibited peasants' owning property, provoked a wave of attacks against plantations. Like countless other peasants, Demetrio worked in the fields. He had no previous military training, but he eventually became a minor guerrilla leader. Through a carefully crafted and well-documented account, the reader witnesses Demetrio's painful farewell to his wife and his child. As the novel opens, he is a fugitive from justice who in the secrecy of the dawn comes to visit his wife and warn her to abandon their home. He has been hiding from the authorities and from his landowner because of his support of the local revolutionaries. As a precaution, he asks his wife to move away with their child. He has decided to leave town and join the revolutionary forces.

Demetrio's departure and separation from his wife early in their marriage is representative of the internal social divisions that the Revolution created. Unlike other narratives, such as *The Flies*, Azuela's *The Underdogs* focuses on the suffering of a humble rural family whose only ambition is a better future for their firstborn infant son. They are the underdogs of this revolutionary saga and pay a high price for their participation in events that will change the national social structure. Yet Demetrio has no choice but to follow his innate desire to seek social justice, the ideological motto of the Mexican Revolution.

Demetrio Macías experiences the revolution both in the physical damage that guerrilla warfare creates in the country and in the psychological effects on the civil population. As he flees his burning home, Demetrio's tortuous future is reflected in the rocky road ahead of him: "When he reached the summit, the sun was bathing the altiplano in a lake of gold. Protruding from the sides of the ravine were huge slabs of rock, outcroppings ridged like fantastic African heads; pitahayas like the arthritic fingers of a colossus, trees jutting down toward the depths of the abyss" (8). The abyss that symbolizes the insurmountable task at hand for Demetrio, a mere peasant, ignorant of the political ideology behind the Revolution, also foreshadows his ill-fated end.

Like many guerrilla fighters, Demetrio Macías eventually becomes a successful revolutionary leader with a substantial number of men under his direction, but he lacks full understanding of revolutionary ideology. His rise to military power is significant, but he is one of many heroes whose contributions will not be recorded fully, unlike those of official revolutionary leaders such as Pancho Villa and Emiliano Zapata. Nevertheless, these underdog protagonists, not the legendary revolutionary leaders, shaped the Revolution's path, often not in straightforward or logical directions.

The Underdogs is, however, a novel of characters, not just a historical rendition of an episode of the Mexican Revolution's lengthy, convoluted battles. The fact that Demetrio Macías is a fictional character indicates Azuela's intention to make his novel a study of human behavior and not a defense of or an attack on revolutionary ideology. Like Altamirano before him, Azuela attempted to incorporate a large constituency of Mexican society into a series of interdependent episodes. The protagonists are common people, mainly peasants; collectively they represent diverse ethnic, social, and economic elements of Mexican society at the time. They are also the unsung heroes and casualties of war.

The characters in *The Underdogs* are unusual because of their strong connection to the beliefs and ways of life of the peasantry. Two types of characters are of particular importance in their depiction of regional culture: the peasants-turned-guerrilla fighters and the women who live in their camps. The fighters within the group are diverse and colorful in their social and ethnic composition. For instance, Venancio, a barber by trade, becomes a makeshift "doctor" because of his hands-on knowledge of removing infected teeth. Unlike most of the men, Venancio can read and write, and he has some literary knowledge, a fact that makes him Demetrio Macías's advisor.

Other colorful characters, such as La Codorniz, "the Quail," show how the popular knowledge inherent in the lower classes comes to play an important role on the battlefield. This is the case when La Codorniz impersonates a priest during an interrogation session of Luis Cervantes, a young captive suspected of being a spy for the federalist forces. The plan, although simple, works. Under threat of execution, Cervantes agrees to undergo confession with the man he believes to be a priest. His "confession" clears Cervantes of any ill intentions against Demetrio's men, and, consequently, he is accepted as a guerrilla fighter. This anecdote is more than a comic literary device. Stories such as this one are present in most Latin American rural societies. The identity of the deceived character changes according to the historical periods. He may be a Spanish conquistador, and the trickster, an Indian. Or a humble peasant may fool an abusive landowner or a greedy American businessman. The message is the same: popular ingenuity confronts organized attempts to corrupt ancient ways of living. Azuela's main contribution to this controversy is the fact that traditional ways may not be necessarily the best option for an emerging modern Mexico.

Another group of Azuela's colorful characters is his collection of women who follow the revolutionary armies, assisting them in domestic chores. The women stand out in an otherwise male-dominated setting. They also represent ancient traditions, mainly as *curanderas,* or healers using herbs, potions, and religious practices. As *curanderas,* such women were often in charge of the revolutionaries' health, especially the care of the wounded. Their presence was necessary because few doctors joined the revolutionary armies, but Azuela held a negative view of the *curanderas'* practice. For example, the following passage describes a *curandera* attempting to heal a serious firearm wound to Demetrio Macías's stomach. Remigia has just killed a pigeon. " 'In the name of Jesus, Mary, and Joseph!' said Remigia, crossing herself. Then, swiftly, she applied the two warm, blood-spurting halves of the pigeon to Demetrio's abdomen. 'Now you're going to feel much better' " (26). Such common practices, Azuela stresses throughout his novel, are indicative of the country's backwardness.

Azuela's documentation of the complex events of the Mexican Revolution (either from the literary or the historical perspective) became a detailed project. His literary production is unusual because the numerous characters he includes represent wide sectors of Mexican society. This is the case in *The Flies,* a short novella that presents stories of various characters such as Pancho Villa and Venustiano Carranza, two revolutionary leaders who were fighting for control of the political leadership of the Mexican Revolution. Neither man appears in the story; instead, other characters represent their political platforms. It is through their anecdotes that the reader is exposed to the ideological complexities behind the various political trends that Villa and Carranza represented. These characters, like Villa and Carranza, represented diverse social groups. Villa's followers, like their legendary leader, belonged to humble social classes, whereas Carranza's followers were mainly rich landowners clinging to their economic power as a source of political control. As the actions of the characters imply, the Villa-Carranza struggle went beyond differences in political views. They also portrayed a battle between good and evil.

The novel's plot presents in a simple literary form the historical characters involved in the fight for political power. Characters in *The Flies* can be divided into two main groups: the wealthy proprietors, who oppose the revolution for fear of losing wealth and prestige. The second group, more numerous and vociferous, comprises characters from the lower classes. Unlike *The Underdogs, The Flies* reveals to the reader upper-class characters, who are presented as parasites and opportunists. These characters are compared with flies, clinging together in an attempt to survive the political and social changes that would destroy their privileged way of life.

The story opens with Carranza's siege of Querétaro, a town north of Mexico City, in his attempt to force President Victoriano Huerta out of power. Querétaro is in shambles, and people desperately attempt to escape the city before the arrival of Carranza's forces. Their only means of escape is by train, and thousands attempt to gain access to a limited number of cars. Among these is an upper-class family: Marta, her two daughters, and a son. Although penniless, they are proficient at the game of social pretension. Through a carefully crafted series of lies, they gain access to a medical car by pretending to have permission from one of the generals in charge. This is the beginning of a series of deceits. They are successful in making the trip safely and without payment. Their most clever strategy keeps the son, Rubén, a young man of military age, out of the national army and from serving in the various revolutionary factions.

As the train heads north, the women become acquainted with key characters, such as General Malacara ("Badface"), whose satirical name suggests the tragic condition of a country consumed in internal military confrontations. At the novella's end, the destitute upper-class family finds a way to survive, as do the military forces, frequently reconstituted in games of political power.

Azuela wrote within the trend of realism, often depicting scenes with great detail and care in faithful reproduction of events he had witnessed. Writing in the style of *costumbrismo,* Azuela reproduces Mexican culture and native characters as he had experienced them in his military expeditions. His literary production is remarkable for its political analysis of the Mexican Revolution and for its usefulness in understanding the emerging twentieth-century Mexican nation. His characters are thus representative of historical protagonists, especially of the peasants who had an important role in the Mexican Revolution. Azuela's fiction documents social and economic changes, including the landowners' loss of political power by the reduction of their property and by the new representation of peasants in local, regional, and national governing bodies. Azuela also wrote about these subjects in many articles for Mexican and U.S. newspapers.

Azuela's style is simple and devoid of complex literary artifice. He was, above all, an activist with obvious ideological sympathy for certain leaders behind the Mexican Revolution. Azuela's point of view of the revolutionary movement is generally positive, in spite of the chaos that it caused. As the Mexican revolution's most famous chronicler, Azuela's well-researched literary works depict the revolution as a historic movement in the shaping of modern Mexico, facing the challenges of the twentieth century.

CRIOLLISMO: THE CALL OF THE LAND

The impact of the Mexican Revolution in Latin America went beyond its strong call for economic justice for the lower classes. The political activism of intellectuals, particularly of writers who associated themselves with social projects, was evidence of an increasing interest in using literature as a vehicle for achieving change. Their highly nationalist spirit led to exploration of national values and identity, as reflected in regional customs.

Writers' quests for traits representative of a national identity took two distinctive directions. First, the process involved a reexamination of the national precolonial and colonial histories, with careful examination of characters associated with key national movements. Such characters, portrayed as native to a specific region, were viewed as a sort of psychological profile, a reflection of broad national values. Second, the characters' setting, the background in which they had developed, became an important component in understanding their behavior and motivation. The expansive Latin American landscape therefore took on an important role in literature.

The literary trend known as **criollismo** explores native traits associated with characters within specific Latin American geographic boundaries. Derived from the widely used term *criollo,* criollismo intended to display native characters as symbols of human ingenuity in overcoming the many natural obstacles in the Latin American landscape. The relationship between characters and nature was the focus of the criollismo movement. In the past, this relationship had often been characterized in negative terms because of the powerful, overwhelming natural elements present in Latin American nature.

Criollista writers actively sought to explore subject matter and characters associated with Latin American local customs or traditions. They were inspired by the realist trend to provide a trustworthy documentation of the background elements that determined their characters' behavior. They were not, however, mere chroniclers of Latin American customs, as their nineteenth-century predecessors had been. Their ideological purpose went beyond the reproduction of folklore in that they intended to transform motifs of Latin American reality into literary symbols and to produce a psychological study of representative Latin American characters.

Criollismo was an extremely popular literary movement. Latin American fiction writers exhibited diverse styles and varying degrees of social and political commitment. They all had in common, however, a deeply felt interest in documenting native elements, which was **autochthonous** of life in their respective countries. The criollista writer was also a committed social activist, who often revealed abuses of the working class by powerful landowners in remote areas of the exuberant Latin American landscape.

The following are three remarkable characteristics observed in criollista writers. One, the characters and their efforts to survive in the overwhelming Latin American nature are central elements of the action line. This struggle, both physical and mental, was the central concern of Uruguayan short story writer Horacio Quiroga, who set his protagonists into direct confrontation with natural forces, including wild animals of the South American jungles.

Two, the protagonist's clashes with the uncontrollable forces of nature, often labeled in terms of **civilization versus barbarism,** serve two purposes. They reflect the physical struggle to convert natural forces into progress by building cities in former wild territories, and they show that out of this struggle certain historical characters arose, such as the **gaucho,** the cowboy of the plains of the Southern Cone countries. His harsh life was a central concern of novelist and short story writer Ricardo Güiraldes.

Three, within the social themes related to the struggle of civilization versus barbarism, the criollista writer fully explores the uncontrolled exploitation of nature. Nature fights back, appearing brutal and often defeating man's projects for development. This trend, known as the **narrative of the land,** in which the landscape takes on central importance in the plotline, is a focus in the work of Venezuelan short story writer and novelist Rómulo Gallegos.

Horacio Quiroga (Uruguay, 1878–1937)

One of the best representatives of the criollismo trend, Horacio Quiroga is also a remarkable literary figure for his innovations in the Latin American short story of the early twentieth century. He was often cited as a literary influence on future Latin American writers such as the Argentines Jorge Luis Borges and Julio Cortázar. They would, in turn, make significant contributions to this genre, now internationally famous.

It is often said that Quiroga introduced into Latin American literature the short stories of Edgar Allan Poe. The influence of the American short story writer is visible in his well-constructed stories as well as in his literary motifs. Poe's exploration of bizarre human behaviors would become a central element of Quiroga's stories; its influence would become apparent in other remarkable Latin American writers as well.

Born in Salto in the northwestern area of Uruguay to an Argentine diplomat father and his wife, Quiroga led a life marked by tragic deaths. Shortly after his birth, his father accidentally shot himself during a hunting trip. Later, his grandfather, committed suicide following a heart attack. As a young man, Quiroga accidentally killed a good friend while examining a gun.

Death is a central concern in Quiroga's short stories. This interest went beyond autobiographical connections. It stemmed from his experiences living in extremely rural, wild areas of Uruguay and Argentina. In Salto, he learned about the difficult life of the **gaucho,** the cowboys of Uruguay and neighboring Argentina who tended the huge cattle industry of these countries. Despite his education in the large cities of Montevideo (Uruguay), Córdoba, and Buenos Aires (Argentina), Quiroga chose to spend extended periods of time in rural regions of varying degrees of wildness.

In addition to his interest in the wilderness, Quiroga was a learned intellectual. In 1900, he made a trip to Paris, where he first encountered photography. Upon his return to Uruguay, he brought with him the turn-of-the-century French literature of the so-called *poetas malditos.* He became an enthusiast of this foreign literary influence, which was highly symbolic and abstract.

His comfortable life in the cosmopolitan city of Buenos Aires, where he was working as a Spanish teacher, suddenly came to an end. In 1903, Quiroga traveled to Misiones in the heart of the Argentine tropical forest, which was the center of the remaining indigenous communities. On this trip, he accompanied the famous short story writer Leopoldo Lugones, who was documenting the indigenous culture of the Guaraní. Quiroga came along as the expedition's photographer.

Their findings about the brutal conditions of life in the Argentine landscape stirred the imagination of the young writer. After that trip, Quiroga attempted to run a family cotton plantation in the Province of Chaco, on the northeastern Argentine region. An area with a strong indigenous Quechua culture, it was also the last Argentine frontier. It attracted thousands of European and Asian immigrants to work in the booming logging and cattle industries. Quiroga failed in his efforts to sustain his cotton plantation, another important source of income in this remote area, but during this period he witnessed the constant abuse of the working class, particularly the indigenous populations, by powerful, unscrupulous landowners.

Quiroga did not give up his idea of living in the wilderness. He returned to Misiones with his wife, who killed herself in an apparent reaction to the primitive living conditions of the area. After a period as a bureaucrat for the Uruguayan consulate in Argentina, he returned to Misiones with his second wife. She abandoned Quiroga for a more conventional life in Buenos Aires. Diagnosed with cancer, Quiroga poisoned himself in a hospital in Buenos Aires.

Quiroga's stories are classic examples of the criollista interest in exploration of the struggle of man against nature. He went beyond mere reproduction of the dangers of life in the South American jungles. His characters' plights are symbolic of internal struggles, often prompted by mental instability. Bizarre behaviors as well as death are Quiroga's favorite literary themes. They are often linked to surprising turns of events and unexpected endings that result in exceptional stories.

Misiones, amid the wilderness of the Argentine tropical jungles, was central to a booming economy throughout the early part of the twentieth century. The area attracted many immigrants from the Southern Cone countries, as well as foreigners from diverse cultural backgrounds. They are the "exiles" in Quiroga's *The Exiles and Other Stories* (1926), characters who, as described by an omniscient narrator, have peculiar behavioral reactions to their experiences living in a wild territory: "Like every frontier region, the province of Misiones—lying between Brazil to the east and Paraguay to the west—is rich in characters who are very picturesque. And the ones who've been born with spin on them, like billiard balls, tend to do remarkably so. They usually hit the cushions and take off in the most unexpected directions" (102).

In the short story "Beasts in Collusion," as one might expect from such a vague title, the characters involved are not animals, at least not in the traditional sense of the word. This is the story of Langhi, a foreigner who arrives at a sawmill located in the heart of the Brazilian Matto Grosso. He comes as a government inspector, there mainly to certify that the mill is recording the right amount of log production for tax purposes. He soon discovers that field workers are abused, paid low wages and often cheated in the weighing of the logs collected. To his surprise, Langhi also learns that previous inspectors knew about this practice and remained silent after receiving bribes from the powerful overseers.

Langhi ignores the warnings of an overseer, Señor Alves, with a criminal reputation and strong control over logging workers. Alves is particularly cruel to Guaycurú, a local native who is among the most productive of the log cutters. Guaycurú, unlike other workers, is mild tempered, a quiet individual who just does his work. When Langhi discovers that Alves had been cheating Guaycurú from profits, he openly accuses the overseer of illegal paying practices.

In such a cruel, barbaric world, Langhi's accusations have no effect. Alves resents the challenge to his authority, so he concocts a brutal revenge. Under the cover of the nearby jungle, he captures both Langhi and Guaycurú and subjects them to terrible tortures. In the end, he blows up Langhi's body and lets Guaycurú die tied to a mound of venomous ants.

It appears that Alves's crimes will go unpunished, that no man in the camp will concern himself with the men's terrible destinies, particularly that of the native's. Suddenly, a puma attacks Alves, killing him. This is an interesting turn of events because the puma, a domesticated pet that belonged to Guaycurú, had never displayed any wild behavior. The meaning of the ambiguous title is now apparent: Alves, a terrible beast, is finally subjugated by a stronger force, and the puma is acting on higher and purer instincts than Alves.

Quiroga's "Beasts in Collusion" is outstanding for its reenactment of the legendary struggle between human beings and nature, reflecting how life in the wild can cause some individuals to become beasts. Ultimately, a wild animal avenges the deaths of Langhi and Guaycurú. The committed friendship between the puma and Guaycurú is revealed in the beast's killing of the more brutal assassin. Nature has its own system of justice. The story uses the setting of Matto Grosso to explore mankind's psychological makeup.

Quiroga explores the human psyche in other macabre stories as well, such as *Cuentos de amor, de locura y de muerte* (*The Decapitated Chicken and Other Stories*, 1917), in which characters face incredible challenges, usually the result of uncontrollable natural forces in their surroundings. His special contribution to Latin American and international literatures is the way in which these characters, although purely South American, acquire a universality as their efforts to control nature become symbolic of a higher, personal struggle.

Ricardo Güiraldes (Argentina, 1886–1927)

Known as Argentina's premier criollista writer, Ricardo Güiraldes made the gaucho a literary character of importance with his novel *Don Segundo*

Sombra (1926; *Shadows in the Pampas,* 1935). Like Quiroga's, Güiraldes's main literary contribution was the development of local, rural characters that reflect the Argentine soul. Güiraldes intended also to create a character of international appeal. Thus, although the gaucho's life is restricted to the environment of the Argentine plains, it became a source of vicarious experiences for any reader who might understand these teachings as a lesson in human behavior.

Born into a wealthy family, he spent the first years of his childhood in France. Upon their return to Argentina, his family spent time in Buenos Aires, the cosmopolitan capital city, as well as on a plantation in the province, where young Güiraldes came into contact with colorful gauchos and life on the pampas. Like other cosmopolitan Latin American writers, Güiraldes's writing expressed a conflict between his knowledge of European culture and his attraction to the rural gaucho.

He produced his first literary work in 1915, although he had earlier associated himself with flourishing literary journals. Among his intellectual associates was the short story writer Horacio Quiroga, with whom Güiraldes had a strong personal and professional relationship. He published a collection of poetry (1915) and two books of short stories (1917) to lukewarm reception. His reputation arose from his work in literary journals. In 1924, along with distinguished poet and short story writer Jorge Luis Borges, he founded *Proa,* a literary publication with international distribution.

Güiraldes traveled extensively through Europe, where he was exposed to innovations of the **vanguard,** an experimental movement. More important, he was a witness to the radical changes in the large European cities that were experiencing the effects of industrialism. He also visited India, Egypt, Japan, and China and displayed an interest in Eastern religions. The influence of these experiences is evident in *El sendero* (*The Path*), a collection of mystical poems published in 1922.

Güiraldes developed a strong literary reputation after the publication of *Don Segundo Sombra* (1927). With this novel he attempted to synthesize the characteristics inherent in the gaucho, and he provided an accurate depiction of the gaucho's adaptation to the rural life of the Argentine pampas. Much like the cowboy of the American West, the gaucho was a central figure in the economic development of the frontier country. Recalling experiences in European cities, Güiraldes was mindful that gaucho life was fast disappearing as technology took over the mighty pampas. From memory he began to write and successfully reproduce sketches of gauchos and the many tasks they performed on the pampas. Through these portraits, and particularly through that of his protagonist Segundo Sombra, the reader learns about local folklore and customs associated with the gauchos. His protagonist's name, "Shadow," appears to be a symbol of the character's present condition; like the remaining gauchos, he is only a memory of a lifestyle in decline.

Don Segundo Sombra offered its readers a multifaceted view of the gauchos' tasks. Güiraldes offered long passages describing the well-known Argentine cattle industry. Some scenes, such as descriptions of the taming of wild horses and the killing of cattle, are among the most colorful renditions of the tasks of these South American cowboys: "Then, taking the blade and making a circle around the joints, he broke the four feet at the hock joints. Between the tendon and the shin he cut a small hole through which he threaded a leather strap, and standing close to a tree, he threw the other end over a branch. I pulled on the strap until the animal was suspended in the air" (*Don Segundo Sombra* 51). Other passages are excellent examples of the crudeness of this rural life, such as depictions of knife fights. This was a realistic illustration of a male-dominated society in which brutal behavior ruled.

Güiraldes's gauchos are well-rounded characters. Critics often praise his ability to offer a complete picture of the characteristics that made them unique. For example, of particular interest to linguists is Güiraldes's careful reproduction of the gaucho language, including the use of colorful idiomatic expressions.

Although Güiraldes was not the first Argentine writer to turn the gaucho into a literary character, his depiction of this gaucho lifestyle is often commended for its successful combining of realism and symbol. Güiraldes was a gifted realist writer who displayed a strong inclination to offer a close-up of his subject matter, both in development of characters and in the depiction of their environment. The gauchos are a central literary component, but they always appear directly within the geographic context of the pampas.

The pampas, a word of Quechua origin meaning "a plain without trees," are an extensive area of fertile land extending between the provinces of Buenos Aires and La Pampa and including parts of the Provinces of Córdoba and Santa Fe. Historically a rural area, the pampas were an important agricultural center for the production of grains, and home to the largest cattle industry in South America. It had also been the border zone between emerging cities like Buenos Aires and the territories formerly controlled by native groups. At the time of the publication of *Don Segundo Sombra,* the pampas were undergoing radical change, leading to industrialization of the area.

Gauchos, among the first adventurers into this wild territory, had gained the reputation of outlaws. Previous literary works had characterized them as free spirits. Güiraldes preferred to build a character worthy of literary interest; his gauchos illustrate old traditions and a way of life that was yielding to modern Argentine values.

Güiraldes's story "The Gauchos' Hearth," published in 1915 in *Cuentos de muerte y sangre* (*Tales of Death and Blood*), is written from the perspective of a lost past, a nostalgia for a dated lifestyle. The story's narrator is witness to a fairly traditional gaucho scene in a pulpería, or country store and meeting place, known mainly for drinking fights. This scene is different, however. As the story opens, it is late at night, and some gauchos are playing cards as others attempt to stay awake. It is a rare domestic scene beside a hearth that keeps these otherwise rough men warm.

One of them is Don Segundo Sombra, well known as a storyteller. Tonight he tells a ghost story: an Englishman, who is a hunter and salesperson on a business trip, hears of a legend about a remote path where the ghost of a man would come to pick up pieces of meat and money that his aging mother left for him on a regular basis. Curious and not a believer in ghosts, the Englishman decided to investigate. He waylaid the ghost, but found that he was not a spirit at all, only a young man who, after struggling with the Englishman, explained the reasons for his disguise. Some time before, he had killed in a fight with the strongman of the area. Fearing for his life, he had decided to hide the corpse and to claim that he had killed himself, that his soul, damned for his suicide, needed to claim meat and money. Since belief in ghosts was a trait of the gaucho, "an integral part of his character" (74), the plan worked. He had survived in the wilderness, supplementing his diet with the meat and saving the money to escape from the scene of his crime. Feeling sorry for the young man's plight, the Englishman left him alone, saying nothing to anyone about the ghost's secret.

This is not, however, the end of the story. Many years later, now an old man, the Englishman returns to the remote area. He is surprised to hear that although the ghost had not been seen, the meat, but not the money, continues to be taken away. Curious about this new arrangement, he decides to investigate and discovers that it is not a ghost, but a family of raccoons that consume the meat.

Aside from Güiraldes's humorous intention, this story is unusual for its nostalgic view of gaucho life. Don Segundo Sombra, like the Englishman at the end of the story, remembers traditional gaucho customs. The young gaucho who had allegedly turned into a ghost may symbolize the collapse of gaucho culture and ways of life. The tradition has not died, Güiraldes seems to say, but remains alive by means of legends such as Don Segundo Sombra's ghost story, as well as by the author's own story of the gaucho as a character of national and international literary value.

Rómulo Gallegos (Venezuela, 1884–1969)

Short story writer and novelist Rómulo Gallegos is recognized as Latin America's most renowned cultivator of criollismo. His writings support his strong political commitment to advance his native Venezuela into a more balanced society, particularly with regard to racial justice and an improved economy. Like other Latin American writers before him, Gallegos's strong call for social equality took him into public office. For his activism, he was forced into voluntary exile; as a result, he gained international exposure.

Born in Caracas into a working-class family, Gallegos embraced education as a way to face the rampant corruption in a government under the control of a military dictatorship. From 1902 through 1905, he was a law student, but he seemed more interested in pursuing a literary career. At the Universidad Central de Caracas, he published articles on literature and on politics in student newspapers. He also came into contact with student political groups and initiated a long career in politics that would culminate with his election as president of Venezuela in 1947.

Gallegos embarked on an active social campaign in the articles he wrote for literary journals, some of which he had helped to found. This was the beginning of his open confrontations with the military government, which often forced closure of such publications. His primary themes, mainly calls for social justice and equal rights for minority racial groups, the Native American communities, and the Venezuelan African diaspora, would be central in his future writings. Also during this period, Gallegos started a teaching career at the secondary level.

His first novel, *El último solar* (*The Last Ranch*), published in 1920, generated much controversy in Venezuela for its open portrayal of the vast government corruption that existed in the early twentieth century. The novel addresses issues clearly observed in the nation's government, under the tight control of the dictatorship of Juan Vicente Gómez. Gallegos was a tireless opponent of Gómez, whose lack of a progressive government and preference for an aging and unjust social system Gallegos criticized as the reason for the rampant poverty in Venezuela, a country wealthy in natural resources.

Gallegos's masterpiece, *Doña Barbara*, became an immediate success after its publication in 1929. The story focuses on a strong-willed woman, Doña Bárbara, who by means of brutal practices rises from humble origins to become a feared landowner in a remote area of the Venezuelan plains. Her powerful handling of her "rancho," the extensive plantation under her total control, can be viewed as representing Gómez's equally strong domination of Venezuela. Indeed, after the novel's publication, Gómez forced Gallegos to accept a post in the Senate, presumably in an attempt to keep the writer under his control. That plan did not work; Gallegos never attended a session, and he left for voluntary exile in the United States.

Gallegos returned to Venezuela in 1935, after Gómez's death. He served in public office in a brief period as head of the Department of Education. His political activities included his close participation in the founding of the Partido Democrático Nacional (National Democratic Party), of a progressive social platform, and his campaign as presidential candidate in 1941. Gallegos, who was running against a strong military candidate, lost that election.

In 1947, Gallegos was again a presidential candidate, this time winning with an overwhelmingly majority. His inauguration ceremony was attended by distinguished, internationally known Latin American writers, such as Cuban anthropologist Fernando Ortiz, Ecuadorian novelist Jorge Icaza, and Americans Waldo Frank and Archibald MacLeish. Also in attendance was Chilean Salvador Allende, who would become the first elected socialist president in Latin American history. Gallegos's electoral triumph was praised as the first democratically elected Venezuelan government in the twentieth century. His government was short lived, however, despite strong popular support; a military coup took place nine months later, in November 1948.

Forced into exile a second time, Gallegos spent the next nine years in Mexico and Cuba, where he continued to publish. He returned to Venezuela in 1958 at the end of the military regime. Although he was appointed a senator, a position adjudicated as a formerly elected president, illnesses prevented his taking on this obligation. He died as a notable political figure whose strong commitment to social issues would characterize the Latin American political arena of the 1960s.

Gallegos's social and political commitment became the inspiration for his criollista fiction. His characters were often drawn from his deep desire to bring his native country's social and ethnic groups into the mainstream historical arena. His novel *Canaima* (1934), translated into English in 1984, offered a panoramic view of national indigenous groups. In *Pobre negro* (*Poor Black Man*, 1937), Gallegos dwelt on the marginal lives of the blacks and the mulattoes, important social components in the historical development of Venezuela's coastal culture. These works reflect the influence of criollismo on Gallegos's works with their reproduction of cultural characteristics, including the speech patterns, of these key social groups.

Doña Bárbara is Gallegos's best-known novel and continues to be read in secondary schools throughout Latin America. This is indeed an honor, because criollismo produced a large number of excellent works of fiction, both novels and short stories, that represent diverse Latin American culture and customs. Gallegos's novel, and especially the character Doña Bárbara, the enigmatic central protagonist, have become associated with two of criollismo's top characteristics: political intention and literary depiction of native characteristics.

The female protagonist of *Doña Bárbara* is central to the understanding of the novel's political statement: the barbarism of life in the remote Venezuelan plains that clashed with new, civilized ways of life. Santos Luzardo, a character of progressive ideas, contrasted with Doña Bárbara's brutal ways of management. Her very name suggests a character that exhibits barbaric behavior. She was an unusual character, because a woman as a powerful and brutal landowner was in contrast to the social reality of the time.

As a young lawyer, Santos Luzardo is eager to put into action new models of management in this remote area. His idealism will soon be confronted by Doña Bárbara's totalitarian control. On the personal level, he also wants to avenge his father, whose mysterious death had prompted Santos's mother to abandon the family plantation for Caracas.

Gallegos's characters have specific roles. They have firm connections to the powerful landscape around them. This is particularly evident in Doña Bárbara. She is a barbarian, her cruel behavior goes against her nature as a woman. Gallegos's novel proposes a closer examination of the impact of nature (in this case the wild Venezuelan plains) on the human psyche. In Doña Bárbara, he portrays the same brutal behavior that readers witness in male characters who fight nature's forces.

Doña Bárbara's story line is simple: raised in a predominantly masculine, riverboat community, Bárbara was sexually assaulted as a young woman. In fury, she promised to revenge herself, so she eventually becomes a powerful landowner and a raging presence against male control of the area. She grows more brutal than any man there, a fact that not even motherhood seems to change. Abandoning her daughter, she chooses to build her reputation as a powerful woman through witchcraft. She gains knowledge of this practice from the indigenous groups living along the mighty Orinoco River.

Doña Bárbara's evil reputation grows, and outsiders to this native "shadowy lore" (37) seem unwilling to challenge her "powers as a sorceress" (44). Her domination comes to an end, however, after the unexpected arrival of Santos Luzardo, a native of the area, whose return comes after he has promised his mother to revitalize the family's abandoned property. To Luzardo's surprise, he soon discovers that Doña Bárbara has illegally taken considerable acreage of his plantation. He immediately decides to fight back.

Luzardo resists Doña Bárbara's control over the superstitious community. Soon he understands that her fame as an "ogress," although based on a series of mysterious circumstances, can be explained as the result of calculation. She has the support of a partner, whose behind-the-scenes orchestrations spread the legends of Doña Bárbara's so-called supernatural powers. Luzardo's target in his attack on Doña Bárbara's power is, however, her illegal appropriation of private property. She has become a wealthy landowner through two activities: illegal appropriation of land and of wild cattle that enter that property. Doña Bárbara bribes local authorities, who overlook these illegalities.

Luzardo decides not to challenge Doña Bárbara's solid reputation as a sorcerer, which the locals leave uncontested. The area is an isolated agrarian community with ample examples of superstitious behavior related to a strong cult rooted in the land. The following passage shows the peasants' view of the power that land exerts on the plantation tasks: "According to an ancient superstition, of unknown origin but common in the Plain, whenever a ranch was established a live animal was buried beneath the posts of the first corral to be built, so that his spirit, imprisoned in the earth of the property, might watch over this and its owners" (78).

The young lawyer chooses instead to fight for what he can prove: Doña Bárbara's violations of legal ownership of property. In the end, she is proven wrong, and a long-awaited fence is built, a symbol of the arrival of a civilized way of life: "The fence-wire, the straight line of man before the curving line of nature, would represent one sole unswerving road towards the future in this land of untold paths where wandering hopes had been lost since time immemorial" (137–138).

Today's reader of Gallegos's novel may question Doña Bárbara's reasons for not fighting Luzardo. The ending seems stereotypical and out of character. Although Doña Bárbara had violated property laws (as did powerful male landowners), she yields to Luzardo because Marisela, her abandoned daughter, has fallen in love with him. Marisela challenges her dreadful mother's power in a scene of high symbolism, as Doña Bárbara prepares to cast a spell on Luzardo. This confrontation, although it implies a clash of good versus evil, comes across as simplistic and predictable.

In her decision to yield the property, Doña Bárbara relinquishes more than her power as a landowner. She allows the two young lovers to be together and thus permits the beginning of a new era, represented by the union of opposing forces: contained nature (Marisela) and dominating control (Luzardo). The reader wonders about the destiny of the many other oppressive, male landowners who will not give up their power so easily for a sentimental reason.

Doña Bárbara is a complex novel. Its omniscient narrator seems to deny the reality of Doña Bárbara's alleged supernatural powers, even though he introduces ample proofs that attest to her use of tricks assisted by loyal workers. The clash of Luzardo's advanced ideas about modern administrative techniques with backward, local ways is highly effective from an activist point of view, but the novel's weakness is in its ideological content. A writer turned politician, Gallegos failed to suggest concrete solutions to the national problem of powerful landowners.

His romantic view of the difficulty of life in the Venezuelan plains, personified in Doña Bárbara, nonetheless continues to appeal to numerous new readers. In 1943, *Doña Bárbara* became a popular movie in Latin America, starring acclaimed Mexican actress María Félix. Today the practice of calling a strong-willed woman a "Doña Bárbara" is a testimony to the impact of Gallegos's novel on Latin American popular culture.

Gallegos continued exploration of strong women as important historical and fictional characters. He drew from documented sources of Latin American folklore, such as legends about the Amazon Indian women. Gallegos's interpretations of the fierce woman as a central character of her own story is an important contribution to the Latin American fiction of the mid–twentieth century.

INDIGENISMO

Throughout most of the nineteenth century and the first part of the twentieth, the Latin American indigenous populations were not considered worthy of literary representation. This phenomenon is particularly noticeable in countries with high concentrations of native groups, peoples who were segregated in inhospitable rural areas and city ghettos. A general characteristic of these ethnic groups was that Spanish often was not their first language, although some of them, usually men, had a working knowledge of the language. Women suffered the greatest hardships; men, either a husband or another family member, controlled most aspects of women's lives. Likewise, illiteracy rates were much higher among women than among men.

Abuse of the indigenous populations took place at various levels—governmental, economic, and in the daily personal contact between people of different races and ethnicities. Negative images of Native Americans caused them to conceal celebrations of their cultural heritage, of ancient traditions, religious practices, and native languages. In the public sphere, most Latin American countries sought to de-emphasize their indigenous past, characterizing it as primitive and backward. The international face that most Latin American countries sought to project was that of modern and developing societies eager to embrace the twentieth century.

Indigenous cultures survived despite overt racism. Perhaps it was because of the rural isolation of some groups, unaffected by mainstream culture, that these native cultures survived relatively undiluted. Of particular importance to students of Latin American cultures is these groups' success in the preservation of oral stories, mainly in the form of religious fables. Other remarkable surviving examples of American heritage include food and clothing. Indigenous cultures thrive today, particularly in Central America and along the northern Pacific coast of South America and in its central Altiplano.

The movement that actively campaigned for improvement of living conditions of Native American populations became known as *indigenismo.* Its ramifications were widespread and highly revolutionary; the movement called for an end to the social, economic, and political mistreatment of Latin American indigenous communities. Much like the U.S. civil rights movement, *indigenismo's* ideal of social justice sought to transform deeply engrained racist views among mainstream societies. Such views were visible in many stereotypical literary portraits of Native Americans, who were depicted primarily in subservient roles or as objects of folkloric interest. As a character, the American Indian often appeared as a primitive. Some literary representations attempted to explore indigenous cultures, but they limited the native characters to an exotic background (for instance, an unexplored natural setting). Their presence had no impact on the plotline, nor did it have a significant literary value.

Latin American writers who produced works with a positive characterization of indigenous cultures can be classified into two major trends. One
found inspiration in the experimental surrealist techniques present in Latin
America, beginning in the 1920s. Although surrealism did not originate in
Latin America, a number of Latin American writers found themselves deeply
involved in the movement because a significant number of them were living
in Europe, particularly in France, during the years between the World Wars.
Known collectively as the **vanguard,** surrealists were part of a fascinating
and complex artistic movement that actively incorporated indigenous cultures, particularly the narrative techniques of oral religious narratives and the
use of a large number of religious symbols. These rich and enigmatic symbols would be praised as the uncontaminated voice of the human spirit.

The second important trend of indigenismo was a highly graphic, realist
approach to depicting the inferior conditions in which native groups lived.
This type of literary work protested the political and social abuses that were
often perpetrated without punishment from authorities. The authors writing
indigenista fiction also depicted racist attitudes against indigenous populations in an open challenge to prevailing social, governmental, and political
institutions. They called for an end to these abuses, a stand that brought
serious problems with governmental powers for some authors.

The *indigenista* movement was popular in countries where natives consti-
tuted a high percentage of the national population. *Indigenista* writers
developed strong, positive indigenous characters who aggressively faced
oppressive figures of sociopolitical power. This is the case of *Huasipungo*
(1934; published in English as *The Villagers* in 1964), a novel by Jorge Icaza
(1906–1978), which first brought into public awareness the abuses perpetrated against the indigenous peoples of his native Ecuador.

Another important feature of the *indigenista* writers was their efforts to
reproduce indigenous cultures from various points of view—social, religious, and economic. They became chroniclers of the often-ignored native
as representative of national values. Native groups became prime literary
material, protagonists of their own lives.

Of the two trends of the *indigenismo* literary mode, the experimental style
inspired by surrealist techniques became associated with the Guatemalan
novelist and short story writer Miguel Angel Asturias, while the open political stand in favor of improvement of indigenous communities found an
advocate in the Peruvian novelist and short story writer Ciro Alegría. These
writers stand out for their unique literary documentation of indigenous cultures. Their works display a balanced view of the Indian, who previously
appeared as a one-dimensional character, a romanticized being comparable
to an inanimate object submerged in the lush Latin American natural world.
Often natives were portrayed as a symbol of incivility, but authors who chose
this perspective opposed the view that the natives' uncivilized customs

explained the backwardness of certain Latin American societies. Both Asturias and Alegría are responsible for the presentation of the Indian as a well-rounded literary character and as a worthy symbol of Latin American identity and cultural values.

Miguel Angel Asturias (Guatemala, 1899–1974)

Miguel Angel Asturias stands out among the first of the Latin American writers to incorporate indigenous folklore into skillful experimental narrative techniques. Asturias was born into a professional family; his father was a lawyer and his mother a schoolteacher. They participated in protests against the dictatorial government of Manuel Estrada Cabrera. Seeking a safer environment, the Asturias family moved to a rural town, where Asturias came into close contact with indigenous communities. His experiences in this environment were pivotal to his decision to study anthropology. He became an active protestor against abuse of native Guatemalan groups, many of whom lived in dire economic and social conditions. As a university student, Asturias was also politically committed. Like his parents, he took part in political activities opposing the aging, tyrannical government of Estrada Cabrera. Following his early political activism, Asturias wrote a ground-breaking dissertation in 1923, "The Social Problem of the Indian."

From 1923 to 1933, Asturias lived in Paris, where he continued his advanced studies in anthropology at the prestigious Sorbonne University. He met Georges Raynaud, a world-renowned anthropologist who had done extensive research on the Maya-Quiché religious belief system and had its sacred text, the *Popol-Vuh,* translated into French. This document, essential to understanding Guatemala's indigenous cultures, aroused immediate interest in Asturias, and he translated Raynaud's French text into Spanish. This anthropological experience influenced the young writer. In 1930, he published his short story collection, *Legends of Guatemala*. Although it was his first book, the short stories, partially inspired by legends from the *Popol-Vuh,* attracted the attention of other experimental writers. The French poet Paul Valéry, Asturias's friend, wrote the introduction to the short story collection.

Upon his return to Guatemala, Asturias worked in two distinct directions. First, he showed a political commitment to and interest in the economic affairs of his native country. The themes appear in his first novel, *The President* (1946), inspired by events during the long, devastating Estrada Cabrera dictatorship. This highly experimental novel is considered the first novel in Latin America to present the figure of the dictator as a literary protagonist. A second important direction of Asturias's narrative is his incorporation of Maya-Quiché religious and popular folk material. Two works in particular are excellent examples of Asturias's political commitment to sociopolitical advancement of native Guatemalan populations: *Men of Maize* (1948) and *Mulata* (1963). His collection of legends, *Lida Sal* (1967), demonstrates that his literary approach to these ethnic characters went beyond anthropological curiosity. In his legends, he carefully represented Maya-Quiché belief systems at an intellectual level equal to that of other world-renowned traditional religious stories. The legends' literary sophistication and the wide use of obscure, challenging religious symbols are Asturias's most notable contributions to contemporary Latin American literature.

Known worldwide for his political stand in favor of native indigenous populations, Asturias received the Lenin Prize in 1966. A year later, he was awarded the Nobel Prize in Literature, the first Latin American writer to be so honored.

Asturias found inspiration for his short stories, or legends, in the *Popol-Vuh*'s stories and in his recording of well-known popular oral traditions. These stories, according to his statement, were easily available; they were transmitted orally, usually by women within a family setting. Asturias insisted that he had heard these stories from a grandmother. His connection with ancient Mayan folklore was important to Asturias, who saw himself as a rightful heir to that rich culture, equated with truly "native" Guatemalan spiritual and cultural values. His legends therefore were his conscious attempt to preserve the oral traditions of indigenous beliefs constantly under threat of assimilation into modern life. They also served as his contribution to a tendency toward experimentation in Latin American literature.

Asturias's interest in developing highly complex stories is particularly evident in two aspects of his work: message and form. In terms of its message, or the lesson that oral traditions inherently present to their listeners, these legends remain closely tied to the highly symbolic Maya-Quiché belief systems. The stories are, however, short and straightforward in their presentation of characters and in the development of the action. The reader's task is to explore new sets of religious symbols, usually drawn from nature. If the stories' exotic symbols fail to arouse the reader's attention, the unusual plots of the legends become then the central point of interest. In terms of form, Asturias's experimental techniques, with his unusual plots and his use of mythical places as settings for his stories contribute to a Latin American–based literary movement known as **magical realism.**

Asturias's legend "Tatuana's Tale" merges a mythical setting with a plot of highly religious connotation. Tatuana is a young woman of rare beauty, who became the slave of a wealthy merchant. Although this plot summary appears simple enough, it is, in fact, the conclusion of a broader story with profound religious symbols. The most challenging symbols are in the action that leads to the purchase of Tatuana as a slave. The message (whether religious or symbolic) is clearly depicted in the fantastic ending, which explains how Tatuana was able to escape from slavery.

The story's setting, as in many traditional religious stories, is mythical: a forest, in which on a vaguely described "one day" Father Almond Tree mysteriously appeared, "without being planted, as though brought there by spirits" (118). According to the native beliefs, "He knew the secret of medicinal plants, the language of the gods that spoke through translucent obsidian, and he could read the hieroglyphics of the stars" (118). Father Almond Tree decides to divide his soul into four parts, symbolically represented as four paths colored white, black, green, and red. These roads appear to be endless, so that the black road, also known as the Sorcerer Night, sells itself to the Merchant of Priceless Jewels in exchange for rest from his endless voyage.

When Father Almond Tree realizes that he has lost one of his souls, he transforms himself into an old man and sets out to seek the Merchant of Priceless Jewels. He succeeds in locating the Merchant, but he fails to convince the greedy man to sell back Father Almond Tree's soul, symbolically described as a jewel of priceless value. Defeated, Father Almond Tree finally abandons his project and begins wandering through the streets; his erratic behavior, like that of a madman, includes his "talking to donkeys, oxen and stray dogs, which, like men, are all sad-eyed animals" (121).

In the meantime, the Merchant has bought a slave girl with Father Almond Tree's jewel soul. The merchant and his newly acquired slave are on their way to his house when a storm takes them by surprise and lightning kills him. Eventually, Father Almond Tree in his endless search finds the young woman, who has taken refuge in the merchant's house. Their happy encounter is interrupted at once; the house is raided, and both are accused of witchcraft. They are sentenced to death.

The end of the story contains a religious lesson set within a fantastic ending. In prison, Father Almond Tree and the young woman share the same cell. The Almighty Spirit communicates to her a plan for deliverance from her imprisonment. After drawing a little boat on her arm, Father Almond Tree provides in words a psychological understanding of the boundaries of reality and imagination as a way to deal with oppressive physical conditions: " 'Tatuana, by means of this tattoo,' he said, 'you will be able to flee whenever you are in danger. I want you to be as free as my spirit. Trace this little boat on a wall, on the ground, in the air, wherever you wish. Then close your eyes, climb aboard and go.' " (121). The girl's wishes come true. The following day, surprised guards find the cell mysteriously empty, and in the center of it lie the remains of a withered almond tree.

Asturias's story draws heavily from the Maya-Quiché religion. Some of the symbols have, however, a universal value represented in characters shared by worldwide religions. For example, the reader understands that Father Almond Tree's knowledge is derived from his intimate knowledge of nature. This metaphorical image is often present in Judeo-Christian traditions and biblical stories. The parallels are striking; for instance, the so-called

Tree of Knowledge was also planted in a garden. Like Father Almond Tree, it had immense knowledge. Other religions also place a theological importance in native trees, and, like Father Almond Tree, through their divine intervention, they cause supernatural events to occur for the benefit of god-fearing individuals.

Other important symbols in "Tatuana's Tale" cannot be interpreted outside the context of Maya-Quiché religious thought and cultural practices. For instance, the colors black, green, red, and white have a central role in the story, although their significance is not apparent. Anthropological research, in particular, examination of the role of colors in today's Guatemalan weavings, suggests possible symbolic interpretations. The weavers of colorful textiles use colors to indicate meaning, such as those in "Tatuana's Tale." The color black is related to war activities; red, to life; and green, to eternity. It is also obvious that the traditional Western associations of colors and human feelings agree with Maya-Quiché interpretations. One example is the role of black to represent death and mourning in association with war, another image of desolation and termination of life.

"Tatuana's Tale" is a prime example of a flourishing, experimental narrative device known in Latin American literature as **magical realism.** This technique presents as either normal or possible unusual events, at times of fantastic nature. In Asturias's tale, Tatuana's miraculous escape can be viewed in two ways. One is a religious level, which presents Tatuana as a god-fearing individual worthy of a miraculous salvation, like many such heroes and heroines in biblical stories. On a psychological level, Tatuana fled from her imprisonment not by means of divine intervention but through her own mental ability to achieve freedom. Slavery becomes a state of mind; Tatuana finds the way to go beyond the physical restraints of an oppressive system. This combination of fantastic plots and an activist message, usually social or political, will become a trademark of magical realism in Latin American literature.

Ciro Alegría (Peru, 1909–1967)

Born in Sartimbamba, a town in the province of Huamachuco in the northern Peruvian highlands, Ciro Alegría had firsthand knowledge of native communities. This was an area with a rich anthropological past; the Wamachucos had a well-developed culture, which had been incorporated into the Inca empire in 1365. At the beginning of the Spanish Conquest of today's Peru, the region was developed after 1551, with the arrival of Catholic missionaries. Today Huamachuco retains a strong religious life, practiced in ceremonies that blend Catholic and Incan religions.

The son of wealthy landowners, Alegría received an advanced education available only to the upper classes. He showed an interest in Peruvian his-

tory, particularly in research of local indigenous customs. He became a political activist during his years at the University of Trujillo. His student
activism, including his vociferous newspaper articles, won him national
recognition as an up-and-coming politician. A further result of his political
commitment was his cofounding in 1930 of the Acción Popular
Revolucionaria Americana (American Popular Revolutionary Action), a
political party that called for immediate improvement of the terrible conditions in which the native groups lived.

Alegría's activism caused his expulsion from college and a series of impris-
onments from 1931 through 1933, during which he was tortured. In 1934,
he left for Chile as a political exile and began writing short stories and novels. Despite a two-year period in a sanatorium for patients of tuberculosis,
he continued his literary production.

Because of his open challenge to the status quo, Alegría spent extended
periods abroad. He was a professor of literature at Columbia University in
New York from 1941 to 1949 and at the University of Puerto Rico from
1949 to 1953. He also lived in Cuba, where he came into contact with the
political ideology of the guerrilla warfare in progress under the leadership of
Fidel Castro. In 1957, he returned to Peru to continue his political career;
he was elected a deputy of the Acción Popular Party in 1963.

His first two novels, *La serpiente de oro* (*The Golden Serpent,* 1935) and
Los perros hambrientos (*The Hungry Dogs,* 1938) began his political denunciation of exploitation of indigenous groups by the Peruvian landowners of
his native Huamachuco. Alegría rejected the common belief that the native
groups' backwardness and poverty were due to their holding on to primitive
cultural traditions and to their refusal to embrace education. Instead, he
openly denounced the illegal practices wealthy landowners used to subjugate
the natives by limiting access to education and financially restricting them to
a convoluted system of salary and compensation.

Another important element in these novels is the role of nature in the
development of the characters. The lush Peruvian highland landscape
becomes an important literary component. It is also symbolic of the workers' plight, particularly that of natives working among the destructive forces
of nature. His novel *The Golden Serpent* depicts the tribulations of workers
on the shores of the Marañón River, a mighty tributary of the Amazon. His
observations in this novel, as in others of his works, were autobiographical;
his family had a small plantation on the shores of this river.

Alegría was a committed activist. His novels can be viewed as his political
manifesto—as a strong call on behalf of indigenous groups and a demand for
an immediate cessation of their exploitation. He soon became well known outside Peru. Alegría's name, especially after the publication of *El mundo es ancho
y ajeno* (*Broad and Alien Is the World*), became synonymous with the denunciation of the open violation of the human rights of Peruvian indigenous groups
by the government and by national and international business interests.

Broad and Alien Is the World, a novel that appeared in English translation in the United States in 1941, is Alegría's most famous work. It soon became a best-seller, the first novel from Latin America well known to American readers. The novel also promoted the pro-indigenous cause in international circles. It gave strength to the *indigenista* literary movement by avoiding one-dimensional characters and heavy-handed symbolism. The reader learns of the terrible conditions of oppressed native groups who struggle to survive in a world of economic and technological change. This image is provided through a series of protagonists, simple representatives of native values in constant clashes with social and political institutions.

Broad and Alien Is the World is a case study of the Peruvian social and governmental institutions' lack of respect for native groups. The novel introduces Rosendo Maqui, mayor of a native community in the Peruvian highlands, who, at the beginning of the novel, attempts to avoid the loss of the communal lands to an unscrupulous landowner, Don Alvaro Amenábar y Roldán. Maqui loses his fight because Don Alvaro has the support of corrupt local government officials.

Rather than work as slaves on their former lands, the community moves to other, less fertile lands. The move splits the community; the lands do not produce enough, so many go to other areas. Their escape is fruitless; Don Alvaro's power catches up with the struggling community, and he manages to imprison Maqui, who is then brutally killed by his jailers. At the end of the novel, a group of the youngest rebels, led by Benito Castro, Maqui's adopted son, take up arms against the authorities. Their protest fails but raises the natives' awareness of the need to organize groups of activists for armed confrontation.

Broad and Alien Is the World offers an insightful view of Rumi, the indigenous community that Maqui headed. Rumi serves as a model for an indigenous political structure of shared living, a system with obvious connections to communist idealism. Maqui is characterized as a just public officer whose power resides not in the office he represents but in the united support of the community that elected him. The novel's strength lies in the efficient portrayal of the characters involved in Rumi's management.

One of Alegría's most important contributions to the *indigenista* movement is a balanced presentation of an indigenous system of government. His views of Rumi's sociopolitical structures are objective, pointing out the positive and the negative elements of this particular indigenous system.

Maqui's relationship with the surrounding Peruvian highlands reflects deep understanding of the indigenous cultures' view of nature. Maqui possesses ancient knowledge of agricultural techniques and of a way to forecast changes in the weather. He is also reverent to gifts from the earth, such as the wheat and the corn that are presented as symbols of "blessed nourishment" (143). Their loss of their community lands is dually important. Their decision to abandon Rumi, their ancestral land, is understood to be a radical position that went against tradition. In the end, they are forced into a "broad and alien world," away from their native land, "which is the man's true navel cord" (433).

Alegría presented a valid picture of indigenous cultures, of a way of life that goes against conventional Western conventions. This clash often results in a rupture of normal indigenous life. In certain instances, the rupture is expressed through the natives' unwillingness to embrace progress. One such incident was the opposition of a community to the widening of a natural drainage ditch for a lake, which would have kept the winter rains from flooding cultivated areas along its bank. Superstitious beliefs stopped a "mayor with progressive ideas" from building the project: "people began to say that the spirit of the lake, in the form of a black, hairy woman, wearing a wreath of rushes in her hair, had appeared to oppose the attempt. The lake of Yanañahui was enchanted" (243). Two aspects are of importance here. First, the natives appear uncensored; their belief system is in plain view. Second, although it may appear to be backward, their decision not to allow an artificial drainage may reflect the native conception of ecological change. This view, although simplistic, addresses the dangers of altering the natural balance of nature.

Alegría's *Alien and Broad Is the World* called for reparation to the Peruvian indigenous communities, affected and often destroyed without due government protection. Amid the destruction, he portrayed the positive contributions of these communities to modern Peruvian society.

Aside from Alegría's strong political activism, his novel was groundbreaking for its literary import. His balanced portrayal of key types of indigenous characters led to a strong movement in Peru and elsewhere in Latin America. One case is that of Peruvian writer José María Arguedas (1911–1969), whose novel *Los ríos profundos* (*Deep Rivers,* 1958) offers a detailed analysis of the natives' psyche within an existential framework.

Above all, Alegría succeeded in creating a balanced depiction of life in an indigenous community. He presented a well-rounded picture of native customs from memories of his experiences growing up in close contact with indigenous groups. His depiction of indigenous lore and religious beliefs remains a model of an effective political protest against imposition of foreign ways of life.

NEGRISMO

Beginning in the 1930s, interest in primal cultures, particularly those from Africa and indigenous America, was strong among **vanguardist** writers. Visual artists, such as Pablo Picasso, produced work that suggested African masks. (Masks had been exhibited in Paris since 1879 at the first ethnological museum of African artifacts.) Following the First World War, numerous important intellectuals had become involved in pro-African or Afro-diasporic movements. Artists of African descent in Latin America and in the United States started to produce work with strong black motifs. The movement, known as *negrismo,* involved all the arts; writers, musicians, and visual artists sought inspiration in rich African American cultures. Of special interest to students of Latin American cultures were artists of the Harlem Renaissance movement of the 1930s; these artists had a strong influence on writers producing in the *negrista* style. African American poet Langston Hughes, among the most famous of the Harlem Renaissance writers, was a particular inspiration for young poets in the Caribbean, especially in Cuba.

This international exposure to African cultures had a significant impact on the literary production of the Spanish-speaking Greater Antilles—Cuba, the Dominican Republic, and Puerto Rico. These islands have only a slight influence from their indigenous cultures in the development of their national identities because their native groups began to disappear early in the mid–sixteenth century. Africans were brought to the islands as slaves, replacing the Indians as laborers in plantations and gold mines. Because of the significantly reduced native population and the massive influx of Africans until the abolition of slavery in the region in 1888, Africans became the foundation of Caribbean popular culture.

The development of Afro-Caribbean cultures did not go unchallenged, and there is a long history of struggle in the Caribbean to gain recognition for the vast contributions of African cultures. The clashes, mainly in social and economic arenas, have taken place among various ethnic groups— blacks, whites, and mulattoes. Such rivalry continues to play an important role in the politics of the area today.

The oldest historical records indicate that in 1502 a handful of Africans arrived as slaves into the Americas on the island of La Española (today the Dominican Republic and Haiti). Their numbers increased dramatically as the Caribbean islands began to develop strong agricultural economies, and the African population often surpassed that of the Spaniards. In San Juan, Puerto Rico, a 1530 census showed 2,292 Africans and 327 white colonialists. La Española listed 20,000 blacks between 1557 and 1564. The combination of Spanish and African cultures within the relatively small confines of the Caribbean islands led to the Spanish Caribbean ethnic groups often referred to as **Creole.** The term, also used in the southern United States, particularly in Louisiana, refers to cultures with roots in both African and European traditions. Neither fully African nor fully European, Creole traditions came to represent cultures that originated in the New World.

Examples of Creole cultures in the Caribbean are extensive and colorful. Some of these traditions, in fact, have gone beyond the specific ethnic background or circumstances that created them to become national traits. An example is music and dance, such as the internationally popular Cuban **mambo,** or the lesser known musical beats of the Dominican **merengue** or

Puerto Rican **guaracha,** rhythms that have African origins. Other aspects of popular culture with an African heritage, such as food, have become so accepted that many citizens are not even aware of their roots.

African religions, particularly the rich and colorful rituals associated with Creole practices, are perhaps the most recognizable products of a Caribbean black heritage today. The strong presence of black religious practices throughout the Caribbean, such as **Voodoo** in Haiti, **Santería** in Cuba, and the **Shango cult** in Trinidad, attests to the importance of native religions for the enslaved Africans and for their descendents. Indeed, religious practices played an important part in the slaves' forced adaptation to foreign soil under the brutal institution of slavery. After the abolition of slavery, many of these religious practices survived and spread into other ethnic segments. Today religion continues to play an important social role in black communities.

Voodoo and Santería are among the best-known black religious practices from the Caribbean. Voodoo, which originated on the island of Haiti, also took root in New Orleans, known as its center in the United States. Voodoo has a strong presence in many Hollywood films. In particular, the allure of "zombies," of the horrific "living dead," has created around this Creole religion an aura of mystery, albeit a negative one. Unfortunately, knowledge of Voodoo in the United States is limited to such stereotypic images, which present a distorted and barbaric impression. For example, the most popular artifact related to Voodoo is the "Voodoo doll," and the image (particularly in films) is that of an aggressive cult that inflicts a painful death on its enemies. Santería, although less known in the United States, has also been characterized as savage by the media, particularly because of its practice of animal sacrifices for ritual purposes.

The *negrismo* movement came to address the lack of in-depth research of black cultures at all levels—social, economic, and religious. In Cuba, it also promoted a literary movement that sought the incorporation of anthropological knowledge within a literary form. Cuban writers became interested in the exploration of Santería traditions, particularly of subject matter that contained literary themes commonly associated with Cuban identity. This was a bold move, because Afro-Cuban cultures and traditions had traditionally been kept marginal to concepts associated with Cubanness. It was also the first time that Afro-Cuban popular cultures had a positive literary depiction.

Writers producing literary or anthropological works on Santería practices found inspiration in various fields. Santería encompasses ways of living that go beyond religious celebrations, and thus writers documented a variety of fascinating data. Some of the engaging subject matter, such as musical performances, are today among the best-known by-products of Afro-Cuban popular culture. The influence of Afro-Cuban musical beats and instruments, particularly of percussion drums, is international, and their presence in U.S. music can be traced in part to national interest in black culture. Cuban bandleader Desi Arnaz, better known as Lucille Ball's husband in the television program *I Love Lucy,* claimed that he first exposed American audiences to Afro-Cuban musical rhythms when he introduced the **conga** into the United States in 1937. This coincides with African American cultural movements, particularly the Harlem Renaissance.

Cuban writers were strongly attracted to Santería religious practices and legends and to historical events associated with its development. They were pioneers; these subjects had rarely been literary motifs and at times had been publicly rejected as barbaric. Their literary importance is solidly based on writers' decisions to use Afro-Cuban motifs and on their contributions to the experimental literary style known today as **magical realism.**

Lydia Cabrera (Cuba, 1899–1991)

Cabrera was among the first Cuban writers to combine in-depth study of Cuba's African culture with interdisciplinary literary and ethnographic projects. She was particularly interested in the compilation of African legends that survived in oral histories in Cuba despite fragmentation of the slave societies. These oral legends, known in Cuba today as *patakí,* are central components of the Afro-Cuban religious system known as **Santería.** The impact of Santería on popular Cuban cultures continues today. It is particularly evident in the music (songs and dances), in dietary preferences, and, principally, in religious beliefs. In fact, a number of internationally known Cuban traditions are of African origin, a tribute to the resilient character of the customs.

In Paris, as a student of art at L'Ecole du Louvre, Cabrera had direct exposure to the European **vanguardist** interest in primal cultures. Her personal research on Afro-Cuban culture would have found sympathetic ears among European painters. Pablo Picasso, the Spanish painter residing in Paris, had started a series of masks, some with clearly African physical traits. Other Latin American writers of the time, such as Miguel Angel Asturias, were involved in the research of their own native indigenous roots.

Cabrera's anthropological research on Afro-Cuban traditions is the theme of her *Cuentos negros* (*Black Tales*), published in 1936 in a French translation. The fact that a reputable commercial press published the work of an unknown author was an indication of the increasing popularity of international black literature. The collection's publication in the thirties also established that decade as the beginning of a strong socioliterary movement within black communities and coincided with the *indigenista* trend.

Cabrera produced an extensive number of publications, both literary and anthropological in nature, based on her field research and on her transcriptions of popular legends from the various Afro-Cuban religious belief systems. Today her books are mandatory reading for the understanding of Cuban black religions, particularly of Santería.

Unhappy with the revolutionary Cuban government, Cabrera left the island in the early 1960s. She moved to Miami, where she continued to write and helped other exiled Cuban writers find publishing avenues for their work until her death.

Intensive research on Santería practices, particularly of its strong attachment to oral legends, was Cabrera's greatest contribution to the *negrismo* movement. Her name became associated with her recording of hundreds of *patakís,* or didactic stories that document, explain, or expand on the complex theology of the many Santería ceremonies. The *patakís,* as international oral histories, have a common purpose or intention, and they share certain characteristics. They are repositories of data on the life and customs of Africans, and many of them describe the painful experiences of slavery. The *pataki* displays a strong didactic nature; an essential message of these stories is the improvement of the reader's well-being. They are, above all, a positive outlook on life, a light of hope and a testimony to the goodness of the human being.

Cabrera's story "Daddy Turtle and Daddy Tiger" is an example of a classic *pataki* in two ways. First, it contains a lesson, valuable for the improvement of one's interpersonal relationships. Second, the story presents mythical characters of importance to the understanding of the religious beliefs of Cuban Santería. This *pataki* also stands out for its interesting narrative structure. It combines two story lines: one takes place in the realm of the divine, a sort of genesis; a second is placed in the animal kingdom, a reflection of certain traits in human behavior.

The use of two independent plotlines (both with pedagogical intentions) reminds the reader of basic narrative techniques, such as the medieval tradition of the **exemplum,** an example of the advantages of good behavior within the socioreligious structures of one's community. The *pataki,* also like the medieval pedagogical story, promotes positive behavior by presenting an example of bad conduct. This makes the *pataki* fun to read, although the characters' conduct should not be imitated; it is an entertaining story about the mischievousness of some and the ingenuity of others in the face of oppression.

The first story line of "Daddy Turtle and Daddy Tiger" takes the reader to a chaotic earth shortly after its creation. Although the newly created earth appears as an imaginary world where impossible natural events take place, the references to nature are real. This is a lush earth, rich in water sources, vegetation, and animal life. The animals are, however, uncertain about their habitat and their function within it. The birds, for example, make nests on the crests of ocean waves.

In this world, mankind is also at the mercy of natural phenomena. They recognize nature's role in their lives and even in their deaths. As an explanation for death, the moon, associated with coldness and, therefore, the termination of life, has a central role in the story. The moon, told by her father that at the end of her cycle she will come back to life, sends a message to men. They, too, according to the moon's hopeful declaration, will be immortal. Unable to deliver the good news herself, the moon uses a hare as a messenger. On his way to meet men, however, the hare gets drunk and delivers the moon's statement incorrectly: " 'I told them: just as I am born, die and . . . never come back, so you shall be born, die and never come back. And they started digging their graves.' " (50). A significant message in Cabrera's *pataki* is the belief that death is not punishment for humanity's weakness (such as is the belief of most Western religious beliefs) but a mere misunderstanding, the result of a chaotic, newly created world. This world, as many *patakís* point out, is in continual change and adaptation.

Cabrera's *patakís* craftily reproduced the oral nature of the original legend. Her style combines narrative techniques that incorporate communicative devices, such as music and dance, with the traditional dialogue. Her stories are therefore highly rhythmic and can be easily transformed into dramatic sketches. Cabrera's *patakís* are crafted within the literary form of the modern short story. They appeal to modern, sophisticated readers despite their strong moral context.

Alejo Carpentier (Cuba, 1904–1980)

Born in Havana, Alejo Carpentier had an unusual upbringing in which he learned foreign languages and gained an appreciation of the fine arts. His French father, an architect, introduced his son to his native language. Also from his father's influence, Carpentier developed a strong interest in the elaborate architecture of his native Havana. The city, an important Caribbean trade center, is among the most beautiful colonial cities in Latin America. Carpentier's mother was a trained musician. Carpentier followed in his mother's footsteps; he became well known for his research on popular Cuban beats, particularly the music of African origin.

The Carpentiers moved to Paris when Alejo was eight years old. There he perfected his knowledge of French. The trip was important in the development of Carpentier's interest in French literature. He continued advanced studies in music, particularly in music theory, and became an accomplished concert performer.

In 1921, Carpentier began to study for a degree in architecture at the University of Havana. He soon abandoned that career for a job as a newspaper reporter. He also started writing literature, mainly short stories for local journals in Havana. Lively intellectual organizations came into being as a result of these publications. These groups were interested in the European **vanguardist** movements, as well as in international political movements.

Carpentier joined some of these political groups, a decision that would lead to self-imposed exile.

Carpentier used his knowledge of French and literature to promote in Cuba the production of experimental literature. He was a key figure in the creation and management of important literary journals known for publication of experimental and vanguardist writing. This was also the beginning of an international readership of Cuban literature, particularly in Latin American countries.

Carpentier maintained an association with the French surrealists and a close friendship with André Breton, founding father of surrealism, whom Carpentier had met in France in 1928. Carpentier's participation in French surrealism was significant. He wrote in French for the reputable journal *La Revolution surréaliste* under Breton's direction. That connection was important in the development of his literary craft. Carpentier's surrealist period was pivotal. It exposed him to the work of other important figures associated with surrealism, Louis Aragón and Tristan Tzara, among others. He also met Pablo Picasso, the experimental Spanish painter. Years later, however, Carpentier adamantly dismissed surrealism as an ineffective vehicle for his literary expression.

Carpentier was also deeply involved in Cuban politics. In 1927, he participated in public demonstrations that would lead to his imprisonment, under the accusation of communism. In jail, he wrote his first novel, *¡Ecue-Yamba-O!* within the *negrismo* trend. When he abandoned Cuba for Paris under an assumed name, he found refuge there in highly politicized surrealist circles.

On his return to Cuba, Carpentier worked in the department of education's radio station, where he broadcasted programs about popular Cuban musical rhythms, and he taught music at Havana's Conservatory of Music. His interest in music, particularly in rhythms of Afro-Cuban origins, led him into serious research on African connections to other Caribbean islands. In 1943, he made a trip to Haiti, where he researched the strong influence of voodoo on that island's history. His novel, *El reino de este mundo* (1949; *The Kingdom of This World*, 1957), was inspired by his findings about the strong relationship between political activism and voodoo.

Because of his political activism, Carpentier lived in Caracas, Venezuela, after 1945. There he worked for radio stations and continued writing literature and working as a newspaper reporter. (Although this was the first time he lived on the continental territory of Latin America for an extended period of time, it was not his first visit. In 1926, he had traveled to Mexico, where he had met Diego Rivera, the famous muralist.) Carpentier took advantage of his stay in Venezuela to travel the continent extensively, including an exploration of the Amazon territory. The trip left a mark on his literary production. A search through the vastness of the Latin American landscape is the theme of his novel *Los pasos perdidos* (1953). This encounter with Latin

American nature had resonance of both literary and philosophical significance.

After the Cuban Revolution in 1959, Carpentier returned to his native island. Because of his former political association with socialist and communist groups, he gained the favor of the new political order. He served as director or board member of various important writing centers and also became a political representative abroad for the revolutionary government. He often represented Cuba on official visits to the Soviet Union, China, and Vietnam.

Carpentier is today among the best-known Cuban writers. His books and stories are widely available in English translations. He received numerous awards, such as the prestigious Spanish Premio Cervantes (1977) and the French Médicis Prix (1979). He was a controversial author, however, because of his strong support of the Cuban revolutionary government. He died in Paris, where he was serving as the Cuban ambassador.

Carpentier's literary contribution to the development of Latin American magical realism arose from the publication of his novel *The Kingdom of This World* (1949; trans. 1957). Its strongly experimental character prompted him to write a prologue to the novel. Today that prologue is considered a manifesto of magical realism in terms of its definition, characteristics, and intention. In the prologue, Carpentier explained his reasons for abandoning surrealist techniques. He was tired of the European tendency to produce unusual images devoid of a real connection with natural sources or historical events. He had become aware of strange realities after a trip to Haiti in 1943, where he had discovered the rituals of voodoo. The widespread practice of voodoo led Carpentier to believe that reality and the fantastic coexisted in the Americas. With his novel, Carpentier set out to document the circumstances in which voodoo played a role in the development of a Haitian emancipatory movement by dissatisfied blacks.

With his novel, Carpentier intended to document complex and unreal events from the history of Latin America. This reality, often unusual, he labeled *lo real maravilloso*—marvelous reality. His theory was that unreal events, unlike the fabricated literary or artistic images of the surrealists, had taken place in Latin America, often within sociopolitical contexts. *The Kingdom of This World* becomes, therefore, just one example of the many instances in which unreal events seem to be at the core of customs native to the Americas, a key to the understanding of national identities.

Carpentier did not intend *The Kingdom of This World* to be a historical text in the traditional fashion, however. Although he based his story on factual events, his aesthetic focus was on reproduction of the underground world of voodoo and its impact on the increasingly numerous slave uprisings. The plot places the characters in real events, as recorded in historical sources, alongside imaginary deeds, as remembered in popular lore. Writing from a chronicler's point of view, the novelist examines the chain of events initiated by Mackandal, a handicapped slave, whose historical uprising had popular appeal among other blacks. He was not like other rebellious slaves; Mackandal used voodoo to produce a myth of invincibility. This incredible belief is central to understanding the uprisings he led. Certain details of Mackandal's plan seem to take the reader to a mythical dimension, a world in which the boundaries between the real and the imagined are blurred.

Carpentier realized that his unique literary style would be controversial. After all, at the time of the publication of *The Kingdom of This World*, most Latin American countries preferred a realistic approach to their national histories. To combat the possibility that his novel might be misunderstood or even rejected as a mere experimental text, he set forth in the prologue a series of reasons for his approach to magical realism. To today's seasoned reader, the unusual events in *The Kingdom of This World* seem normal, acceptable as plausible or, at least, explicable within a literary framework drawn from the genre of the fantastic. In fact, current editions of the novel usually do not carry Carpentier's 1949 prologue.

In *The Kingdom of This World*, Carpentier attempts to document the presence of magical realism as it relates to the era of slavery, among the most important of the historical periods in the development of today's Latin American countries, especially those within the Caribbean basin. Carpentier characterizes slavery as a social and political institution that displays repressive elements. Exploration of the complex world of slavery, particularly the brutal means to control slaves, is Carpentier's literary aim.

Carpentier's novel sets out to delve into the defense mechanisms that slaves were forced to use in reaction to official oppression. He chose a series of Haitian slave insurrections beginning in 1757 that challenged the supremacy of white plantation owners and eventually led to organized revolutionary movements. Unlike other acts of protests, such as traditional guerrilla warfare, resistance in Carpentier's novel includes a major role for faith in supernatural events.

The Kingdom of This World's story is simple. Mackandal, a young slave on a wealthy sugar cane plantation, loses an arm after a terrible accident while working at the mill. Unable to perform heavy work, he is made responsible for the plantation's cattle and is left unsupervised and in remote fields. The reader is warned that Mackandal would not stay put and be content in this idyllic setting. He was a Mandinga, of people who came from the African nation of Angola. As a group, the Mandingas were known for their rebellious spirit and for having participated in numerous slave revolts. Unlike previous uprisings, Mackandal's insurrection would not be an armed movement.

In the fields, bored with tending the cattle, Mackandal soon discovers that his animals avoid certain plants and mushrooms. He takes a collection of the specimens to a local *yerbera,* an old black woman with extensive knowledge on the area's vegetation. Mackandal witnesses the *yerbera's* supernatural powers when she dips her hand and arm into boiling oil without suffering harm. After undergoing mystical training in the secrets of voodoo with the *yerbera,* Mackandal begins his deadly campaign against white plantation owners.

Mackandal's plan has no supernatural connotation. He had discovered a potent poison in a certain type of mushroom and made it available to blacks serving the nearby plantations. The poison is administered so successfully that the authorities are baffled. Many people die, and the responsible parties remain unknown. Mackandal, who had gone underground, coordinates the distribution of the deadly poison.

Eventually, after a terrible torture session, a slave reveals that Mackandal is responsible for the deaths. A huge search party is organized, but Mackandal's followers are not worried about his capture. A common belief among the blacks had transformed Mackandal into a powerful voodoo leader, whose supernatural powers included an ability to transform himself into animals. This belief is corroborated by sightings of animals with unusual coloration or shapes and by the birth of a child with the head of a boar. At the end of the novel, Mackandal is captured and sentenced to death by the colonial authorities.

His death is controversial, however. Mackandal promises to escape and return from his death by fire. This seems to happen, at least in the eyes of the slaves who witness the events. The narrator, who until this point seems to believe in Mackandal's powers, dismisses this possibility. For the slave population, although Mackandal disappears, he will return to provide for their political liberation: "Endowed with supreme authority by the Rulers of the Other Shore, he had proclaimed the crusade of extermination, chosen as he was to wipe out the whites and create a great empire of free Negroes in Santo Domingo" (36).

Mackandal's story is pivotal in the understanding of the colonial history of the Americas. In *The Kingdom of This World,* Carpentier chose to document unusual events that took place at the peak of slavery. He drew from ancient African beliefs, present in the Americas and especially in Haiti: "the Mandingue Negro would tell of things that had happened in the great kingdoms of Popo, of Arada, of the Nagos, or the Fulah. He spoke of the great migrations of tribes, of age-long wars, of epic battles in which the animals had been allies of men. He knew the story of Adonhueso, of the King of Angola, of King Da, the incarnation of the Serpent, which is the eternal beginning, never ending" (13). These oral and indigenous folk and religious practices found an important role in the development of Caribbean national identities.

Carpentier's novel is also an important political text. Although Mackandal's approach to political discontent appears basic to the modern reader, it was revolutionary in terms of the way that he procured the few tools available for effective insubordination. He was ingenious in his choice of weapon. A mere cattle caretaker, Mackandal's use of poisonous mush-rooms reveals his strong desire to achieve liberty. The irrepressible urge for personal and political freedom becomes the novel's main theme. Mackandal's story, in terms of Carpentier's strong political activism, represents the struggle against Latin America's long history of foreign domination.

Carpentier's contribution to today's widely practiced magical realism is his conviction that the fantastic happened (and still takes place) in the convoluted history of Latin America. Carpentier was also a committed activist. His incorporations of aesthetic experimentation and political intention are the most celebrated characteristics of *The Kingdom of This World*.

BIBLIOGRAPHY

Alegría, Ciro. *Broad and Alien Is the World*. Trans. Harriet de Onís. New York: Farrar & Rinehart, 1941.

Altamirano, Ignacio Manuel. *El Zarco, the Bandit*. Trans. Mary Allt. London: Folio Society, 1957.

Arguedas, José María. *Ríos profundos*. Trans. Frances Horning Barraclough. Austin: University of Texas Press, 1978.

Asturias, Miguel Angel. *Men of Maize*. Trans. Gerald Martin. New York: Delacorte Press, 1975.

———. *The Mirror of Lida Sal: Tales Based on Mayan Myths and Guatemalan Legends*. Trans. Gilbert Alter-Gilbert. Pittsburgh: Latin American Literary Review Press, 1997.

———. *Mulata*. Trans. Gregory Rabassa. New York: Delacorte Press, 1967.

———. *The President*. Trans. Frances Partridge. Prospect Heights, IL: Waveland Press, 1997.

———. "Tatuana's Tale." Trans. Patricia Emigh and Frank MacShane. *The Eye of the Heart. Short Stories from Latin America*. Ed. Barbara Howes. New York: Bobbs-Merrill, 1973: 118–122.

Azuela, Mariano. *Two Novels of Mexico: "The Flies" and "The Bosses."* Trans. LesleyByrd Simpson. Berkeley: University of California Press, 1956.

———. *The Underdogs*. Trans. Frederick H. Fornoff. Pittsburgh: University of Pittsburgh Press, 1992.

Cabrera, Lydia. "Daddy Turtle and Daddy Tiger." Trans. Susan Bassnett. *The Voice of the Turtle: An Anthology of Cuban Stories*. Ed. Peter Bush. New York: Orove, 1997: 49–71.

Carpentier, Alejo. *The Kingdom of This World*. Trans. Harriet de Onís. New York: Noonday Press, 1989.

Gallegos, Rómulo. *Doña Bárbara*. Trans. Robert Malloy. New York: Peter Smith, 1948.

Güiraldes, Ricardo. *Don Segundo Sombra*. Trans. Patricia Owen Steiner. Pittsburgh: University of Pittsburgh Press, 1995.

————. "The Gauchos' Hearth." Trans. Patricia Emigh. Ed. Barbara Howes. Indianapolis: The Bobbs-Merrill Co., 1973: 73–78.

Quiroga, Horacio. *The Exiles and Other Stories.* Trans. J. David Danielson. Austin: University of Texas Press, 1987.

————. *The Decapitated Chicken and Other Stories.* Trans. Margaret Sayers Peden. Austin: University of Texas Press, 1976.

SUGGESTED READINGS

Callan, Richard J. *Miguel Angel Asturias.* New York: Twayne, 1970.

González Echevarría, Roberto. *Alejo Carpentier, the Pilgrim at Home.* Ithaca: Cornell University Press, 1977.

Leal, Luis. *Mariano Azuela.* New York: Twayne, 1971.

Nacci, Chris N. *Ignacio Manuel Altamirano.* New York: Twayne, 1970.

Previtali, Giovani. *Ricardo Guiraldes and Don Segundo Sombra; Life and Works.* New York: Hispanic Institute in the United States, 1963.

Shaw, Donald. *Alejo Carpentier.* Boston: Twayne, 1985.

Chapter 3
The Coming of Age of Modern Latin American Literature: The Boom

THE BOOM: A DEFINITION

Latin America's best-known international literature came into being during the 1960s in a movement known today as the Boom. Novels and short story collections from various Latin American countries were published in large numbers. They were writings of exceptional quality, characterized by highly innovative and experimental forms. Today this production is considered the beginning of a modern Latin American literature with strong international appeal. A tribute to the Boom authors' importance is the fact that forty years later they continue to write best-sellers, and they are often cited as literary mentors by up-and-coming international writers.

Although the production of the Boom writers is large and explores diverse subject matter and literary themes, the works so classified share common essential characteristics. The Boom writers display a strong interest in breaking away from narrative devices associated with highly traditional literature, especially a realistic approach, produced throughout most of the twentieth century. The literary experimentation of Boom writers takes various forms, but the authors' inspiration was European and American literature produced during the First and the Second World Wars. This literary period, often referred to as the **vanguard,** was highly experimental, a fact that became an inspiration for Latin American writers.

The Latin American Boom writers experimented not only because of their strong connections with European literatures but also because they had as literary models innovative Latin American writers, especially the surrealists. As discussed in the previous chapter, one important innovation of surrealist fiction writers Carpentier, Cabrera, and Asturias is their handling of native cultures. Although influenced by surrealism, they concentrated on Latin American societies and offered in-depth analyses of native cultural substrata (African-Cuban history in the cases of Carpentier and Cabrera) and the rich indigenous mythology (such as Asturias's documentation of the Maya-Quiché popular oral traditions). These writers are also significant because, unlike the older French surrealist models, their writings retain a fresh outlook, perhaps because of their strong basis in Latin American cultures. They continue to be models for generations of young Latin American writers.

The writers of the Boom were influenced directly by European literature. Many Latin American writers spent extended periods of time living in Europe, particularly in France. Like Latin American vanguardist writers before them, they were fluent in French and in English and were particularly influenced by the French literature produced during the New Novel period, an experimental literary movement of the mid-1950s and early 1960s. The New Novel opposed the traditional structure of the novel, especially the restrictions of the realist style. It also had a new approach to the role of the narrator and the development of character.

Three characteristics associated with the Boom can be traced to literary echoes of specific European and American writers. First, the Irish novelist James Joyce became one of the first literary models for Latin American writers in the early twentieth century. The influence of his novel *Ulysses* (1922) on up-and-coming Latin American writers was the motivating factor in their exploration of two important literary components: use of language and psychological depiction of characters.

Second, the influence of French existentialist Jean Paul Sartre is apparent in the characters' approach to the often absurd conditions of their troubled existence. Latin American characters experience serious crises in nightmares that blur the line between reality and imagination. The characters' behavior in the face of unusual events leads to the development of experimental plots, the bases for movements related to the fantastic or to magical realism.

Three, the characters are set within the unique coordinates of Latin American geography. Unlike previous protagonists, such as those of the criollistas, they are not trapped, however, by a wild environment that limits their psychological development. As in the literary setting of the American writer William Faulkner, the Latin American landscape becomes a symbol of the characters' personal or psychological struggles. The creation of mythical settings associated with Latin American cultures is among the most important characteristics of the Boom. Latin American settings became symbols that explored the development of culture from sociopolitical viewpoints.

Along with their evident efforts to take literature to experimental levels equal to those of international literature, the writers of the Boom displayed an interest in Latin American societies. Depiction of complex Latin American political and economic structures, explored by criollista writers, became for this newest generation an ideological goal of high importance. It was more than just a realistic reproduction of folklore or a photographic approach to social ills. Contemporary Latin American writers had a more cosmopolitan view of their native societies, including the exploration of cultural icons specific to native backgrounds. Their characters, inspired by real social and political figures, would become known internationally as representatives of Latin American cultures.

Latin American writers continued the documentation of their national histories, placing emphasis on significant events that shaped cultural or social identities. On the other hand, and of great interest to international readers, this historiography became part of the ongoing analysis of the development of humanity, a subject matter previously left understudied by both international historians and literary critics. Latin American historical events became a central component in the development of a complex narrative structure, starting with the **novel of the Mexican Revolution.** Latin American history attained worldwide importance and became an integral factor in the understanding of the complex Latin American social systems. This is one of the most important contributions of Boom literature: portrayal of Latin American society went beyond the anecdotal dimensions of previous works and became part of a more metaphysical and psychological approach to the exploration of the human psyche.

With this examination of Latin American society came a reinterpretation of the historical development of various components in the national psychological profile. A central theme was the analysis of the so-called national identities, including issues at the core of the sociopolitical and economic structures, often examined from the vantage point of several historical times. This renewed interest in historical periods also provided opportunity for the development of characters that had been either ignored in formal national historiography or that had not found a literary voice because of previous traditional aesthetics. The characters, unusual in their erratic behavior or in their unique place in national institutions, became protagonists or antagonists. They are, however, usually representative of modern Latin American societies, and they present a lesson in the development of social structures.

Unlike their previous, realism-based generation, Boom writers sought to explore Latin American reality by means of experimental narrative forms. This break with traditional aesthetics introduced several radical elements, such as the development of an unusual story often experienced by a less than credible protagonist or featuring a narrator who may or may not be trustworthy. These changes were made possible partially because of writers' exploration of literary modes associated with European vanguardism. They are the fantastic and the magical realism movements, today essential elements of Latin American literature, the preferred approach for experimental writers.

Latin American Boom writers depicted national historical events by means of narrative devices that used the fantastic. In a departure from realistic, concrete, logical literary techniques, their approach was both experimental and symbolic. Authors were interested in breaking away from the traditional Latin American literary scene. Working with the fantastic, they sought new approaches to basic components of narrative structures, such as the reliability of the narrator, the changing perspectives or points of view in various narrators, and fragmentation of the time frame of events. Such changes made Latin American literature intellectually more challenging; it departed from previous realist literature, which had presented symbols that they considered too concrete, simple, or obvious.

Fantastic narration is often defined as alteration of the physical world, particularly of the laws that regulate and control world events from natural and rational perspectives. From the scientific point of view an event such as a person's flying is irrational and physically impossible. In a fantastic narration, this event is plausible and symbolic. This is the core of the fantastic: the development of irrational events that take place within settings that are both imaginary and highly metaphorical. The way characters react to fantastic occurrences that are often outside their experience or that take place without warning becomes central to the psychological study of the protagonists. At the core of the characters' personification is their approach to making sense, rational or irrational, of the events that they are experiencing. The reader is left with the task of finding symbolic values in these bizarre events.

An extraordinary approach to the fantastic narration in Latin American literature is magical realism. Latin American writers of the Boom produced a style known today as Latin America's contribution to the postvanguard, an international movement heavily involved in literary experimentation. Magical realism came into vogue after the publication in 1966 of Gabriel García Márquez's novel *One Hundred Years of Solitude*.

Two Latin American writers had a particular influence on the Boom: the Argentine Jorge Luis Borges and the Mexican Juan Rulfo. They are analyzed here as antecedents to the Boom and as masters of the experimental techniques that later writers would make their own literary trademark. Borges is considered today the father of the modern Latin American short story. He provided midcentury Latin American literature with a complex approach to Latin American societies from an intellectual point of view. Juan Rulfo displayed an earthbound approach to rural societies, in particular, their belief in supernatural events.

The aesthetics of magical realism shared by Boom writers provided cohesion to a best-selling literary movement with a Pan-American approach and international appeal. The appeal of magical realism to both Latin American and international readers is in its highly cultural, social, and religious-bound components. Like realist writers, the Boom fully explored Latin American reality and history.

These writers were fascinated by unrecorded native history, particularly from the point of view of the common people—peasants or common city dwellers. They were not interested in a rational approach to official history, however, but in a number of documented unusual occurrences that gave Latin America an aura, a mystique. They did not have to look hard; evidence of the unusual nature of Latin American reality was plentiful in colonial chronicles and in modern stories about social and political personages, such as the totalitarian dictator.

The major appeal of the Boom writers may be, however, their documentation of native Latin American culture, particularly depiction of life in the countryside. As large cities became important technological centers in most Latin American countries, elements of rural life became literary themes. Rural culture, with its ingrained religious components, helped to shape national identities and often determined certain historical processes. Native belief systems, many writers insisted, are often unconscious and rise into conscious recognition during fantastic events. These occurrences are highly symbolic and, as with the fantastic genre, of Pan-American and international appeal.

The writers of the Boom discussed here are the Argentine Julio Cortázar, the Peruvian Mario Vargas Llosa, the Mexican Carlos Fuentes, and the Colombian Gabriel García Márquez. All have strong thematic connections with Latin American cultures or sociopolitical institutions. One reason Cortázar's short stories became known throughout the Americas is his aesthetic experimentation with narrative devices. He was also among the pioneers in Latin America who explored the fantastic as a reflection of privileged mental states of mind. Often drawing from Latin American cultural components, Cortázar's stories delve into the experience of unusual, uncanny events.

Vargas Llosa's interest in the oppressive military presence in his native Peruvian government illustrates the degree of political involvement of the Boom writers. He explored the military as both a "native" character of importance in Latin American social fabrics and as a literary symbol that addresses issues of interest to worldwide contemporary societies. Vargas Llosa's detailed historical approach to Peruvian national values makes him an innovator of the historical narrative genre, a style very much in vogue in Latin America throughout the late nineteenth and the twentieth centuries.

The writings of Carlos Fuentes and of Gabriel García Márquez display characteristics associated with the fantastic and with magical realism. Although the terms are often interchangeable because of similarities in aesthetics, it is apparent that these two authors use the genres with specific ideological purpose. Fuentes's approach to the fantastic leads him into research of Mexico's indigenous anthropology. His unusual plots invite the reader to examine bizarre behaviors that result from rejection of native cultures.

García Márquez is the Latin American writer who best exemplifies the aesthetics of **magical realism,** a style that today is integrally characteristic of literary production from Latin America. The national and international appeal of magical realism may lie in its close association with Latin American cultures, both rural and urban, indigenous and modern. These are societies that since their foundation have defied control by logic, societies in which unusual events have been historically common occurrences. García Márquez skillfully recreates Colombian society; he is, like the native colonial chroniclers, a self-made historian who traces the particularities of Latin American cultures. Those peculiarities appear in his examples of magical realism.

This chapter ends with an analysis of *En Chimá nace un santo* (1964; *A Saint Is Born in Chimá*, 1991) by Colombian fiction writer Manuel Zapata Olivella. This novel uses experimental techniques similar to those associated with magical realism. García Márquez created Macondo and Zapata Olivella created Chimá, each a village on the Colombian coast. Chimá is an imaginary place, a landscape with a strong role in the development of extraordinary characters and plots. It has a mythical value, with characters that represent a variety of social and economic aspects of life in a small, isolated town on the Latin American coast. The characters, following Rulfo's literary model, display uncommon behaviors and are at the mercy of local religious beliefs. Their interaction and their handling of unusual events that suddenly plague them, as in other novels of the "Boom," represent Zapata Olivella's comments on the Colombian political condition.

ANTECEDENTS OF THE BOOM

Jorge Luis Borges (Argentina, 1899–1986)

Jorge Luis Borges, poet, short story writer, and essayist, is known for his radical renovations to the aesthetics of the short story. An inspiration to Latin American and to international short story writers, he is the intellectual father of a new approach to the genre. His contribution to modern Latin American literature goes beyond his revolutionary narrative style, however. Borges was well read; he became a literary critic whose encyclopedic knowledge included interdisciplinary fields such as philosophy, religious studies, mathematics, and world history. This vast scholarship has a prominent place in his stories, which are often allegorical.

Borges was also a polyglot. His profound interest in ancient and modern languages is evident in his short stories, which often display obscure references to exotic cultures, foreign to his native Argentina. A gifted translator, he translated into Spanish stories of Kafka, a writer whom he admired. Other translations into Spanish are of works by English-speaking writers of international fame, such as Virginia Woolf, William Faulkner, and Oscar Wilde. In particular, his Spanish translation of James Joyce's *Ulysses* is considered a masterpiece.

Borges was born in Buenos Aires into a family involved in key events in Argentine history. His paternal grandmother was an English woman, part of a booming European immigration wave that was transforming Buenos Aires into a cosmopolitan city. Other historical connections included family members in governmental posts after the war of independence in 1816. If the reader takes some of his short stories as partially autobiographical, an ancestor of Borges died fighting rebellious Indians in a period around the middle of the nineteenth century.

From his father, an English teacher, young Borges inherited a liking for English literature. He had learned the language as a child. He was a voracious reader. His list of favorite writers in English was long. Among others, there were Mark Twain, Edgar Allen Poe, Emily Dickinson, Lewis Carroll, Walt Whitman, William Faulkner, and Virginia Woolf. His knowledge of English literature earned him a post as professor of English and American literatures at the University of Buenos Aires. He wrote poetry in English. His main literary language, however, was Spanish.

Borges's literature, both poetry and short stories, reflects influence of vanguardist movements that he experienced in Europe. At age fifteen, he traveled with his family throughout Europe, and he lived in Geneva, where he attended school for some years. He learned Latin, French, and German. As a young adult and an aspiring poet, Borges spent time in Spain. There he started writing vanguardist or experimental poetry. He also met distinguished Spanish intellectuals through his contacts with literary journals that were publishing his poetry.

Borges's first short story collection, *A Universal History of Infamy* (1935), was revolutionary in its departure from traditional realist techniques. Two of its characteristics were unusual plots and the reactions of odd characters to actions that went beyond their control. The stories are examples of a new genre, the **fantastic,** which attempts to explore a series of abstract or metaphysical subjects. Borges found inspiration for his strange characters in several cultures, such as a slaver, a nineteenth-century New York mobster, and a samurai in ancient Japan. The characters become trapped in plots that encompass metaphysical considerations. Among his important literary motifs is his conception of time; actions from the past and the future occur simultaneously in an immediate present. Borges also showed a particular interest in human destiny, mainly in death, and in the ways in which individuals seem to delay it or invent an alternate destiny to replace a mundane one. His penetrating idea is that human existence is really a dream. Borges's central concern was the existential anguish of modern man immersed in the twentieth-century quest for personal identity.

He published his best-known stories in *Ficciones* (1944) and in *The Aleph* (1949). They appeared in English translation in the United States in 1966 amid highly positive critical reviews. In 1961, he received the prestigious Formentor Prize, which he shared with Samuel Beckett. Borges's reputation outside Argentina was almost instantaneous. He toured the United States that year for the first time, and in 1967 he held the Charles Eliot Norton Chair of Poetry at Harvard University. By the end of the 1960s, he was probably the best-known Latin American writer. He continued a full working and learning program despite having lost his sight in the late 1950s.

Borges's fame and his worldwide literary significance are based on short stories with a metaphysical basis, with a message that appeals to international readers. These stories are not set in Argentina and the characters are not Argentine. In them the reader is exposed to a variety of ideas central to Borges's opinion of the purpose of literary work. His decision to address such issues in an international literature and not by means of "local" characters and settings was controversial in his native Argentina.

In his article "The Argentine Writer and Tradition," Borges addressed the issue of what constitutes Argentine culture and how to reproduce it within the context of Argentine symbols. He challenged the traditional critical position that defined Argentine culture in the figure of the **gaucho,** the cowboy of the pampas, the wild plains of the Province of Buenos Aires. According to that strict definition of national values, the austere life of this national hero was considered a metaphorical reflection of the psychological makeup of Argentina as a modern nation. According to Borges, the gaucho's main concern, as reflected in the formal literature written about these colorful characters by learned writers, reflected three general themes: "the pangs of love and loneliness, the unhappiness of love" (*Labyrinths* 178).

Borges's article challenged two main conceptions about the constitution of national Argentine literature. First, Borges proposed that, although limited to the wild, rural setting of the pampas, the gaucho's metaphorical preoccupations would have gone beyond the subjects of loneliness and the impossibility of love. He also proposed that other characters, including figures of international significance, could represent Argentine national values, most importantly as literary symbols of "being Argentine without abounding in local color" (*Labyrinths* 181). He went straight to the core of the argument and challenged the traditionalist stand on native Argentine literary motifs, limited "to a few impoverished local themes, as if we Argentines could only speak of *orillas* [river banks] and *estancias* [plantations] and not of the universe" (182). With his references to *orillas* and *estancias,* Borges pointed to the limited settings available to Argentine writers if they were to remain within the traditional conception of national literature, closely related to and therefore limited to, readers interested in those literary symbols.

Borges did produce short stories about gauchos, setting them within a time of importance in the development of modern Argentine identity.

Written within the confines of the national trend of the so-called **gaucho literature,** Borges's stories "Streetcorner Man," "The Life of Tadeo Isidoro Cruz (1829–1874)," and "The Dead Man" present the gaucho as a protagonist. He is characterized, however, as an outlaw, marginal to societal expectations of civility. Metaphysically, Borges's gauchos, including his characters living on the fringes of the law, take the reader into a mythical space where rational thinking is replaced by primitive, and therefore primal, motivation and behavior.

Borges's interest in tough men with criminal backgrounds and unrepentant, violent behaviors is evident in "Streetcorner Man." Unlike most of Borges's stories, this is a simple narration, devoid of experimental narrative devices. The narrator, vaguely referred to as "the Kid," is both a witness and a participant in the action that he narrates to a listener, addressed as Borges. Through the kid's narration the reader meets the main protagonists: Rosendo Juárez, known as the Slasher, and Francisco Real, an equally evil character with a bloody nickname to prove it—he's known as the Butcher. The setting of the action is a dance hall in the outskirts of Buenos Aires, in a neighborhood of ill repute where all kinds of men come to drink and dance the tango.

Although he's within a marginal setting conducive to irrational behavior, Rosendo does not accept the Butcher's challenge to a knife fight, an action that surprises the Slasher's friends, particularly the narrator, the Kid. The tough man has been the Kid's role model, and the Kid imitates Rosendo's behavior down to the most insignificant details, even the way he spits. After Rosendo walks away from the fight, the Butcher appears happy, perhaps satisfied that he has proven his unchallenged supremacy. This display of macho bravery is short-lived, however. Outside the hall, the Butcher is knifed by an unknown attacker. Fatally wounded, he comes inside the bar and dies among drunkards, a pathetic end for this self-proclaimed hero.

Death, not characters or action, was Borges's central concern. One of the witnesses expresses the story's motif, the existential significance of death: "All it takes to die is being alive" (*The Aleph* 41). The story's surprising ending, with its subtle hint that the Kid could be responsible for the Butcher's death, seems to support Borges's conceptual approach to death's immediacy, even when circumstances appear to conspire to keep it away.

Death and the destiny of outlaw characters are the main themes of "The Life of Tadeo Isidoro Cruz (1829–1874)" and of "The Dead Man." The stories have in common male antihero protagonists, who find themselves facing consequences of their irrational behavior. Both of them, particularly at the moment of their death, come to understand their destiny. Tadeo Isidoro Cruz is the more sympathetic character of the two men. The illegitimate son of a gaucho who had been forced into a militia group, Cruz appears to have decided not to become a soldier. He is working as a gaucho when, without cause, he is forced to kill a man. Although he tries to escape the authorities, they finally capture him. His penalty is, as in his father's case, military service.

Tadeo Isidoro, unlike his father, appears satisfied with his forced destiny. He successfully fights in civil wars and serves in military campaigns against rebellious Indians. In the end, as a sergeant appointed to a local police force, he finds himself involved in a search for a fugitive who, much like himself years before, has killed a man. The surprising ending, when Tadeo Isidoro turns against his own men and begins to fight alongside the fugitive, is described within the context of the revelation of his own destiny: "He understood that his real destiny was a lone wolf, not a gregarious dog. He understood that the other man was himself" (*The Aleph* 85).

A twisted plotline with a consequence fatal for the protagonist is the central action of "The Dead Man." As in "The Life of Tadeo Isidoro Cruz (1829–1874)," young Benjamín Otálora is forced to become a fugitive from justice after he kills a man. He seeks the help of a powerful strongman, Azevedo Bandeira, whose gang he hopes to join. He has with him a letter of introduction from a local gangster to facilitate entrance into such a secretive group. Otálora sets out on his search and, by mere coincidence, stumbles into Bandeira in a bar. There Otálora stops one man from knifing another, who is Bandeira himself. Otálora then becomes part of Bandeira's group, quickly learning the tasks of gauchos, including the illegal activities associated with this nomadic life, such as cattle smuggling.

Although it appears that Otálora has a guaranteed future, he seeks to take over Bandeira's leadership and enlists the aid of other gauchos. He finally appears to have gained control, but his friends turn against him and give information to Bandeira. Like the protagonist of "The Life of Tadeo Isidoro Cruz (1829–1874)," at the moment of his execution, Otálora analyzes the events that precipitated his demise, a moment that also verbalizes as the story's message: "Otálora realizes, before dying, that he has been betrayed from the start, that he has been sentenced to death—that love and command and triumph have been accorded him because his companions already thought of him as a dead man, because to Bandeira he already was a dead man" (99).

Borges's international appeal may lie in his carefully sought balance between philosophical concepts and the intricate structure of his short stories. His stories are examples of innovative narrative techniques stemming from a vanguardist mode present in Latin America since the early 1920s. Borges was a literary model for Boom writers of the 1960s. Today he is one of the most frequently translated Latin American short story writers and a significant literary figure of international acclaim.

Juan Rulfo (Mexico, 1918–1986)

Juan Rulfo is considered the last writer of the movement of the **novel of the Mexican Revolution.** He displayed a persistent interest in the literary depiction of issues relating to that eventful sociopolitical movement. Rulfo's style is innovative, and it is a direct antecedent to the experimental style of the Boom writers. He broke away from the strong realist approach of pre-ceding writers of the literature of the Mexican Revolution and favored an abstract presentation of Mexican society. His choice of a mythical setting and of strange characters that experience unusual events has been an inspi-ration for magical realist writers, particularly Gabriel García Márquez.

Rulfo was born in a small town in Sayula, in the state of Jalisco, some three hundred miles northwest of Mexico City. His father, a wealthy landowner, lost his money and land after the Mexican Revolution. In 1925, his father was assassinated during the armed conflict of the Cristeros revolt. That civil confrontation was in opposition to federal regulations that placed heavy restrictions on the celebration of religious events, mainly Catholic, and limited the influence of the Catholic Church in civil affairs. The warfare had particularly devastating effects in Jalisco, an area already badly affected by battles at the end of the revolution. It was also a terrain that was suffer-ing terrible effects of erosion, including years of droughts. The arid terrain sent many campesinos into involuntary immigration, particularly through Tijuana, on the border with the United States.

The revolutionary and civil wars in Jalisco are prominent in Rulfo's short stories. He was moved by the many shocking stories resulting from those conflicts. In Rulfo's own case, his family lost members in the war, and he spent part of his childhood in an orphanage, after his mother's death from a heart attack. He would have bad memories of his life in the orphanage of boys, run by French nuns of the Josephine Order; he often referred to it as a correctional facility.

He moved to Mexico City at age fifteen. The capital city left a strong mark on the rural teenager. He entered the university to study accounting and lit-erature, but, because of financial difficulties, he did not finish a degree. He held a series of jobs, including working as a bureaucrat for the Department of Mexican Immigration and as a salesperson for the Goodrich Rubber Company. His work with the Immigration Department allowed him to travel extensively through Mexico and to come into contact with a variety of people of different socioethnic backgrounds. In 1962, he joined the National Institute for Indigenous Studies. His passion for the documenta-tion of Mexico's rich anthropological past would curtail his own literary pro-duction.

Among the youngest Mexican writers to produce experimental literary work, Rulfo also had active participation in the national intellectual scene. In 1944, he founded *Pan*, a journal devoted to promoting the newest gen-eration of Mexican writers. He joined efforts with up-and-coming writers, particularly short story writer Juan José Arreola (1918–2001), who was *Pan*'s cofounder. True to its symbolic title, the journal became a "bread loaf," nourishment for young writers in the midst of a literary scene con-trolled by realist writers. Thus, both Rulfo and Arreola published their first short stories in *Pan*. Their innovative styles would soon capture the attention of national literary critics.

The publication of Rulfo's first and only short story collection, *El llano en llamas y otros cuentos* (1953; *The Burning Plain and Other Stories*, 1967) marks the beginning of a trend in Latin American literature in which the character faces the forceful reality of the Mexican rural landscape in the midst of unusual events. This juxtaposition of the real with illogical or absurd occurrences would become one of his contributions to the future magical realistic production. Rulfo's deeply felt exploration of the Mexican landscape would also affect the Boom literary production, particularly in his creation of villages with ancient anthropological and mythical values. The characters that inhabit these villages are symbolic and display an existentialist dilemma of international appeal.

Rulfo's literary reputation rests, however, on a single novelette, *Pedro Páramo* (1955). The story is simple: after his mother's death, Juan Preciado, a young man, sets out to Comala, his mother's native village, in search of his father, Pedro Páramo. This travelogue of an ordinary protagonist undergoes a sudden and interesting turn of events when Preciado realizes that he and the characters he meets in Comala are dead. They are the narrators of the events that led to Pedro Páramo's destruction of Comala. Comala, like García Márquez's future Mancondo, becomes a mythical landscape, one in which Rulfo explores ingrained Mexican socioreligious beliefs.

Pedro Páramo also offers a strong political reading about Latin America's strongmen, the so-called ***caciques*** or ***caudillos.*** These powerful landowners had almost unlimited political control over small towns and villages. Rulfo's psychological profile of the caudillo goes beyond the characterizations of previous realist writers, such as Rómulo Gallegos. In Rulfo's caudillo readers find a well-rounded character, whose control over Comala is possible through the existing local sociopolitical institutions. Thus, although a despicable character, Pedro Páramo is also brilliant in his handling of political institutions. Such literary characterization of the caudillo will appear in future novels featuring Latin American dictators.

Rulfo was also a photographer and screenplay writer. A prolific photographer, he continued his project of documenting rural and ancient Mexican landscapes. A land of enormous geographic and socioeconomic contrasts, Mexico for Rulfo is both nurturing and punishing. The most striking of his photographs are those of the sparse, arid terrain of his native Jalisco. The desolate landscape and the abandoned villages share the haunting, eerie quality that is also characteristic of his writings. As with the criollista writers before him, Rulfo shows a deep impact by the Mexican landscape; however, a more important contribution was his uncanny depiction of the strong relationship in Latin America between man and nature.

Rulfo's photographs also reveal an interest in capturing images of cities. They are alluring reproductions of impersonal spaces, particularly of Mexico

City, which become symbols of an industrial wasteland. Rulfo often made negative statements about Mexico City, today the world's largest city. He preferred, however, to set his literary characters in the rural areas that he knew intimately as a child. In a way, it seems that Rulfo held the cities responsible for the demise of village life because workers preferred the sheltered spaces of the city to the punishing natural elements of the countryside.

Rulfo was also an active participant in Mexico's booming film industry. In 1955, the film *Talpa,* based on a short story by Rulfo, was produced. He wrote screenplays during the 1960s, at the peak of Mexican cinema, which had yet to feel the threat of Hollywood. His short story "El gallo de oro" ("The Golden Cock") was made into a film in 1964, with a screenplay written by Carlos Fuentes and Gabriel García Márquez. In 1967, his novel *Pedro Páramo* appeared in a film scripted by Rulfo. A collection of Rulfo's stories written for films is available in Spanish: *El gallo de oro y otros textos para cine* (*The Golden Cock and other texts for the cinema;* 1980). These texts speak about the use of cinematic techniques in Rulfo's writing.

Important literary personalities recognized Rulfo's *Pedro Páramo* as a masterpiece of Latin American literature. Two were the Argentine short story writer Jorge Luis Borges and the Mexican poet and essayist Octavio Paz. Rulfo received distinguished honors and awards in Mexico and abroad. He was awarded two Rockefeller grants in 1953 and 1954 and a Guggenheim fellowship in 1968, the same year he received Mexico's highest literary recognition, the National Prize for Letters. In recognition of his literary production, he was elected to the Mexican Academy of the Spanish Language in 1980. He was also granted Spain's distinguished Príncipe Asturias Prize in 1983.

Rulfo's short story collection *The Burning Plain* strongly influenced Mexican and Latin American literatures of the mid-1950s. This was a decade of literary change, particularly the rejection of the realist model in the depiction of the Latin American reality. Like Borges, Rulfo attempted to create new aesthetic approaches to the exploration of native histories, characters, or landscapes. Their differences lay in their experimentation with reality, which in Rulfo's work retains a degree of social activism, a characteristic of novels of the Mexican Revolution.

The stories in *The Burning Plain* are brief, intrinsic to Rulfo's concise style, built on short, to-the-point sentences. This element in itself is a striking change from the style of previous Latin American short story writers. The succinct quality of his stories contributes to the development of strong characters and a stern setting. Rulfo, following the realist Mexican tradition of documenting sociopolitical discontent, merges the newest trends of aesthetic experimentation with the social denunciation that is characteristic of Latin American literature of the mid–twentieth century.

Rulfo's writings display three striking elements: creation of a surreal rural landscape, desolate characters, and undetermined or ambiguous endings.

Although these elements are experimental, they stand out because of their close attachment to Mexican culture and indigenous belief systems. Despite their closeness to the world of the Mexican campesino, characterized as humble and destitute, the stories possess worldwide appeal because the characters become symbols of the convoluted life typical of the mid–twentieth century, which demanded that traditional ways of life give way to modern concepts. As Rulfo's text explores such changes, they are depicted as difficult but often welcome because rural traditions are not always positive.

The landscape is perhaps the most dazzling feature of Rulfo's stories. It stands out because of its mysterious and alluring nature, and the reader is often uncertain whether the place is real or a figment of an unreliable narrator's imagination. This is the case in the story "Luvina," named for a town supposedly located in an uncertain area in "the mountains in the south" (283). It is a mysterious town, more so because the protagonist, a man on his way to Luvina, never makes it there. He is in a bar, speaking to an unidentified old man who has a grim opinion of Luvina. It is a remote, inhospitable village where there is never a blue sky: "The whole horizon there is always a dingy color, always clouded over by a dark stain that never goes away" (284). It is also dry, a land perpetually castigated by drought.

This information comes from an old man, who has been drinking at a bar with the traveler, who is resting during his long trip to Luvina. The old man tells a series of stories about his experiences while living in Luvina. His characterization of the village is heightened to maintain the traveler's interest so that he will continue to buy drinks for the old man. The old man creates an environment of mystery around Luvina's desolate and arid geography. Nature has a strong grip on its scattered inhabitants, who are at the mercy of strong, dry winds.

The literary depiction moves away from the traditional and concrete approach of the **novela de la tierra.** This is a land, like that in many other places in Latin America, where nature exerts tremendous control because of its strength. Unlike previous realist approaches, in "Luvina" the setting takes on a mysterious aura as the ceaseless wind is personalized to represent death and despair: " 'The people from there say that when the moon is full they clearly see the figure of the wind sweeping along Luvina's streets, bearing behind it a black blanket; but what I always managed to see when there was a moon in Luvina was the image of despair—always' " (285).

In an interesting turn of events, the explanation for this terrible feeling of despair has a logical explanation. The desolation of Luvina came about after the village lost its natural resources (the reader assumes that this is partially the result of erosion and drought). Men of working age had to leave to find jobs. The ghosts, perhaps exaggerated by the narrator's heavy drinking, were indigenous women who avoided him, as the local culture expected of them. In the ambiguous ending, the narrator does not fully explain the reasons for his leaving Luvina.

There is, however, a component of political activism. The old man insists that he had attempted to provide solutions for Luvina's aging population. Yet the indigenous women laughed at his advice that they should appeal to the government for help; their comment about authority, which they call the "lord," goes to the core of the abuse to indigenous communities: "That lord only remembers them when one of his boys has done something wrong down there. Then he sends to Luvina for him and they kill him. Aside from that, they don't know if the people exist" (289).

The use of characters based on unusual rural protagonists supports the depiction of a mythical Mexican landscape. "Macario" is the story of a boy, the title character, who is narrating his life story. He, like the old man in "Luvina," is an unreliable narrator; the reader soon learns that he is mentally retarded and he is the town target of jokes and physical abuse. As the story opens, he is sitting quietly by the sewer waiting patiently for frogs to come out. Although this is an unusual activity, he soon explains his reason: his grandmother hates their croaking sounds and is often kept awake at night. Macario, who loves her tenderly, has decided to kill any frogs that may leap out of the sewer that night.

While Macario patiently awaits the frogs, he thinks about his life in a straightforward stream of consciousness. He is an orphan, with no information about his parents. He has been raised by a woman named Felipa and his grandmother, who remains unidentified by name. Although Macario appears to love both women, Felipa is Macario's substitute mother, providing the physical care that he does not receive from his grandmother. This is a story about wanting love, represented by Macario's whining about his constant hunger. According to his story, he is often hungry, despite the fact that his grandmother and Felipa provide him with enough to eat.

Macario, both a tragic figure and a social outcast, is trapped in a dismal existence with no way out. Like the nameless indigenous women in "Luvina," Macario is marginal; unlike those women, his limits are not ethnic but physical because his disability is the target of the town's open aggression. Also like the indigenous women, Macario has no exit from his existential dilemma. Luvina's women refuse to leave on religious grounds: they cannot take the remains of their ancestors with them. Macario, playing with crickets, finds himself playing the same role as the insects: "The day there are no more crickets the world will be filled with the screams of holy souls and we'll all start running scared out of our wits" (298). These popular religious beliefs are important because they inject a reason for being into an otherwise meaningless existence.

Pedro Páramo is Rulfo's most famous work of fiction. Critics often list this highly experimental novella as the beginning of the aesthetics of magical realism. García Márquez stated that he could not have written his masterpiece, *One Hundred Years of Solitude*, without Rulfo's model, specifically the particular literary treatment of the landscape, and the creation of Comala, the prototype of a rural Mexican village. Comala, like Luvina, has an important role in the development of characters who, like earlier protagonists, are symbols, often parables; their behaviors are lessons to be learned. In line with Rulfo's activism, the message is strongly political. Rulfo was also interested, however, in the exploration of the human psyche, using characters who are witnesses to passionate events. This is the Rulfo of international appeal, as reflected in the many translations of *Pedro Páramo*.

As in most of Rulfo's stories, the landscape and the village of Comala are central elements in a story that is interesting because of its gathering of unusual characters. *Pedro Páramo* is a simple novel from a narrative point of view: Juan Preciado, having learned from his mother at the time of her death the identity of his father, sets out to meet him. In the mode of a travelogue, Juan Preciado records his impressions about changes in the landscape as he approaches Comala for the first time. Once in Comala, he meets a number of characters that fill in the voids of his personal story.

Comala is a mythical place. Its association with intense heat is apparent in its name, a *comal* in Mexican cooking is an iron plate used to cook tortillas at high temperatures. Another indication of this is that the action takes place in August, the so-called dog days. It is, therefore, a village that suffers the consequences of intense weather conditions. The characters' behaviors have been predetermined by geography, living as they do in a rural and isolated village, one where the oppressive heat can often lead to irrational behavior.

Upon Juan Preciado's arrival in Comala, he finds it in shambles; nothing resembles his mother's loving memories of her beloved birthplace. The village is dead. Few people are willing to tell him Comala's story or his own family history. To his surprise (and here begin dazzling experimental narrative devices), Juan Preciado suddenly realizes that he and the few people with whom he has come in contact are dead. Their fragmented stories about the destruction of Comala at the hands of the local *cacique,* Pedro Páramo, constitute the novel's most important narrative element.

Death is a symbol that plays two distinctive roles. The belief in ghosts or in the possibility that the soul remains active after death is a strong feature of Mexican religious lore. In *Pedro Páramo,* the characters' immortality is restricted to the confines of Comala, a sort of purgatory. This adds suspense to the otherwise simple story of Pedro Páramo, the aging political *cacique* of a remote, impoverished village. The characters appear to have been condemned to being eternal narrators, offering a lesson with a moral ending. The historical accounts disclosed by Comala's inhabitants and, more important, their own reactions to these often terrible events have an international appeal.

The most significant character in *Pedro Páramo* is its protagonist, the powerful landowner who in spiteful revenge against the township had set up the terrible events that brought about Comala's financial demise. Pedro Páramo's hatred for Comala started when the inhabitants openly celebrated the death of Páramo's beloved wife. *Pedro Páramo* can be read as an early novel of a genre within the trend known as the **novel of the dictator.** Several characters that had had direct contact with this terrible *caudillo* produce information about him. Their multiple points of view about the possible reasons for Pedro Páramo's fatal decision make up most of the novella's plot.

Pedro Páramo's end, like that of other notorious Latin American dictators, is predictable: a violent death. An illegitimate child of Pedro Páramo, a strong-willed man who had survived the Mexican Revolution, assassinates his father. The culmination of a life characterized by violence and death is narrated in the concise style so characteristic of Rulfo: "After a few steps he fell; inside, he was begging for help, but no words were audible. He fell to the ground with a thud, and lay there, collapsed like a pile of rocks" (124).

Juan Rulfo's experimentation with narrative devices, including multiple points of view and the lack of a reliable narrator, influenced early production of the Boom. His view of Mexican society from the perspective of dead characters was a change from the monotonous approaches in realist writings of the second half of twentieth-century Latin American literature. Above all, his direct and concise style and his political platform for socioeconomic change would appeal not only to the Boom writers, but also to the most recent Latin American writers, some of whom have declared him their literary model.

WRITERS OF THE BOOM

Julio Cortázar (Argentina, 1914–1984)

A prolific writer and the author of numerous short stories, novels, poetry, and literary criticism articles, Julio Cortázar was born in Brussels to Argentine parents. Two years later, the family moved to Switzerland, where young Cortázar began learning French, a language that he would master as an adult. When he was four years old, the Cortázars arrived in Buenos Aires and established themselves in a working-class neighborhood on the outskirts of the city. Buenos Aires appears often in Cortázar's literary production.

Shortly after their arrival in Argentina, Cortázar's father abandoned the family. The children, young Julio and his sister, were placed in the care of an aunt and a grandmother. The absence of his father would be reflected in Cortázar's work, particularly in his often murky characterizations of father figures.

Literature was important to young Cortázar. He was shy and often sick, especially from asthma, and so he became a voracious reader. During this period, he developed a taste for novels of adventure, particularly those of Jules Verne. A precocious child, he was, according to his own statement, nine years old when he wrote his first novel. In 1928, he enrolled in a

Normal School and received teaching certification in 1932. Three years later, he obtained a teaching degree in literature.

Cortázar began studying literature at the University of Buenos Aires but was interrupted within a year because of his family's precarious finances. He made teaching his choice of career. He worked in several rural schools in the province of Buenos Aires, areas that he considered representative of true Argentine culture. Meanwhile he wrote short stories and poems in his spare time, although his work was not published until 1938.

By 1941, he had published poetry and short stories in student literary journals. After a public confrontation in opposition to a newly elected president of Argentina, military strongman Juan Domingo Perón, Cortázar left his post as professor of French literature at the University of Mendoza. This was only the first of his confrontations with military governments, in Argentina and elsewhere in Latin America. Cortázar would not teach in Argentina again.

In 1946, he gained national recognition with the publication of his short story "Casa tomada" ("House Taken Over") in *Los Anales de Buenos Aires,* a literary journal edited by the famous short story writer Jorge Luis Borges. This was his first published story and his first meeting with Borges, whose reputation gave Cortázar an edge in a competitive national and international literary market. The influence of Borges's literature on Cortázar's production is significant both thematically and aesthetically, but whether Borges became Cortázar's literary mentor is still a matter of controversy. Cortázar never acknowledged a direct influence of Borges on his work. He did, however, attend a series of presentations by Borges that revealed the latter's extensive knowledge of medieval English literature.

Cortázar's literary reputation solidified following the publication in 1951 of his short story collection *Bestiario* (*Bestiary*). The stories draw heavily from the genre of the fantastic with characters facing unreal events that often speak about their heightened state of mind. He continued to be a contributor to literary journals. One in particular, *Sur,* edited by the distinguished writer Victoria Ocampo, gave Cortázar an international reputation.

To make ends meet, Cortázar became a translator of literary works written in French and English. Among the authors he translated into Spanish are André Gide, G. K. Chesterton, Daniel Defoe, and Marguerite Yourcenar. One writer in particular, Edgar Allan Poe, was to have an especially strong influence on Cortázar's stories. Critics today consider Cortázar's Spanish translation of Poe's short stories (University of Puerto Rico Press, 1956) a masterpiece and an example of skillful translation. His in-depth knowledge of European and American literature is reflected in his own literary production. He also wrote critical pieces on both Spanish American literature and works from other countries. His articles, especially those concerning aesthetics of the short story, are important tools to the readers' understanding of his own literary production.

In 1951, he received a fellowship from the French government. He lived in Paris and worked as a freelance translator for the United Nations Educational, Scientific and Cultural Organization (UNESCO). Despite his international reputation as an up-and-coming Latin American writer, Cortázar would consider his work as a translator (of nonliterary material) his main profession. His work with UNESCO provided him opportunities to travel freely throughout Latin America and Europe.

Cortázar made Paris his permanent home because of his public opposition to military regimes in his native Argentina. In 1981, President François Mitterrand granted Cortázar French citizenship. Cortázar insisted on keeping his Argentine citizenship as well, however, an action of importance because he considered himself a devoted Argentine despite having spent his professional life in France.

In 1963, Cortázar became a novelist of note with the publication of *Rayuela* (*Hopscotch,* 1966). This novel placed him into the highly experimental trend of Latin American Boom writers and earned him readers across the Americas. The novel became a bestseller in Latin America and a model of a new experimental form.

His international fame reached its peak with Michelangelo Antonioni's critically acclaimed film *Blow-Up* (1966), based on Cortázar's short story "Las babas del diablo" ("Blow-Up"). Like the works of other Boom writers, his literary production often appeared translated into English shortly after its original publication in Spanish.

As a distinguished writer Cortázar began a busy schedule of international visits. For example, he became closely associated with cultural institutions in revolutionary Cuba. Throughout his career Cortázar displayed a public approval of socialist governments. Besides his visits to Cuba and his articles in support of the Cuban revolutionary government, he also visited Chile in 1970 in support of President Salvador Allende. He favored other incipient socialist-oriented movements, such as that of the Nicaraguan Sandinista rebels. After the triumph of the Sandinista revolution in 1979, Cortázar visited Nicaragua several times. He produced a travelogue, *Nicaraguan Sketches,* a collection of essays that depicted the Sandinistas in a positive light.

His reputation was also strong outside Latin America. In 1973, *Libro de Manuel* (*A Manual for Manuel;* 1978) earned him the French Médicis Prize. In keeping with his strong call for political activism and his hatred of military dictatorships, he donated the prize money to the United Chilean Front, which opposed the rise to power in Chile that year of General Augusto Pinochet. In *A Manual for Manuel,* Cortázar explored the underground world of guerrilla fighters and the terrible torture they faced from Latin American military dictatorships. In the "Note to the American Reader" of the English translation, Cortázar states his intention that *A*

Manual for Manuel provide a "testimony of torture" at the hands of the Argentine military junta under General Jorge Rafael Videla (5).

Cortázar became an active speaker against the crimes committed under military dictatorships. In 1983 he made an appearance at the United Nations on behalf of the thousands of *desaparecidos*—activists who had disappeared. Most of the *desaparecidos* were young people who were kidnapped in Latin American countries under military dictatorships during the 1970s and the 1980s and tortured as punishment for their participation in underground movements against the illegal governments. Many of the activists never returned to their homes; their whereabouts remain unknown, and their bodies have never been recovered. Cortázar also spoke on behalf of his native Argentina, which had been in the grip of a terrible military dictatorship since 1976.

Cortázar became a well-known literary figure in the United States. As early as 1960, he frequently appeared at academic conferences. In 1975 he visited the University of Oklahoma and Barnard College in 1980.

Cortázar made an enormous contribution to the development of the Latin American experimental short story of the mid–twentieth century. A master of the short story form, his stories are perfect examples of this genre's tight construction of plot. Unusual elements of Cortázar's stories, including his preference for unexpected endings, make reading his stories an uncanny experience. His name is linked to the genre of the **fantastic,** an aesthetic style that attempts to examine the Latin American environment from a different perspective, one that emphasizes surreal events. His work as an avantgarde writer has been recognized as a key to understanding the experimental literature produced by other Boom writers. Perhaps the strongest testimony to the importance of his literary production is the influence it exerts on today's writers. He is often listed among the most important international short story writers of the twentieth century.

Cortázar's short stories reflect a variety of styles, themes, and characters. Unlike other Latin American writers, he places his characters within numerous environments, often foreign to the traditional locales of Latin American cities or the geography of the Latin American countryside. Perhaps because Cortázar spent so many years of his life as a permanent resident in France, his literature displays his interest in European themes. Some of his stories take place in French settings, usually Paris. There is a strong tendency as well to attempt an examination of reality from a European perspective and from the point of view of themes associated with city life. His characters, who are often Latin Americans, find themselves trapped in a city that restricts their behavior. The plight inherent in an urban experience—such as the big Parisian metropolis—became one of Cortázar's trademarks and a literary model for Latin American writers who had started literary documentation of the growth of their large cities, particularly of the capitals.

Despite his exile in France, Cortázar produced a number of stories that take place in Latin American settings. These short stories reveal a twofold interest: first, Cortázar provides an anthropological exploration of the Latin American psyche from a historical perspective; second, he skillfully offers a sociological approach to understanding national governments, their frequent experiences of political havoc, and their effects on the common citizen.

One factor in Cortázar's international reputation is a strong influence of surrealism, particularly in his use of the fantastic. Speaking about his attraction to the fantastic, Cortázar pointed to the genre's uncanny ability to produce in the reader a reaction of shock, an uncommon effect in a more passive reading experience: "something grabs us by the shoulder to throw us outside ourselves" (*Around the Day* 30–31). That element of surprise and the lesson learned from events associated with it are Cortázar's main interest in the fantastic.

Cortázar's exploration of native Latin American settings and characters from a fantastic perspective are evident in the short stories "House Taken Over," "Axolotl," "The Night Face Up" (*Blow-Up and Other Stories*), and "Apocalypse at Solentiname" (*We Love Glenda So Much*). They stand out because of their different approaches to unreal situations and for their depictions of Latin American characters faced with these unusual events. In "Apocalypse at Solentiname," for example, strange events take place in Latin America within the complex politics of the military.

Cortázar's interest in exploring Latin American society by means of symbols associated with cultural icons is evident in "House Taken Over." In this simple story, an unnamed man and his sister, who live in the huge house of their ancestors in a historic neighborhood in Buenos Aires, attempt to combat boredom by performing ordinary domestic tasks. They live without financial worries; as absent landowners, their earnings are plentiful enough to allow them to enjoy their hobbies. This peaceful life comes to an unexpected halt, however, when the brother announces without explanation to his sister, " 'They've taken over the back part' " (13) of the house. His solution is to close up that section of the house. The party responsible for taking over the house remains unknown to the characters, to the reader, and to the narrator.

The events that follow relate to the characters' efforts to lead normal lives despite the unwanted guests, who are kept away from the protagonists' living quarters by safely secured doors. They are not successful in keeping the forces at bay, however, and are forced to abandon the house, room by room, as they are chased out by mysterious "noises, still muffled but louder" (16). The ending, as the siblings leave the house, features the brother's last, puzzling statement about his behavior: "I locked the front door up tight and tossed the key down the sewer. It wouldn't do to have some poor devil decide to go in and rob the house, at that hour and with the house taken" (16).

The influence of Edgar Allan Poe is clear. The siblings are not central to the plotline. The house, much like its counterpart in Poe's "The Fall of the

House of Usher," is the protagonist. It influences the behavior of the characters, who, as they point out, find themselves irremediably tied to that house. The taking over of the house remains unexplained.

On the other hand, these protagonists belong to an important social class: absent landowners whose easy life, as they comment, comes from the earnings of a land that they are not working. Their story therefore takes on a political reading: the "they" who take over the house suggests the destitute, lower classes claiming for themselves a place in the aging national social system. As the purposely open ending of the story stresses, there is uncertainty of the future in the face of such a radical transformation, at least from the protagonists' point of view. They have lost control over their aged house, a symbol of a backward Argentina, clinging to colonialist ways of living.

Cortázar's interest in the exploration of metaphysical or philosophical concepts from a Latin American point of view is evident in "Axolotl." The story takes place in Paris, in the city's Botanical Gardens, where a man, unidentified by name or national origin, discovers a water tank containing the axolotls. The protagonist becomes obsessed with these strange-looking creatures and starts researching their origin. Half-fish and half-amphibians, the specimens are Mexican, nine of them, cramped in a tank where they desperately spend countless hours, "looking with their eyes of gold at whoever came near them" (4). Those inquiring, mysterious eyes captivate the character's attention. He starts to visit the axolotls on a daily basis. At the end of the story, there is ambiguity about who is inside the tank and who is the narrator, the man or the axolotl.

There is an important mythological component to this story. In the Mexican Toltec and Aztec religious belief systems, the axolotl was the animal representation of Xolotl, the so-called Vigilant, a god whose role included his guiding the dead in their final, dangerous voyage to the underworld. Cortázar's story recognizes the axolotl's role as a guide for humanity, with the character's fixation on the creatures' enlarged eyes and their reciprocal gaze in a "hopeless meditation" (7). The protagonist's inference that he has become an axolotl, whether in physical or metaphysical terms, is left to the reader's interpretation. The message of the story seems to point to the character's newly developed role, that of seer, a task that has been denied to the axolotls, restricted by captivity in the tank and reduced by modern life to mere objects of curiosity.

Cortázar's interest in ancient Mexican native religions is again evident in "The Night Face Up." The protagonist is an unnamed young man who, at the beginning of the story, is pleasantly riding his motorcycle in an unidentified city. After an unavoidable accident, he enters a hospital where he undergoes serious medical procedures. He starts having nightmares that lead to a second story: an unidentified young man is fleeing from hunters of human beings. He is an Indian, running in the wilderness, trusting that his intimate knowledge of the jungle will keep him safe from his pursuers. Despite his efforts, the young man is captured and sent into a temple where he will be sacrificed to the gods. At the end of the story, the reader understands that these two characters are really one: the Indian has been dreaming of a more humane death, choosing to die in a modern time and in a hospital, not at the hands of priests who are about to sacrifice him to the gods.

Unlike "Axolotl," "The Night Face Up," although drawn from Aztec religious beliefs, does not intend to communicate a metaphysical message. Here Cortázar places religious behavior in a negative light. This is evident in his detailed account of the "War of the Flowers," the military's capture of prisoners intended for human sacrifice, of which his Indian character was a victim. At the level of a political reading, therefore, "The Night Face Up" displays a strong attack against organized religion, which among the Aztecs had the support of the highly organized military social class. Cortázar appeals to today's reader to engage in an analysis of the strong historical association between the military and the Church in Latin American societies.

The military's imposition of power is the central concern of "Apocalypse at Solentiname." The story centers around an unnamed Argentine writer who, while on a visit to Costa Rica, has the opportunity to travel to neighboring Nicaragua. There he is taken to Solentiname, a peasant commune organized by Liberation Theology priest and poet Ernesto Cardenal. Written in the travelogue style of a diary, the Argentine writer fully describes the flourishing and inspiring community, praising not only its natural beauty but also the highly sophisticated intellectual life that he witnesses among the humble inhabitants.

The historical background of the plot is autobiographical. Cortázar traveled to Nicaragua in 1976, during a revolution against the dictator Somoza. The guerrilla group, known as Sandinistas, had been in existence since 1961, inspired in part by the success of the Cuban Revolution. Cortázar, an admirer of the Cuban socialist project, visited Solentiname, an agrarian religious community that had become internationally known because of Cardenal's reputation as a poet. Founded in 1966, the village of Solentiname brought together peasants and fishermen into a self-sufficient unit, which promoted a way of life shown in biblical and socialist texts. Independent from the fame of its distinguished founder, Solentiname had international exposure because of its primitive art paintings, poetic production, and their collective interpretation of the New Testament scriptures, which placed Solentiname within the trend of Liberation Theology. This innovative religious thought proposed that equal treatment for all is not only political justice but also a religious mandate reflected in Jesus Christ's teachings. Because of Solentiname's direct involvement in the Sandinista warfare, Somoza's military forces brutally attacked the inhabitants and dismantled the commune in 1977.

Despite the story's strong historical background, including the introduction of guerrilla figures such as the poet Tomás Borge who befriends the

Argentine writer and narrator, "Apocalypse at Solentiname" retains some of Cortázar's experiments with the fantastic. On returning to Paris, the Argentine protagonist takes his photos to be developed. To his horror, instead of seeing the friendly faces of the Solentiname peasants, he had been transported to the future; through his pictures, he becomes the sole witness to the massacre of the village. It is an **omen,** an important element in Cortázar's stories. Only the narrator has had this privileged vision of the future. Even a friend who looks at the photographs sees only the beauty of people and the lushness of Solentiname of the early days.

Cortázar, a representative of the Latin American Boom period, stands out because of his complex literary technique. A master of the genre of the fantastic, Cortázar displayed a particular interest in exploring surprising elements: "I have always known that the big surprises await us where we have learned to be surprised by nothing, that is, where we are not shocked by ruptures in the order" (*Around the Day* 31). Unlike other writers of the fantastic, for Cortázar these surprises, or "ruptures in the order," were plentifully available in Latin American history, and particularly evident in the excesses of military power.

Thus Cortázar considered his literary work a tool of political discontent. He was, however, mindful of the delicate balance between message and aesthetic experimentation. Although often inspired in real events, his short stories were not intended as historical documentation in the traditional sense. This is the case, for example, in "Meeting" (*All Fires the Fire*), a tribute to guerrilla fighters Fidel Castro and Ernesto (Che) Guevara. In this story, these key figures in the triumph of the Cuban Revolution appear as mysterious characters who, against all odds, triumph in an almost lost cause. Many young writers today imitate Cortázar's unusual characters and plot lines. Above all, his political reading of Latin American societies continues to resonate at the international level because these issues, faced in Latin America at that time, are still unsolved, and similar conditions exist in other countries as well.

Mario Vargas Llosa (Peru, 1936–)

Novelist, short story writer, playwright, journalist, literary and political critic, Vargas Llosa exemplifies the writer's multifaceted role as an intellectual and a social commentator in Latin American societies. His interest in literature is profound, as is evident in his writing within several genres. This is a common practice among Latin American writers, who often experiment with blending literary techniques from various genres. Writers' intentions, in addition to their attempts to create new ways to narrate a story, are to engage the readers' active participation. This approach, although complex, appeals to a more interdisciplinary market, to modern readers who are interested in exposure to a variety of literary techniques and modern thematic approaches to unusual plots.

Vargas Llosa adds to his work a cry for social justice. In particular, his commitment to the advancement of the Peruvian indigenous populations has become his most important political cause. As a public figure, he has also taken upon himself an active role as commentator on the complex world of contemporary Latin American politics.

Born in Arequipa, on the Peruvian highlands of the Andes, Vargas Llosa spent the earliest part of his childhood with his mother's family because of his parents' separation before his birth. His upbringing took him to the Cochabamba in Bolivia and to Piura, a northern Peruvian town, among the first Spanish colonial establishments in the mid–sixteenth century. In this rich cultural and ethnic area, he came in contact with Quechua indigenous populations and learned firsthand about their ancient traditions. The influence of these memories, as he has pointed out in his essay collection *Making Waves,* is pivotal in his earliest literary production ("The Country of a Thousand Faces" 1–15).

Vargas Llosa was ten years old when his parents reconciled and moved to Lima, the capital of Peru and the country's cultural and literary center. The change was abrupt in terms of physical location, because Lima is a coastal city. He attended several private Roman Catholic and military schools and then studied literature at the University of San Marcos in Lima. In 1959 Vargas Llosa received a grant to do graduate study in Spain for his doctorate in Latin American literature. He welcomed this opportunity because he was beginning a career as a newspaper reporter; he had recently married and was barely making ends meet. That same year, he published his first short story collection, *Los jefes* (*The Cubs and Other Stories;* 1979), which won a literary prize.

To earn his doctoral degree, Vargas Llosa wrote a dissertation on Colombian novelist Gabriel García Márquez; it was published in book form in 1971. His profound knowledge of literary criticism is evident there and in another of his books, *The Perpetual Orgy: Flaubert and Madame Bovary* (1986). Vargas Llosa has continued producing critical analyses in numerous articles, mainly for journals and newspapers, using multidisciplinary angles in studies of the complex character of Peruvian and other Latin American cultures.

In 1960, Vargas Llosa moved to Paris, where he worked as a teacher of Spanish for the Berlitz Schools. He also wrote news from Latin America for the Agence France Presse and for Radio Télévision Française. His stay in Paris gave him an opportunity to improve his writing skills and to meet important literary figures of the time. He also read French literature in the original, particularly the works of vanguardist authors such as Jean Paul Sartre and Camus.

In 1964 Vargas Llosa embarked on a trip into the Peruvian Amazon. This was his second excursion there; already in 1958 he had explored the region of the Marañón River, an important tributary of the Amazon. He had come into contact with indigenous groups of the Aguaruna and the Huambisa, known for their strong desire to remain faithful to their tribal customs and traditions. In his explorations of the Marañon River, he experienced life in the primitive villages in the Peruvian basin of the Amazon. An area of considerable extension, located in the eastern part of the country, it makes up 60 percent of the national territory. Until then, Vargas Llosa pointed out in *A Writer's Reality,* his view of this extensive region and of its inhabitants was "a world I sensed only through reading Tarzan and seeing certain movie serials" (65).

Vargas Llosa's experiences on the Amazon have found a place in his literary production. He saw in the Amazon peoples' primal way of life, violent and brutal, a symbol of Peruvian society and an exciting literary setting. He wrote, "on the one hand all that barbarity infuriated me; it made my country's backwardness, injustice, and lack of culture even more evident. On the other hand it all fascinated me; what formidable material to narrate!" (72). Like other Latin American writers, he would return to the extreme rural conditions of the Amazon where the modern and the primitive coexist in a constant struggle. Also of importance is his depiction of indigenous characters in a positive light. This was despite the traditional negative or stereotypical representation of such characters in Latin American literature. His experiences in the Amazon, as he remembers in his autobiography *A Fish in the Water* (464–65), were the "raw material" for his novels *The Green House, Captain Pantoja and the Special Service,* and *The Storyteller.*

In 1963, Vargas Llosa published *La ciudad y los perros* (*The Time of the Hero,* 1966), his first novel. This began his international reputation as one of the youngest of the experimental Latin American novelists. Immediately he became a literary best-seller in Latin America and Europe. In the United States, Vargas Llosa's novels appeared in translation within a few years after the publication of the Spanish original. His two novels published in the 1960s, *La casa verde* (1966; *The Green House,* 1968) and *Conversación en la catedral* (1969; *Conversation in the Cathedral,* 1975), earned him a reputation as a skillful experimental Boom writer He has taught at prestigious U.S. universities, such as Columbia, Harvard, and Princeton.

Between 1967 and 1974 he traveled extensively throughout Europe while working as a translator for UNESCO. He lived in several important cities, centers of European culture such as Paris, London, and Barcelona. In this period, his international reputation also peaked. In 1973, he published *Pantaleón y las visitadoras* (1973; *Captain Pantoja and the Special Service,* 1978), a funny but critical novel about the sexual tensions among soldiers in a remote Peruvian town and the peculiar and efficient way the military leaders resolved the problem. The novel became a successful film in 1999.

Other highly praised novels of Vargas Llosa include *La tía Julia y el escribidor* (1977; *Aunt Julia and the Scriptwriter,* 1995) and a partially autobiographical novel, and *La guerra del fin del mundo* (1981; *The War of the End of the World,* 1985), a historical account of religious fanaticism and governmental dictatorship in late-nineteenth-century Brazil. His interest in the historical narrative is evident in his most recent novel *La fiesta del chivo* (2000; *The Feast of the Goat,* 2001), which centers around the figure of Rafael Leónidas Trujillo, military dictator of the Dominican Republic from 1930 to 1961.

Vargas Llosa has successfully experimented with two other narrative genres: the detective novel in *¿Quién mató a Palomino Molero?* (1986; *Who Killed Palomino Molero?* 1987), a genre of increasing popular demand in Latin America; and the erotic novel in *Elogio de la madrastra* (1988; *In Praise of the Stepmother,* 1991) and *Los cuadernos de don Rigoberto* (1997; *The Notebooks of Don Rigoberto,* 1999), works about sexual taboo, which is seldom explored in Latin American literature.

In 1990 Vargas Llosa ran for president of Peru. This was a surprising political move, because he had had little experience in the political arena. His opponent, Alberto Fujimori, won the elections and became the first person of Japanese descent to hold the Peruvian presidency. After his defeat, Vargas Llosa abandoned Peru and established residency in Spain. In 1993, he received Spanish citizenship.

In 1993 he published *El pez en el agua* (*A Fish in the Water,* 1994), his memoirs of losing the race for president in 1990. Beyond the political significance of the text and its highly analytical look at contemporary Peruvian politics, *A Fish in the Water* is an important work because Latin American writers seldom produce formal autobiographies. In this memoir, Vargas Llosa remembers his strained relationship with his father, a man who had abandoned Vargas Llosa's mother before his birth and who surprisingly came back into their lives ten years later. He also made public declarations about domestic physical abuse against him and his mother. This is indeed a controversial subject, because the borderline between physical discipline, such as spankings, and abuse of children is often blurred.

Vargas Llosa has received many national and international awards. His prizes include Spain's premier awards, the Príncipe Asturias (1986) and the Cervantes (1994). In 1995, he became a member of the renowned Royal Academy of the Spanish Language, an honor granted only to intellectuals reputed to be among the best in their command of the Spanish language. He has also received national literary prizes in Italy, Switzerland, Israel, and Germany. He is an international literary figure; his works have appeared in translation in many languages, including Rumanian, Russian, Turkish, Japanese, Chinese, and Korean.

In his voluminous literary production, comprising predominantly novels, Vargas Llosa uses numerous themes and displays an interest in analyzing facets of Peruvian society. He reproduces Peruvian lifestyles from diverse points of view. His characters represent the multiple levels present in the complex Peruvian society, which is sharply divided into social, racial, and professional classes. This sociopolitical approach is a strong contribution to the documentation of Peruvian societal cultural patterns. With his characters, representatives of social groups that often find themselves in open clashes, Vargas Llosa shows the tensions present in any modern society. For Peruvian society in particular, Vargas Llosa portrays characters that historically have had a major role in the development of modern Peru.

Men in the military are a significant character type in Vargas Llosa's narrative. For Vargas Llosa, the military's political power over the Peruvian government and societal behavioral patterns can be traced to important historical periods. The military characters are set within their specific code of behavior. Although they are trained in the strictest ethical codes, Vargas Llosa emphasizes that they are responsible for imposing military traits on contemporary Peruvian society that go against acceptable ethical behavior.

Vargas Llosa offers a detailed analysis of the military as strongmen. Imposing and powerful figures, Vargas Llosa's military characters are examined from a historical point of view, and they reflect his own experiences with military men. He confronted military politicians as a newspaper reporter and as a presidential candidate. This interest has led him recently to offer a historical approach to the rise of the military strongman as the prototype of the Latin American dictator.

Vargas Llosa carefully illustrates in his novel *The Feast of the Goat* that the military man has in-depth knowledge of social and political structures, which he uses masterfully to his advantage, thus gaining a dictatorial control. The Dominican dictator Trujillo's control over the country illustrated an extreme use of power, both physical and psychological. It also included imposition of personal ethical values by means of distribution of economic advantages to those who followed his ideals. These characteristics are at the core of Vargas Llosa's *The Feast of the Goat,* which presents a Machiavellian dictator, able to maintain control of the country's government despite his open abuses of power. If economic bribe did not work, the military dictator's main tool was the strength of the military forces. Violence and acts of aggression, including torture, were preferred methods to eliminate voices of dissent. Military persecution could take place even outside the native country. This was the case in the disappearance in 1956 of Jesús de Galíndez, a Dominican exile who, from his teaching post at Columbia University, had started a campaign in the United States against the Trujillo dictatorship.

Vargas Llosa's interest in the military extends from Peru's historical involvement in warfare after the wars of independence in 1821. Two wars are important for understanding the role of the military in the development of Peru's contemporary national identity. The first was the War of the Pacific (1879–1883). In this war, an armed conflict between Chile and Bolivia over the Pacific commercial trade, Peru suffered considerable material loss, including the siege of Lima by the Chilean forces.

The second interventions of importance here are the clashes with Ecuador over national borders; these disputes arose from ancient historical misunderstandings of these Andean countries' borders on the Cordillera del Cóndor. After armed attacks in 1941, 1981, and 1995, the struggles ended in 1998 with official treaties. The solution to the conflict included an ecological park administered by both countries. Scientists hope that such a protected park will benefit the delicate environment of the Andean highlands.

Military forces continue to exert a tremendous influence on the Peruvian government. In 1968, a military coup ended the presidency of Fernando Belaunde Terry and led to a dictatorship headed by General Juan Velasco Alvarado. The military intervention lasted until 1980, when General Francisco Morales Bermúdez, who had replaced Velasco Alvarado, allowed national elections. Balaunde Terry was reelected.

In 1983 Vargas Llosa found himself involved in the complex political arena when the reelected president Belaunde asked him to chair a national commission investigating the crimes of eight reporters under the military dictatorship (*Making Waves,* "The Story of a Massacre," 171–99). One may assume that the results of Vargas Llosa's investigation prompted his decision to run for the country's presidency in 1990. He ran as a representative of a new era for Peru, one with modern intellectual trends, one open to foreign ideas. His defeat, unexpected by many of his followers, has been attributed to the control of the military, who feared Vargas Llosa's damaging information about underground activities during its dictatorship. The power of the military in Latin America often produces radical changes in national political structures.

Another reason the military has a prominent role in Vargas Llosa's fiction is that he studied at the well-known military school Leoncio Prado from 1950 to 1952. As a teenage boy from the Peruvian sierra, newly arrived in the capital city, he came into close contact with children from other geographic areas and from varied social and ethnic backgrounds, allowing him to move beyond the social and racial divisions apparent in Peruvian society at large. As he has indicated, because it was a state school with minimum tuition fees and an ample fellowship program, "Enrolled there were youngsters from the jungle and from the highlands, from every departamento [a Peruvian state], every race, and every economic stratum" (*A Fish . . .* 100). Their inevitable interactions, which often resulted in physical aggression, were daily occurrences at the school. Vargas Llosa also learned about military discipline and governance, in-depth knowledge that would be useful to him later as a political candidate.

The short story "Los jefes" ("The Leaders"), published in the collection *The Cubs and Other Stories,* is Vargas Llosa's earliest attempt to explore his memoirs about his experiences in the Leoncio Prado military school. Set within an unnamed military school, the action begins at the moment when upper-level students are plotting against the school's director, Mr. Ferrufino, who had recently ruled that older students would not receive a schedule for their upcoming final exams. This was punishment for an unstated violation and also a warning to the younger classes that misbehavior was not tolerated by his administration. The punished students, however, do not take the ruling lightly, and as the story opens, they openly express their disagreement with Ferrufino's decision.

When more sanctions are brought against them, the students decide to organize a massive protest that will keep all students out of the classrooms. Who will carry out the ambitious plan, and how to do so, is the short story's major concern. In the end, although it appears that the plan may work, the school's student body overcomes the few students who guard the school's gate, ending the strike. The strike leaders enter the school, well aware that there will be consequences for their rebellious behavior.

"The Leaders" introduces the reader to a series of characters, students, faculty members, and administrators who are typical of military life. Their behavior represents aspects of the military code of conduct, which not only limits their behavior but also restricts their options in the event of conflict. Because the story takes place in a military school for boys, the obvious interpretation is that this locale is symbolic of Peruvian society at large and that the reader witnesses military training of boys of various ages and backgrounds. Incidents reveal the oppressive tactics available to the military in an all-male environment, away from the civilized manners of modern society.

Within the restrictive arena of the military school, where all faculty members are military, Ferrufino is the most important character. He appears on few occasions, however, and his dialogue is brief. The reader learns about his personality through indirect characterization; students speak about him as a strong-willed administrator. Like a political dictator, Ferrufino does not listen to the students' complaints, despite the fact that they have sent a polite representative to his office. Ferrufino's refusal to reverse his decision or to consider another form of punishment forces the students to boycott classes.

Ferrufino is representative of the figure of the Latin American dictator, who, like this intransigent administrator, often comes from the military. He does not appear to fear the students' insubordination; he controls by means of totalitarian practices available to him in a military setting. Vargas Llosa's message, both ideological and social, is his analysis of the impact of the strongman on military-oriented Latin American societies. Although it may appear at first that the military's strength lies merely in physical superiority, this is only a partial explanation for its successful overthrow of democratic governance. As one unidentified character points out, Ferrufino's reasoning for punishing the students is based on a long sermon "about God, about discipline and the supreme values of the spirit" (48). Therefore, just like the political dictator, Ferrufino works with well-known ethics, and his use of punishment is acceptable to conservative social institutions.

Vargas Llosa's contributions to contemporary Latin American literature are remarkable. His approach to portraying Peruvian society, especially his realistic depictions of social and political constituencies, allows for an analysis of current national conditions. His diverse characters reflect Peruvian cultural patterns and also represent worldwide values, given that other societies are based on similar definitions of power structures according to strict racial and gender parameters. Given today's rise of the military in settings around the world, Vargas Llosa's psychological profile of this character type becomes of particular significance to international readers.

Carlos Fuentes (1928–)

A multifaceted intellectual, Carlos Fuentes is among the most important Mexican political activists. Two groups have gained his critical attention: his native country's marginalized indigenous communities and so-called illegal aliens in the United States, mainly *braceros*—fieldworkers who cross the U.S. border by means that may cost them their lives. Fuentes's literary production is extensive, covering diverse genres: short stories, novels, plays, screenplays, and essays on literary criticism and sociopolitical issues. He is an important critic of Mexican and Latin American cultures, with many publications on historical, social, and anthropological topics. Today he is Mexico's best-known spokesperson, and the international media often call on his expertise in Mexican issues and in immigration trends.

Fuentes was born in Panama City to a Mexican diplomat father, but he had an international childhood. He spent extended periods of time in important Latin American cities, such as Quito, Montevideo, Rio de Janeiro, and Buenos Aires. His departures from a Mexican way of life and his immersion in diverse Latin American cultures stimulated his interest in examining the "Pan-American" identity, the cultural values that are shared by most Latin American countries. Even as a child, he had a keen eye for cultural differences. His strong interest in Mexican and Latin American histories, particularly the complex period of the Conquest, may also have begun during his childhood.

Fuentes was six years old when his father was transferred to Washington, D.C. For the next six years, he attended Henry Cooke public school, becoming immersed in American culture and fluent in English. Although an upper-class Mexican, Fuentes must have had experiences similar to those of Spanish-speaking immigrants. Mexican *braceros* were beginning to arrive in considerable numbers into the United States in the late 1930s. Their struggle was complex, and their presence brought change to the monolingual American society. They also opened up discussion of racial issues.

Fuentes has commented about his "American" experience. He seemed to have learned English fast and fairly well, in fact, according to his own testimony, so well that he did not suffer racial discrimination. He was popular among his peers and behaved like a typical American child. The successful process of incorporation into a foreign culture came to a halt, with Mexico's controversial decision in 1938 to nationalize foreign oil companies in Mexican territory. The reaction in the United States was negative, reflected in the harassment that many Mexican immigrants endured. Fuentes, as the child of a Mexican diplomat, became the target of his peers' scorn.

In reaction to the anti-Mexican sentiment, Fuentes began a serious study of Mexican culture. Until then, Mexico had been just an object of curiosity for this wandering diplomat's child. As a preteen, he was already struggling with the issues of individuation that are so common among adolescents. For many immigrants, belonging to a nonmainstream culture can be shameful. Anti-Mexican sentiments merely increased Fuentes's interest in Mexican and Latin American cultures, however.

Fuentes's father's diplomatic career took him to Santiago, Chile, in 1941. This move was fruitful in Fuentes's literary development. He started writing short stories that were published in his school's student newspaper. He also showed interest in poetry, perhaps inspired by the distinguished Mexican poet Alfonso Reyes, who had been the Mexican ambassador to Brazil. Fuentes's father had served as Reyes's secretary. The boy's experiences in Chile and later in Argentina were productive, and they helped him to improve his linguistic skills in Spanish.

Back in Mexico in 1944, Fuentes came into permanent contact with Mexican culture. It was a process of cultural adaptation, similar to his assimilation of native customs during his previous experiences abroad. Until then, his contact with Mexico had been minimal, limited to his readings and to summer family vacations. His immersion into Mexican culture was intense, and included his learning the linguistic patterns of Mexican Spanish. It was at this time that he fully discovered Mexico for the first time.

In 1948, following in his father's footsteps, Fuentes studied law at the prestigious National University of Mexico. He underwent further advanced studies in international law in Geneva. He mastered French by translating works by the novelist Balzac into Spanish. His future literary production would display a strong influence of French literature, particularly of the vanguardist movement of the New Novel.

Fuentes was an early trendsetter in the growing Mexican literary scene of the 1950s. In 1953 he published his first short story collection, *Los días enmascarados* ("The Masked Days," translated in 1980 as *Burnt Water*), which displays his interest in Mexican indigenous belief systems as literary themes. He was also active in Mexico's intellectual life. In 1955 he founded the *Revista Mexicana de literatura* (Journal of Mexican Literature), which published the works of international personalities such as the Argentine fiction writers Jorge Luis Borges and Julio Cortázar. This was an impressive endeavor in which he joined forces with Octavio Paz, a major Mexican poet much respected in Latin American literature.

Fuentes's earliest novel, *La región más transparente*, 1958; *Where the Air Is Clear*, 1960) and *La muerte de Artemio Cruz* (1962; *The Death of Artemio Cruz*, 1964) earned him an immediate international reputation. It is particularly telling that the English translations appeared within only two years of their original publication. He was soon hailed as one of the top Latin American writers of the 1960s and stood out as a young writer particularly interested in producing radical changes in the traditional and realistic Latin American literature. Fuentes also became known for his activist "Mexican-ness," a subject of importance not only in his literary production but also in his abundant academic articles.

Fuentes's works of fiction are extensive. In 1975, by then an established writer of the Boom, he published *Terra Nostra* (in English translation in 1976), a highly experimental novel that explores Spanish and Mexican histories. In 1985, he published *El gringo viejo* (*The Old Gringo*), a novel about the death in Mexico of the American writer Ambrose Bierce. It became the first novel written by a Mexican to appear on the *New York Times* best-seller list. With the release of an American film production of the novel in 1989, Fuentes's reputation in the United States was solidly established. Another critically acclaimed novel of his in the 1990s was *Diana, o, La cazadora solitaria* (1994; *Diana, the Goddess Who Hunts Alone*, 1995) in which Fuentes displays his strong interest in the American and the Mexican film industries. In the short story collection *La frontera de cristal* (1995; *The Crystal Frontier*, 1997), Fuentes uses a realist approach in depicting the oppressive conditions of Mexican migrant workers in the United States.

Fuentes has served as a professor of Latin American literature in prestigious universities such as Columbia (1978) and Harvard (1987). He has received a number of international literary honors, among them, the UNESCO's Picasso Award (1994), and in Spain the prestigious Premio Miguel de Cervantes (1987) and the Premio Príncipe de Asturias (1994). He was named Doctor Honoris Causa by the National Mexican University (UNAM) in 1966 and by Cambridge University (1987).

Today Fuentes's insight into the often-contentious relationship between Mexico and the United States makes him an important spokesperson. One of his academic publications, *The Buried Mirror: Reflections on Spain and the New World* (1992), is an impressive video documentary with a book that traces the development of Latin American cultures from their Spanish roots to modern times. Recently Fuentes, as a member of the Mexican Commission for Human Rights, has spoken in direct terms of racist practices against Mexico's indigenous communities, often visible in the few, weak government programs specifically designed to improve the financial condition of those groups. Popular approval of Fuentes in Mexico is strong. Evidence of this is, for example, Subcommandant Marcos's statement that Fuentes is his favorite author. (Marcos is the head of the Zapatista Army of

National Liberation, known as Zapatistas, the group that currently seeks autonomy for indigenous groups in Chiapas, a state in Mexico's southeast.)

Fuentes's fiction displays a distinctive trend. Mexico's indigenous backgrounds, primarily Aztec, Toltec, and Mayan, are rich sources for his experimentation with the limits between reality and imagination. Well versed in local religious legends, Fuentes places his characters in modern Mexico, but they are often haunted by their pasts. Like other writers of the Boom, he is interested in the fantastic. Fuentes's approach to native Mexican religious practices lies within this context, often related to unusual events of magical realism. His stories are not an anthropological exploration of Mexico's past, a purpose of the *indigenista* writers. Instead, he intends to present the indigenous heritage as part of Mexico's psychological profile. His characters face unreal events that often parallel national events. Their destiny, like that of Mexico, is irremediably linked to the nation's precolonial past.

Fuentes's short story "Chac-Mool" (1954) develops two distinguishable characteristics of the fantastic story. He presents realistically a common character, and this character suddenly finds himself the victim of unreal events. This is the story of Filiberto, a forty-year-old man who drowned in Acapulco as he attempted to take a long swim in the ocean at midnight. As the story opens, a friend has traveled from Mexico City to the boarding house where Filiberto had been staying. He takes his friend's body to the capital by bus and, in the meantime, he reads Filiberto's diary. The diary is the main part of the story and the center of the plot.

Filiberto, a rather colorless character, was an office bureaucrat, with a deep interest in Mexico's anthropology. He was a collector of reproductions of idols. Self-taught in Mexico's history, he perfected his knowledge of Mexican cultures with frequent trips to the archeological sites of Teotihuacán, an important Toltec religious city northeast of Mexico City, and of Tlaxcala. The latter was home to a cultural group that, despite military aggression, had resisted incorporation into the Aztec empire. At the beginning of the story, Filiberto, the amateur anthropologist, has been looking for a "reasonable replica" of an ancient god, Chac-Mool. When he finally finds it, strange events start happening around it.

Chac-Mool, a deity for the Toltec, Mayan, and Aztec civilizations, appears in temples throughout Central America. In Mexico, the odd figure, a man in indigenous attire, partially lying down while holding a vase on his stomach with his hands, is present in Mayan statues found in Chichén Itzá, on the Yucatán Peninsula, and in the Great Temple of Tenochtitlán. His role in the complex Central American religious system is not completely known, but for the Maya he was the god of rain. Another theory attributes to Chac-Mool the role of messenger; with his vase, he may have been taking offerings to the gods.

Filiberto displays serious interest in Chac-Mool. The life-sized statue joins his collection in a dark basement of his house, a sad destiny for a god of rain.

Almost at once, the house's pipes unexpectedly burst, flooding the cellar and soaking the statue. The powerful god of rain required ample amounts of water. When the pipes continued to break and terrible sounds kept coming from the cellar, Filiberto begins to worry. Eventually, Chac-Mool comes to life, which does not surprise Filiberto.

Chac-Mool becomes a demanding and threatening presence in Filiberto's life. Finally Filiberto loses his job and escapes to Acapulco, a land of plentiful water. There, however, he meets his death at sea; he appears to have sacrificed himself to Chac-Mool's thirst for water.

This ending, a surprising turn of events, takes the reader into a mythical dimension. His best friend goes to Filiberto's house, and "a yellow-skinned Indian" (14) opens the door, announcing that he already knew about Filiberto's death. The Indian politely asks him to carry Filiberto's coffin to the basement. The basement's underground image is a symbol of Mexico's collective unconscious. Finally, Filiberto's friend faces the past, which, until that point, he had thought was mere fantasy.

"Chac-Mool" is a significant story in its symbolic exploration of the Mexican indigenous background. In a psychological reading, these ancient cultures possess Filiberto at a subconscious level. He places an object of mere curiosity in his basement, but Chac-Mool does not remain passive. The protagonist hears ancient stories from the statue, "wonderful stories about the monsoons, the equatorial rains, the scourge of the deserts; the genealogy of every plant engendered by his mythic paternity: the willow, his wayward daughter; the lotus, his favorite child; the cactus, his mother-in-law" (11). In the conclusion, the old Indian that receives Filiberto's friend was the representation of an aging cultural memory, defying national forgetfulness; it will not die so long as it is part of a collective unconscious.

Fuentes is also a committed activist writer. One of his most important contributions is his painstaking documentation of the current living conditions of thousands of Mexican workers in the United States, often transported there in inhuman, unsanitary, and even dangerous conditions. As media coverage indicates, these workers sometimes suffer painful deaths in their desperate attempts to enter the United States to work. Fuentes has become these immigrants' vociferous ally. In his short story collection *The Crystal Frontier,* his style takes on a realistic, often crude tone in revelation of the many faces of Mexican immigration. He approaches this delicate subject by giving a face and a name to characters who represent the many types of people forced by poverty to leave their country, even against their will. The many characters in *The Crystal Frontier* are young and old, workers of all types, men and women desperately attempting to improve their own lives and the lives of their families.

In *The Crystal Frontier,* Fuentes explores the complex processes leading to a substantial Mexican migration into the United States. Unlike other, fictional accounts, this collection draws heavily from various historical and critical points of view. In addition, he looks into American and Mexican histories, particularly the expansionist policy of Manifest Destiny of the 1840s, which led to the U.S. incorporation of roughly 50 percent of Mexican territory. Fuentes's critical standpoint goes beyond that of a historian. Rather than dwell on the reasons for the Mexican-American War, he prefers to explore the collective psyche of a nation forced to live in subservient conditions, as a character declares, "a poor country . . . next to the richest country in the world" (239).

Fuentes's characters represent many faces and many generations of Mexican migrant workers. Their stories are as diverse as their reasons for coming to the United States. The migrant workers' poverty is their compelling need; however, in Fuentes's characterizations the reader sees their existential struggle, which goes beyond financial distress. Fuentes's characters are not the traditional migrant workers performing agrarian tasks. He has preferred to examine a more modern view of Mexican migration, particularly because of changes in technology and in immigration laws that have affected both the American and Mexican economies.

One important change in immigration patterns is the presence of female workers. Fuentes presents the financial contribution of migrant working women. Thousands of them work in *maquilas* along the U.S.-Mexican border. They provide cheap labor for American companies. Usually referred to as "sweat shops," as the story's narrator says, they had been operating since 1972, and by 1994 they amounted to some 200,000 jobs. Such an economic boom became possible because of working practices that would be illegal in the United States, but it provided the possibility of financial independence to Mexican women. That liberty comes at a price, however. Women often come from distant areas and are separated from husbands and families; their supervisors often abuse them physically and sexually.

Fuentes displays a strong interest in exploring the lives of migrant characters affected by changes in immigration laws, created by fluctuations in the U.S. economy. For example, in "The Crystal Frontier" Mexican workers fly into the United States, unlike migrants in other stories. Although the scene is presented as normal, it is unusual because the men will be working in New York City, but for only one weekend. They are to clean the glass in the interior of high buildings, work for which it is cheaper to hire Mexicans than unionized workers. Fuentes's metaphor for the U.S.-Mexican border, a "crystal frontier," is a strong comment on the often controversial and adversarial relationship between the two countries. The border, which until recently was limited to the boundaries of the Río Grande, symbolically extends into any American city because modern technology can transport workers anywhere into the United States. The presence of the Mexican worker is, therefore, not only useful but unavoidable.

Although it may appear at first that Fuentes's characters are victims, they fight against the terrible conditions that they face in the United States. This is an important contribution to a subgenre that could be labeled "immigration literature." This literary production serves two purposes. One, it seeks to document Mexican migrant patterns and the development of the so-called Mexican-American migrant culture, known also by names such as Mexicano and Chicano. Two, it creates literary characters out of migrant workers, people who are often left without a name or a past in migration data. These "ethnic characters" often come into contact with other groups. Their confrontations, friendships, and alliances are yet another important angle in this genre.

In the story "Las amigas," Fuentes communicates his views about the positive contributions of Mexican migration to American society. It is a simple story of an elderly widow from the "Old South" who finds herself unable to maintain her big house. Because she does not want to live in a nursing home, a nephew convinces her to find live-in help. She does so against her will, and soon the black employees must quit because of the old woman's rampant racist comments. Her attitude changes radically with the arrival of Josefina, a young Mexican woman, forced to perform domestic work because her husband has been jailed illegally. Josefina, unlike the other maids, resists Miss Amy's constant personal attacks. In the conclusion, Josefina wins her employer's affection when the two women discover that both suffer from a broken heart.

Fuentes's stories in *The Crystal Frontier* are powerful statements of the strength of human will to survive. In a direct, realist style, his characters try to reflect the faces of thousands of Mexican workers, many of whom are commonly portrayed by the media as fruit pickers, house cleaners, or mere statistics related to the complex Mexican and the American national economies. The characters are well-developed personalities who face conflicts in their daily lives in a foreign country. The characters' lessons in the true meaning of life, in the function of material goods in one's well-being, and in the importance of family are transmitted as messages to all readers, regardless of their ethnicity or cultural affiliation.

Gabriel García Márquez (Colombia, 1928–)

Considered Latin America's most prominent fiction writer, Gabriel García Márquez produces works representative of magical realism. Like other writers of the Boom, he is a multifaceted intellectual, a novelist, short story writer, essayist, and scriptwriter. He is also well known as a political commentator on current conditions in his native Colombia. His leftist political views are often controversial, particularly his public support of Fidel Castro's political system. García Márquez is nonetheless a figure of international importance. His books are often on best-sellers lists in Spanish-speaking countries and in the United States.

García Márquez was born in the small village of Aracataca on the Colombian northern Atlantic coast. He is a ***costeño,*** as the inhabitants of the coast are known in Colombia. The tropical landscape and especially its unique culture had a strong influence on his literary production. Life in a remote town with many colorful characters and unusual living arrangements provided inspiration for his early short stories. García Márquez created the literary setting of Macondo, an imaginary Latin American coastal town. It reflects social, economic, and political problems and the way of life in an isolated village on the Colombian Atlantic coast. Macondo is also a mythical landscape representing the development of society's values. The town and its people have worldwide appeal.

Other important childhood memories are associated with his maternal grandparents, with whom García Márquez spent the first part of his childhood. From his grandfather, Nicolás Ricardo Márquez Mejía, a retired colonel and one of Aracataca's founders, García Márquez learned about Colombia's convoluted political history of the early twentieth century. From him, García Márquez heard testimonial accounts of Colombia's cruel civil wars and of the effects of American economic intervention on the Colombian coast. His grandfather's historical stories served as inspiration for García Márquez's military characters, who represent several political periods in the development of modern Colombia.

García Márquez's grandmother, Tranquilina Iguarán Cotes, was also a figure of importance in Aracataca's history. From her, García Márquez learned colorful family anecdotes featuring unusual characters. These also appear in his earliest short stories. A natural storyteller, García Márquez's grandmother revealed to her grandchild the rich local folklore, including indigenous and black religious practices and popular beliefs. In his autobiographical book *The Fragrance of Guava,* García Márquez described them succinctly as his "grandmother's phantoms, portents and invocations" (17), stories that haunted his nights as a child. In tribute to Tranquilina Iguarán, the matriarch character of his masterpiece novel *One Hundred Years of Solitude* bears the name Ursula Iguarán.

Family memories and Colombian national history from social, economic, and political angles are important components of García Márquez's fiction. He describes incredible anecdotes dealing with governmental repression, such as workers' bloody demonstrations that, although kept alive by popular memory, are stricken from official historical accounts. García Márquez's colorful family's history, especially the unusual love stories of relatives, has become part of the signature of his plots. Such details are rich and often contain incredible turns of events.

His life in Aracataca ended after his grandfather's death, when he went to live with his parents for the first time, at age ten. He did not spend much time with them, because he went to a boarding school in Barranquilla, the largest city on the Colombian Atlantic coast. At age twelve he received a scholarship to study in a private school in Zipaquirá, a city in the outskirts of the Colombian capital of Bogotá. This was García Márquez's first exposure to the culture of the Andean high plains. He was an outstanding student there, despite his humble family and his regional upbringing.

After graduation García Márquez stayed in Bogotá as a law student at the prestigious National University. He did not fully enjoy his chosen studies and had already decided to embark on a literary career. His decision to enroll in law school was a way to please his father, from whom García Márquez had always felt estranged. He did not complete his law degree.

García Márquez's first literary publications were short stories published in 1945 in "El Espectador," a newspaper in Bogotá. By 1950 he was working as a newspaper reporter, a career that would broaden his view to the whole nation. In 1952 he published a chapter of his novel *La hojarasca* (*Leaf Storm*), which three years later would become his first best-seller in Colombia. Like his Macondo-based fiction, this work explores the effects on the Colombian Atlantic coast, of the banana plantations, controlled by American export companies. In incipient political activism, García Márquez's novel documents exploitation of the local workers by the Americans, supported by the oppressive Colombian government. Political issues are lively in García Márquez's work, particularly with regard to his demand for social justice for the Latin American working and peasant classes.

This initial period was decisive in García Márquez's literary career. Joining up-and-coming writers, he initiated a self-taught literary training. During this period, he discovered the Czech writer Franz Kafka. From Kafka García Márquez learned that "many other possibilities existed in literature outside the rational and extremely academic examples I'd come across in secondary school textbooks" (*The Fragrance* 31). Other literary influences on García Márquez's earliest writings were Ernest Hemingway, James Joyce, and Virginia Woolf. He also showed interest in classical tragedies, particularly in Sophocles's plays *Oedipus Rex* and *Antigone*. A voracious reader, like many other Latin American writers, he also became captivated by the complex narrative structure of *A Thousand and One Nights*.

Further acquaintance with avant-garde literature took place during his stay in Europe. García Márquez was in Paris in 1955, where he started writing his novel *El coronel no tiene quien le escriba* (*No One Writes to the Colonel*), a short novel partially inspired by his grandfather's memoirs about Colombia's complex history of civil wars. Despite his limited budget, he took advantage of his stay in Europe. He traveled extensively, including visits to communist countries. His personal witness of life under communism would influence the young writer, who was beginning to show leftist inclinations.

During this formative European period, García Márquez also studied film in Rome. He began to write newspaper film reviews and eventually wrote screenplays during his stay in Mexico in the early 1960s. His interest in film-making has continued. He has written numerous screenplays and has taught screenwriting in Mexican and in Cuban film schools. An important collaborator was the Mexican writer Carlos Fuentes, who, like García Márquez, worked in the Mexican film industry. Although some of his published stories, such as *La increíble y triste historia de la cándida Eréndira* (*Innocent Eréndira,* 1972), became successful films, García Márquez is said to have rejected numerous times the suggestion of a film version of his masterpiece, *Cien años de soledad* (*One Hundred Years of Solitude*).

García Márquez built a literary reputation around a series of short novels and short stories that deal with distinctive characters located on the Colombian Atlantic coast. He was living in Mexico when, in 1961, he finally published *No One Writes to the Colonel,* followed in 1962 by *Los funerales de Mamá Grande* (*Big Mama's Funeral*). In the latter collection of short stories, both characters and setting are central elements of plots that often take an unusual turn. García Márquez's Macondo is similar to his native Aracataca. Like Faulkner's depiction of Yoknapatawpha, a rural American town as the heart of Southern culture, García Márquez's Macondo is a mythical representation of Latin American society. He also draws heavily on both national history and his family memoirs to produce a plot that surprises readers because of the author's ability to combine techniques of realism and the fantastic.

In the story "Big Mama's Funeral," García Márquez created a character, Mama Grande, who is a giant figure representative of Latin America's prevalent matriarchal system. Echoes of García Márquez's grandmother are evident here. She, like Mama Grande, was a central figure of a large family, and she also had influence in the management of her remote Colombian village. García Márquez has often acknowledged her as one of his favorite models for a literary character and as a teacher of storytelling techniques. As a rural woman, she believed in ghosts. Her stories about supernatural beings that García Márquez heard as a child were always presented within a realist frame. Her acceptance of the most unreal events as real and, above all, her telling the stories from a credible point of view, are visible in García Márquez's narrative techniques of magical realism.

True to the aesthetic principle that unreal events can take place in Latin America, Big Mama's funeral presents for "all the world's unbelievers" the matriarch's fabulous funeral, which was attended even by the Pope (*Collected Stories* 184). The story, which is written as a formal, newspaper article, is also a satire of the power that certain families with extensive land ownership exert upon small Latin American villages. Mama Grande was, like Gallegos's Doña Bárbara, a feared figure with a strong control over a region's economic structure, described in the exaggerated terms characteristic of García Márquez's magical realism: " . . . no person who lived in a house had any property rights other than those which pertained to the house itself, since the land belonged to Big Mama, and the rent was paid to her, just as the government had to pay her for the use the citizens made of the streets" (191). Another political attack on the government's fear of such controlling rural personalities is Mama Grande's listing of her properties. In her dying delirium she made a lengthy list of "[the] wealth of the subsoil, the territorial waters, the colors of the flag, national sovereignty, the traditional parties, the rights of man, civil rights . . . (192).

One Hundred Years of Solitude appeared in 1967, and it became an instant best-seller, with thousands of copies sold every week. Critical reviews by important writers, such as his friend Carlos Fuentes, were extremely positive. He had created perhaps the first literary work recognized as a masterpiece in all Latin American countries. This was also the peak of the Boom period. The unusual events in *One Hundred Years of Solitude* became synonymous with magical realism. He also provided Latin American literature significant international readership, reflected in the numerous translations of his novels into foreign languages.

Gabriel García Márquez's extensive literary production is extraordinary because of its superb literary quality and because of its exploration of diverse characters and literary motifs. In his novel *Crónica de una muerte anunciada* (*Chronicle of a Death Foretold*, 1981), García Márquez experimented with the narrative techniques of the detective genre. In the novel *El amor en tiempos del cólera* (*Love in the Time of Cholera*, 1985); he offers an unusual love story, based loosely on his parents' idealized, romantic courtship against the wishes of his mother's parents. He has also worked with various types of characters, particularly historical figures of importance to the understanding of Latin American societies. This is the case of *El otoño del patriarca* (*The Autumn of the Patriarch*, 1975), a novel about a fictional, aging Latin American dictator, and *El general en su laberinto* (*The General in His Labyrinth*, 1989), a tribute to Simón Bolívar, the liberator of several Latin American countries from Spanish control in the early part of the nineteenth century.

García Márquez's worldwide reputation as a best-selling writer continues. International writers, such as the Nobel Prize–winning novelist Toni Morrison, often cite him as an important literary mentor. His international reputation reached a peak in 1982 when he received the Nobel Prize in Literature by unanimous decision.

Today García Márquez is a spokesperson for leftist and socialist governments, such as Cuba's model of communism. In his native Colombia, he has had an active role in national politics, particularly in his role as an impartial mediator between the government and officers of the national guerrilla group known as the Revolutionary Armed Forces of Colombia.

García Márquez is Latin America's most popular literary and public figure. This fact was fully evident upon his publication in 2002 of *Vivir para contarla* (*Live to Tell*), the first volume of his autobiography, which sold some 500,000 copies in Latin America and Spain within forty-eight hours of its release. In the United States, in an unusual editorial move, Alfred A. Knopf, the prestigious publishing house, sold the Spanish edition before the forthcoming English translation. To no one's surprise *Vivir para contarla* also became a best-seller in the United States. This is a tribute to García Márquez's influence in the important U.S. market, as well as to his appeal to an increasingly large Latino readership.

One Hundred Years of Solitude is García Márquez's most famous novel. It appeared at the peak of the magical realism trend and today represents that avant-garde technique, widely used during the Boom period. Unlike similar experimental techniques, such as the fantastic, García Márquez's version of magical realism retains realism, and therefore credibility. This he achieves primarily through depiction of real-life characters, inspired in economic and political figures from the Colombian social structure. These characters symbolize the values shared by other Latin American cultures, and thus their appeal extends beyond the confines of Colombia.

One Hundred Years of Solitude depicts the story of a family, the Buendías, whose members have various social and economic functions in the small town of Macondo. They are products of several historical periods; the title points to one hundred years in the lives of five generations of male Buendías. García Márquez writes from the point of view of a modern chronicler; his characters are not only historically accurate but also symbolize gender and social roles prevalent in Latin American societies. The characters are far from predictable, however; female protagonists in particular challenge traditional Latin American societal expectations. These colorful characters and a complex plot make the novel a timeless classic with international appeal.

García Márquez's approach to Latin American society is grounded in his exploration of the role of the countryside in the development of Colombian national values. Following the literary model of the **novela de la tierra,** the Colombian landscape is central to an understanding of his characters' often peculiar behavior. He did not reproduce a real area, however, as realist novelist Rómulo Gallegos did with his depiction of the Venezuelan plains. The Macondo of *One Hundred Years of Solitude* is a fictional town, although with definite echoes of his native Aracataca. Macondo's ambivalent atmosphere, where real and unreal events seem to coexist, is García Márquez's impressive contribution to new experimental narrative techniques in Latin America. A tribute to his literary craft is the fact that readers in other parts of Latin America have seen Macondo as a symbol of their own national values, despite geographic, cultural, and historical differences.

One explanation of García Márquez's popular appeal is his ability to present uncanny events as normal—or at least possible. Macondo's history, from its founding to its demise, is, much like Latin America's genesis, a compendium of events that often defy logical explanation. A young couple founds Macondo, echoing the biblical story about the creation of the world from the book of Genesis. José Arcadio Buendía, who had recently married Ursula Iguarán, is forced to defend his family's honor. After he kills a man in a duel, he and Ursula decide to leave their village to found a new one. Other young couples follow them. After getting lost in a wild area, they end their quest. There they establish Macondo, a town so new that "many things lacked names, and in order to indicate them it was necessary to point" (1).

José Arcadio Buendía does not reflect the basic characteristics usually associated with city founders. He is instrumental in the initial phases of the construction of Macondo—for example, in deciding the placement of streets and in designing the houses' architecture—but otherwise he is presented as an idealist and a dreamer. His childlike fancy increases after a troupe of gypsies discover the remote town and become the town's only connection with the outside world. From a wise gypsy, Melquíades, José Arcadio buys trinkets, such as magnifying glasses, that capture his overactive imagination. The gypsies also bring other incredible items, such as flying carpets, to the delight of children and adults.

After José Arcadio buys a portable lab intended to transform gold into more gold, he abandons to Ursula the raising of their two children, Aureliano and José Arcadio. The boys are the first generation of Buendías, whose future actions will have dramatic effects on Macondo. Aureliano will become a colonel of regional importance; his brother, José Arcadio, will become an oppressive landowner. Their opposing points of view about Macondo's management represent often extreme opinions in Latin American political and economic issues.

Female characters have an important role in *One Hundred Years of Solitude*. For example, Ursula presents a contrast to José Arcadio, whose characteristics are typical of Latin American men in rural communities. This strong-willed woman takes charge of both family and local issues. Above all, she maintains the family's reputation. She is particularly vigilant to avoid a dreaded curse: the birth of a child with a pigtail. This deformity, according to a widespread rural belief, can take place among those who marry close relatives. (The reason José Arcadio had killed a man was that he and Ursula were cousins, and the man had made derogatory comments about their marriage.)

As Ursula raises her family, she is always mindful of the threat of a possible fulfillment of the family curse. This is the core of the novel's plot, its thematic center. The Buendías are descendents of the visionary ancestor José Arcadio. His two sons, José Arcadio and Aureliano carry with them memories of their father's psychological makeup. Some of those inherited images arise during his conversations with Melquíades, the wise gypsy, who introduced to José Arcadio ancient mysteries such as alchemy and chemistry. There is tension between rational thought, which Ursula represents, and José Arcadio's fantasy, reflected in flying carpets and other trinkets that the gypsies bring into Macondo.

One Hundred Years of Solitude is a modern interpretation of the development of Latin American culture in isolation from major restrictive social institutions such as the Church or the government. The reader is a witness to Macondo's founding by a handful of families and to its development into a booming town, mainly because of the establishment of banana plantations. The process toward achieving civilization has at its center a member of the Buendía family. García Márquez constantly insisted the unusual events that plagued the Buendía generations were not fantastic or imaginary: "I wasn't inventing anything at all but simply capturing and recounting a world of omens, premonitions, cures and superstitions that is authentically ours, truly Latin American" (*The Fragrance* 59).

Inspired by his grandfather's detailed description of his family's participation in Colombia's complex political history, García Márquez's novel offers a powerful statement about the military's power in Latin America. As Macondo becomes a village of considerable size, it attracts the attention of the government, which forces the inhabitants to adopt national laws and regulations that are not suited to the peaceful life of a small village. Macondo's rebellions, led by Aureliano Buendía, represent Latin America's guerrilla warfare; they are often the only solution to disagreement with highly structured political systems. García Márquez seems to state that the division between political discontent and resistance to oppressive dictatorial practices is blurred. Guerrilla fighters turned into political leaders can be as oppressive as deposed elected officers. These ideological divisions are present within the Buendía family, as family members take opposite sides. Political activism is a male activity; women are marginal to Macondo's intense political life. Even so, Ursula openly opposes her sons' dictatorial control of Macondo. This is an isolated case, because her control over Colonel Aureliano Buendía comes from her privileged position as his mother.

Another strong social statement in *One Hundred Years of Solitude* is García Márquez's depiction of the power of the Roman Catholic Church. It is evident that, as in the case of the government, the Church comes to Macondo only after the town's size makes it profitable. That comment goes to the core of the history of the Church in Latin America, where traditionally it has held control only in large, inhabited areas, particularly in the capital cities. Under this arrangement the rural areas, free of the Church's direct influence, retained native religious beliefs. García Márquez took an even stronger stand against the Church's policy of nonintervention in the national political scene. He went straight to the point that often the Church aligned itself with the political status quo.

García Márquez's most direct political attack and one of interest to an American reader is his depiction of the arrival in Macondo of U.S. banana import companies. They were an important industry for Aracataca, but by the time of García Márquez's birth, the American companies had left the town impoverished. Physical reminders remained as evidence of the financial boom. The plantations had been built segregated from the rural inhabitants who came to the banana fields as workers. The latter had no right to use the facilities built for the American managers. American families had no contact with the locals; the companies built their own schools, social and entertainment centers, and food facilities. In other words, it was a replica of American-style, upper-class living.

García Márquez masterfully links belief in the supernatural, associated with magical realism, to historical events from an equally incredible perspective. For example, he reproduced details of an actual massacre in 1929, when hundreds of workers went on strike against the United Fruit Company, located near Aracataca. Although it was a real event, specific details about the government shooting the strikers were eliminated from official sources, and the facts became confused in multiple popular versions. This happened, a fact to which reliable sources have attested despite official disapproval of their testimony. One such source was García Márquez's grandfather, from whom he heard details of the event.

The ending of *One Hundred Years of Solitude* is captivating and representative of García Márquez's hallmark of magical realism. Aureliano, a fifth-generation Buendía and its only survivor, discovers to his horror that his newborn child, also named Aureliano, was born with the dreaded pig's tail. While reading an old manuscript written in the ancient language of Sanskrit, left behind by the omniscient narrator Melquíades, Aureliano is surprised to find, after much decoding, that it is the story of the Buendía family. Melquíades is the author of this manuscript, which was written "not . . . in the order of man's conventional time, but had concentrated a century of daily episodes in such a way that they coexisted in one instant" (421).

The final episode, the destruction of the family house and the end of Aureliano's life, is drawn from a biblical conceptualization of Macondo's rise and fall. As in the biblical apocalyptic predictions of the end of the world, Aureliano's deciphering of Melquíades's manuscript means that "everything written on them was unrepeatable since time immemorial and forever more, because races condemned to one hundred years of solitude did not have a second opportunity on earth" (422). Readers are left to interpret, therefore, the Buendías's behavior and the messages inherent in their existence, marked by unusual events symbolic of their privileged existence. Melquíades becomes, therefore, a chronicler of Macondo's history; the unusual episodes at the heart of magical realism represent his abstract interpretation of real events. At the end of the novel, the reader suddenly finds out that the one hundred years of solitude is a metaphor for the history of the Buendía family and the fulfillment of the dreaded curse.

García Márquez's literary appeal lies in his brilliant merging of earthy characters, a distinctive Latin American landscape, and unusual plots. His characters come from the real social structures of Latin American working or rural communities. Their attraction for a non-Colombian reader is perhaps that as character types—rural, religious, or political figures—they would have equivalents in other societies. García Márquez stated in his introductory essay to *For the Sake of a Country: Within Reach of the Children,* a book for children on Colombian history and social culture, that his writings promote a society that is "kinder to itself; that makes full use of our endless creativity and devises an ethic, and perhaps an esthetic, for our overflowing, legitimate eagerness to improve ourselves" (12). Above all, they illustrate a variety of sociopolitical concepts, particularly family values and the roles of the government and the church.

Manuel Zapata Olivella (Colombia, 1920–)

Manuel Zapata Olivella is one of the best Latin American fiction writers who deal with subjects pertaining to the Afro-American heritage in Latin American coastal societies. As a descendent of African slaves, Zapata Olivella displays a strong interest in Afro-Colombian traditions, with special emphasis on religion and music. He is also a committed political activist; he has stood in opposition to violation of the human rights of indigenous populations and to racist practices against blacks in his native Colombia.

Born in Lorica, on the Caribbean coast of Colombia, Zapata Olivella, like García Márquez, is a *costeño.* This geographic area has a solid African heritage, and the merging of indigenous cultures has a distinctive Creole character. The blend of native cultures with black and European traditions, known as **syncretism,** created unique popular traditions.

Zapata Olivella has commented about the effects of nature on the inhabitants of Lorica, a small Colombian coastal town. Having grown up near the Sinú River, he remembers his childhood in bucolic terms: "I could distinguish which bird was singing, to which species an eggshell belonged that I found" ("Quijote" 1). Childhood memories became inspiration for *Tierra mojada* (1964); *Damp Earth,* a novel that explores the vegetation and the animal life of the Colombian coast. Like the criollista writers, he was influenced by the lush coastal landscape; its effect and its value as a literary symbol are evident in his mature literary production. During his youth, he came into contact with a number of typical coastal personages that would appear as characters in his short stories and his novels.

The son of a university professor, Zapata Olivella became a physician and psychiatrist in 1948. On professional trips, he traveled to Mexico and Paris in the 1940s and 1950s. Like the writers of the Boom, he reflected these travel experiences and literary contacts in his writings. As a journalist, he also came to know up-and-coming writers in Colombia or during his trips abroad. One of them, Gabriel García Márquez, became one of his closest friends.

Literary echoes of García Márquez's earliest short stories are evident in Zapata Olivella's early work. The presence of a coastal landscape and the creation of fictional villages are shared characteristics. They both developed characters whose socioethnic traits are traced to coastal Colombian roots. Their writings led to an increasing interest in literary works with the Atlantic coast as the literary setting. Until then, with the exception of Cuban writer Alejo Carpentier, the literature produced by Atlantic writers in Latin America had not had international exposure.

In 1946 Zapata Olivella visited the United States. He explored the border towns along the Río Grande and the cities of Los Angeles, Chicago, and New York. He also toured the pre–civil rights movement South, where he learned about the social injustices that African Americans endured. In New York, Zapata Olivella met Ciro Alegría, the distinguished Peruvian novelist and political activist. Following Alegría's advice, Zapata Olivella started writing fiction. Before that time, he had written articles for Colombian newspapers.

His visit to New York had another positive result; Zapata Olivella met the celebrated African American poet Langston Hughes, who became his literary model. Zapata Olivella had literary mentors among other important black Latin American writers, such as Cuban poet Nicolás Guillén. In 1930, Hughes had met Guillén in Havana, and they had become good friends. According to Guillén, Hughes was the inspiration for his *son,* the black-inspired poetry that became his literary trademark. Hughes translated Guillén's poetry into English, making it available to the flourishing, black Harlem Renaissance movement. Zapata Olivella became an outstanding scholar on the cultures produced by the African diaspora.

Zapata Olivella is a multifaceted writer, having written short stories, novels, and plays. He is best known for his novels, which he began writing in 1947. A committed activist and a spokesperson against the rampant racism of Colombia, he published *Chambacú, corral de negros* (1963; *Chambacu, Black Slum,* 1989). A year later, *En Chimá nace un santo* (1963; *A Saint Is Born in Chimá,* 1991) appeared in the midst of the Boom movement. This novel dwells on the development of religious cults in Latin America based on the assumption that miracles can happen through the intervention of a blessed person.

Zapata Olivella did not write another novel until the publication of *Changó, el gran putas* (1983), which remains without an English translation. It is an important work because it explores the complex Afro-Colombian religious belief system of the Yoruba African tradition of the *orishas.* The *orishas* are powerful deities; like the gods of Greek mythology, they are symbolic representations that attempt to explain mysteries of the universe and of the human psyche. His most recent novel, *Hemingway, el cazador de la muerte* (*Hemingway, the Hunter of Death,* 1993), not yet available in English translation, is partially inspired in the American novelist's fascination with Africa. This is also Zapata Olivella's tribute to Hemingway's influence on Latin American writers of the 1960s.

An activist and politician, Zapata Olivella served in 1999 as the chargé d'affaires in the Colombian embassy on the Caribbean island of Trinidad. He has also served on numerous occasions as a spokesperson against institutionalized racism in his native Colombia. To that effect, he was among the organizers of the First National Conference on Afro-Colombia in 2002. This conference, part of an emerging movement toward implementation of legal procedures for the protection of human rights for the large Afro-Colombian community, produced a declaration that was distributed nationwide. The statement, which Zapata Olivella signed, demanded from the Colombian government reparation for damages caused by racism and exploitation. In his well-researched *Las claves mágicas de América Latina* (*The Magical Keys to Latin America*, 1989), an anthropological study on the history of slavery, Zapata Olivella demonstrated that Afro-Latin American communities have suffered terrible experiences at the hands of governments. This book is also an important research tool, because it offers a positive view of the development of Afro-Latin American cultures.

Zapata Olivella's writings explore Afro-Colombian popular and Creole cultures. His literary approach to this subject shows two trends. First, unlike the writers of the Boom, he is a consummate researcher, having spent years of intense fieldwork both in Colombia and in African countries. Second, his characters, well grounded in local cultural patterns of behavior, represent aspects of sociopolitical life in Colombia. Through his characters, Zapata Olivella provides a voice that is both proud of these social classes' cultural achievements and politically demanding of their claims for the betterment of their sociopolitical conditions.

Zapata Olivella's interest in rich Colombian religious beliefs is evident in *A Saint Is Born in Chimá*. A highly symbolic novel, it draws heavily on coastal popular cultures. Its characters are representative of lifestyles native to this geographic area. The setting is Chimá, a small fishing village in an irregular landscape that has historically isolated its inhabitants from major urban centers. They are, therefore, accustomed to deciding their own destiny in their approach to legal and religious matters. In a way, it is Zapata Olivella's version of García Márquez's Macondo; Chimá, with its distinctive indigenous name, is depicted as a mythical place.

The residents of Chimá do not question the most unusual of events, particularly those of a religious nature. One example of the people's faith in the supernatural is the town's devotion to a wooden carving of Saint Isidore, who was born in Cartagena, Spain. In a curious historical connection, his cult came to the city of Cartagena in Colombia. A native carving of Isidore was immediately believed to have had a miraculous origin. The town's carver, Remigio, according to his testimony, had gotten lost in the forest while looking for wood for his craft. Miraculously, he found the saint's image placed in the fork of an olive tree, known in the region as the wood that Noah used to build the ark. The statue guided Remigio into the town.

This legend, with only one witness, Remigio, created a devotion because the statue was believed to have supernatural powers. During the hottest and most severe days of drought, the statue, when submerged head down in water, would induce plentiful rains. In the torrential and damaging rainy season, hanging it by its feet would halt the rains. Not surprisingly, Remigio eventually became well known in the area because of his many reproductions, which he sold in Chimá and other nearby towns. These images, according to popular belief, had the same miraculous powers as the original.

In this background of strong popular devotions, the novel opens on the Day of the Dead, a significant celebration in most Latin American countries. The popular religious celebration has gathered the small population of Chimá in the local cemetery, a dark setting: "The burning candles intensify the whiteness of the lime, still damp on the tombs. The paper roses, black and purple, are stuck to the wooden crosses like enormous bottle flies. The gathering of country people overflows the small cemetery: a patch of high ground in the middle of the swampy plain" (1). The cemetery is a privileged setting in the sense that, if any unusual event takes place, it will be considered normal. The dual pagan-Christian nature of the cemetery also allows for the celebration of certain religious acts not permitted in other traditional settings, such as churches. This has an important implication, because it stresses that the local villagers have maintained their own religious customs, often independent of mandated Roman Catholic rituals. Chimá's inhabitants are, indeed, rebellious. Despite their religious zeal, they have created their own rituals, such as their worship of the statues of Saint Isidore.

Zapata Olivella offers a detailed description of the All Souls Day, a ceremony celebrated on the night of November 2, with the sanction of the Roman Catholic Church. In Chimá, the ceremony has an eerie feeling of the supernatural, reinforced by dark and mysterious descriptions of the cemetery at night. Although a priest is in charge of the rituals, the gathering is like an ancient pagan religious celebration in which the congregation openly speak to the dead as they lay paper wreaths on the tombs. It is, according to popular belief, a day when the dead can hear their relatives' prayers and requests. The inhabitants of this impoverished village often asked for better living conditions. This dual religious element, incorporating popular practices into mainstream Roman Catholic orthodoxy, will play an important role in the incredible event that is about to happen.

It is a stormy night, "the traditional rainstorm of the Day of the Dead, as certain as death itself" (2). Padre Berrocal is hurrying to finish the prescribed rituals when a lighting bolt starts a fire in a nearby wooden hut. It is the humble home of Domingo Vidal, a young man suffering from a severe case of microcephalia. He had been left there alone. Because of his physical condition, Domingo has retained the features of a small child, although his head is unusually large. Because of a severe mental handicap, Domingo is unable to move on his own and is, therefore, trapped in the burning house. When the crowd arrives at the hut, the fire has engulfed it; there seems to be no way to rescue Domingo. When Padre Berrocal enters into the flames, the crowd goes wild and attempts to stop him. He is successful in saving Domingo from the fire, however.

This event can be considered a miracle in itself. The events that follow give the impression that something extraordinary has just happened. To the eyewitnesses' surprise, Padre Berrocal survives when the roof caves in, and neither his clothes nor Domingo's have been burned. Domingo does not have any visible burns, nor is his hair burned. Worried because the frenzied crowd, believing that there has been a miracle, has already started to reach out for pieces of Domingo's clothing, the priest takes him into the church. The crowd roars for Domingo: "God has designated Dominguito with a bolt of lightning!" (4).

Despite Padre Berrocal's attempt to explain the unusual circumstances, Chimá's inhabitants proceed to declare Domingo a miraculous religious figure. The facts that the fire took place on the Day of the Dead and that Domingo was thirty-three years old (Jesus Christ's age at the time of his death) seem to support the popular belief that this event was, indeed, of a supernatural character. By sheer strong belief, other minor events confirm that a miracle had happened. On his return to his family, Domingo starts drawing crude lines and scribbles, an activity that is surprising because of his handicap. Chimá's inhabitants believe the drawings to be portraits of divine figures and declare them blessed relics.

Soon, Domingo's fame creates a cult that spreads to nearby populations; large numbers of people come to Chimá to ask Domingo for divine intervention. Constant rains swell the river so that it threatens to flood the impoverished village. Just as the Catholic Church allows public parades of religious icons in cases of extreme emergency, Domingo's followers carry him in a procession, against the wishes of his mother, who is concerned about her son's health. The crowds hope for a miracle. It seems to happen because, although the rain continues, the dreaded floods do not take place. As a consequence of his getting wet and of rough physical handling, Domingo dies of pneumonia.

With Domingo's death, Padre Berrocal hopes for an end to the cult. He was wrong, however, and the cult persists. Domingo's followers decide to ask the Church for his beatification. One important factor behind Domingo's cult is his local origin. He is not an imported saint of foreign extraction, as Saint Isidore is. Domingo has a strong appeal for Chimá's starving native population because he shares a racial connection with his followers; they, like him, are Creole, in this case, a mixture of indigenous and black cultures. He becomes, therefore, a direct link to local groups, much like the strong association that dead relatives exerted on the living. As the reader witnesses, the cult of the dead makes them more effective intercessors of divine power.

Another characteristic behind Domingo's rapid rise as a religious figure is the emergence of a "prophet," a figure who plays an important role in organizing the cult, with its considerable number of followers. Jeremías, Chimás's sacristan, takes it upon himself to organize Domingo's followers against the Church's wishes, represented in Padre Berrocal's open opposition to Domingo's burial in the church. The people represent popular animosity toward organized religion, in this case, the mainstream teachings of the Catholic Church, particularly the Church's stand against idolatry.

The tensions inherent in the ease with which popular lore transforms personages into objects of worship are also sociopolitical. It is clear that, given a choice, Chimá's inhabitants prefer faith in Domingo, an underprivileged local figure, to a foreign religious doctrine, that of the Catholic Church. There is also a political aspect to the story, in that the Church often fails to protect locals from the injustices of the political system.

Like Domingo, Jeremías is a complex figure, whose motivations seem not to be entirely religious. Before Domingo's death, he becomes known as Domingo's "apostle" and, as such, he assumes strong messianic behaviors. He openly acts as Domingo's right arm and the interpreter of his wishes (since the young man was physically limited in his ability to speak coherently). Even after Domingo's death, despite a lack of proven miracles, Jeremías increases the number of Domingo's followers. Thus, Jeremías becomes a religious leader of a prosperous cult. At the core of Domingo's worship is the people's natural dislike of the Catholic Church's monopoly of sanctioned devotion and their need for a local religious hero.

Jeremías represents other religious figures from Latin American history that played important roles in local sociopolitical arenas. Strong-willed characters have used religious practices as a political weapon since the arrival of the conquistadors. In modern times, religion continues to influence the constitution of social groups in Latin America. On one hand, rejection of mainstream Catholic practices and incorporation of native religious forms can be construed as an expression of political discontent and a return to authentic Latin American cultural values. On the other hand, the power of a single individual to organize crowds around a religious practice is a characteristic of cult figures in Latin America and elsewhere. As is often the case, these personages have power that goes beyond the religious realm to extend into political arenas.

Padre Berrocal is the novel's most fascinating character. It is interesting that Domingo's miraculous rescue from the fire and later the procession that leads to his death occupy only a few pages. The novel's main action relates Padre Berrocal's opposition first to Jeremías's blasphemous religious practices and eventually to Chimá's inhabitants' determination to observe public worship of Domingo in the local church or cemetery. This was against Padre Berrocal's racial and religious background; like Chimás's inhabitants, he must maintain control so as not to succumb to the practice of local religious beliefs.

Padre Berrocal is a mulatto, the child of runaway slaves. An extremely devout Catholic, he characterizes Chimá's cult of Domingo as "satanic deceptions" (26). Remembering his childhood in the area, he sees that the new cult corresponds to other "superstitions," such as the local belief in witches that drain the blood of newborns by sucking their umbilical cords or the headless horse that appears at midnight. Although Padre Berrocal successfully buries Domingo's corpse in the cemetery despite the township's desire for burial inside the church, he is not able to stop Jeremías from becoming a well-known prophet. As Padre Berrocal suspects, Jeremías's interest in Domingo's miracles is financial; the man soon starts receiving considerable donations.

The novel's climax comes two years after Domingo's burial, at the peak of an extensive pilgrimage to his tomb. It is Easter Sunday, and Jeremías's followers decide to rescue the saint's remains. They claim that the corpse is uncorrupted, a sign that would corroborate Domingo's divine nature. They march toward the church and occupy it. Claiming a miracle, they are hopeful that this is the ultimate proof that will lead to Domingo's beatification.

In the end, Domingo's followers are twice defeated. Padre Berrocal comes to the church and defies the exultant members of the congregation, who force him out. Under the cover of night, he steals the body and, in a macabre scene, cuts it to pieces and buries it again. In a surprising twist, convulsions paralyze Padre Berrocal's body shortly afterward, and he dies on Domingo's tomb where his followers have taken him, hoping for a miracle.

The collapse of Domingo's cult does not come, however, from the fate of Padre Berrocal but from the regional political authorities. In a scene reminiscent of the conquistadors' brutality against native cults, police forces break into the church and kill Jeremías. The organized cult comes to an end, or so it seems. Upon learning that the leader of the cult is dead, the police abandon the church despite the numerous congregants who are protesting Jeremías's brutal death. An omniscient narrator explains the reason for the withdrawal: "They understand that the people need only a pretext to fight and with those machetes and shotguns they would be capable of carrying out greater prodigies than all the miracles attributed to Domingo Vidal" (109). This comment goes to the core of the powerful influence of religious practice in Latin America.

Zapata Olivella made great contributions to the emerging aesthetics of magical realism. Like Rulfo and García Márquez, he developed simple characters with deep ideological characteristics that speak about Latin American sociopolitical structures. Based on native coastal and ethnic elements with which he was familiar, Zapata Olivella's characters in *A Saint Is Born in*

Chimá represent issues inherent in the often murky balance between religious practices and political governance. His contribution here lies in his skillful treatment of magical realism in descriptions of Domingo's alleged miracles. In the end, just as in biblical stories, the reader is left wondering whether the events took place or were the result of a skillful and deceptive narrator. The message is, however, the same. Zapata Olivella dwells on the power of religious practice in Latin American societies and its extraordinary impact on political structures.

BIBLIOGRAPHY

Borges, Jorge Luis. *Ficciones.* Trans. Anthony Kerrigan et al. New York: Grove Press, 1962.

———. *Labyrinths: Selected Stories and Other Writings.* Ed. Donald A. Yates and James E. Irby. New York: New Directions, 1962.

———. *A Universal History of Infamy.* Trans. Norman Thomas di Giovanni. New York: Dutton, 1972.

Cortázar, Julio. *Around the Day in Eighty Worlds.* Trans. Thomas Christensen. San Francisco: North Point Press, 1996.

———. *Bestiary: Selected Stories.* London: Harvill Press, 1998.

———. *Blow-Up and Other Stories.* Trans. Paul Blackburn. New York: Pantheon Books, 1967.

———. *A Manual for Manuel.* Trans. Gregory Rabassa. New York: Pantheon, 1978.

———. *Nicaraguan Sketches.* Trans. Kathleen Weaver. New York: Norton, 1989.

———. *"We Love Glenda So Much" and "A Change of Light."* Trans. Gregory Rabassa. New York: Vintage Books, 1984.

Fuentes, Carlos. *Burnt Water.* Trans. Margaret Sayers Peden. New York: Farrar, Straus & Giroux, 1980.

———. *The Crystal Frontier. A Novel in Nine Stories.* Trans. Alfred Mac Adam. New York: Farrar, Straus & Giroux, 1997.

García Márquez, Gabriel. *The Autumn of the Patriarch.* Trans. Gregory Rabassa. New York: Harper & Row, 1976.

———. *"Big Mama's Funeral." Collected Stories.* Trans. Gregory Rabassa. New York: Harper & Row, 1984.

———. *Chronicle of a Death Foretold.* Trans. Gregory Rabassa. New York: Ballantine Books, 1982.

———. *For the Sake of a Country within Reach of the Children.* Bogotá, Colombia: Villegas Editores, 1996.

———. *Innocent Eréndira and Other Stories.* Trans. Gregory Rabassa. New York: Harper & Row, 1978.

———. *Love in the Time of Cholera.* Trans. Edith Grossman. New York: Knopf, 1982.

———. *No One Writes to the Colonel.* Trans. J. S. Bernstein. New York: Harper & Row, 1968.

———. *One Hundred Years of Solitude.* Trans. Gregory Rabassa. New York: Harper & Row, 1961.

"Quijote mestizo, El." http://elpais-cali.terra.com.co/historico/mar172003/ EVE/A1017N1.htm. March 17, 2003.

Rulfo, Juan. "Luvina." Trans. George D. Schade. *The Penguin Book of Latin American Short Stories*. Ed. Thomas Colchie. New York: Viking Press, 1992: 283–290.

———. "Macario." Trans. George D. Schade. *The Eye of the Heart*: 295–299.

———. *Pedro Páramo*. Trans. Margaret Sayers Peden. New York: Grove Press, 1994.

Vargas Llosa, Mario. *Aunt Julia and the Scriptwriter*. New York: Farrar, Straus & Giroux, 1982.

———. *Captain Pantoja and the Special Service*. London: Faber & Faber, 1978.

———. *Conversation in the Cathedral*. New York: Harper & Row, 1975.

———. *The Cubs and Other Stories*. Trans. Gregory Kolovakos & Ronald Christ. New York: Harper & Row, 1979.

———. *The Feast of the Goat*. Trans. Edith Grossman. New York: Farrar, Straus & Giroux, 2001.

———. *A Fish in the Water: A Memoir*. Trans. Helen Lane. New York: Farrar, Straus & Giroux, 1994.

———. *The Green House*. Trans. Gregory Rabassa. New York: Harper & Row, 1968.

———. *Making Waves*. Ed. and trans. John King. New York: Farrar, Straus & Giroux, 1996.

———. *Notebooks of Don Rigoberto*. Trans. Edith Grossman. New York: Penguin Books, 1998.

———. *The Perpetual Orgy: Flaubert and Madame Bovary*. Trans. Helen R. Lane. New York: Farrar, Straus & Giroux, 1986.

———. *In Praise of the Stepmother*. Trans. Helen R. Lane. New York: Farrar, Straus & Giroux, 1990.

———. *The Time of the Hero*. Trans. Helen R. Lane. New York: Grove Press, 1966.

———. *The War of the End of the World*. Trans. Helen R. Lane. New York: Penguin Books, 1997.

———. *A Writer's Reality*. New York: Syracuse University Press, 1991.

Zapata Olivella, Manuel. *Chambacu, Black Slum*. Trans. Jonathan Tittler. Pittsburgh: Latin American Review Press, 1989.

———. *A Saint Is Born in Chimá*. Trans. Thomas E. Kooreman. Austin: University of Texas Press, 1991.

SUGGESTED READINGS

Bell-Villada, Gene. *García Márquez: The Man and His Work*. Chapel Hill: University of North Carolina Press, 1990.

Brody, Robert, and Charles Rossman. *Carlos Fuentes, A Critical View*. Austin: University of Texas Press, 1982.

Captain-Hidalgo, Yvonne. *The Culture of Fiction in the Works of Manuel Zapata Olivella*. Columbia: University of Missouri Press, 1993.

Castro-Klarén, Sara. *Understanding Mario Vargas Llosa*. Columbia: University of South Carolina Press, 1990.

Guzmán, Daniel de. *Carlos Fuentes*. New York: Twayne, 1972.

Jackson, Richard. *Black Writers in Latin America*. Albuquerque: University of New Mexico Press, 1979.

Mellen, Joan. *Gabriel García Márquez*. Detroit: Gale Group, 2000.

Peavler, Terry J. *Julio Cortázar*. Boston: Twayne, 1990.

Pelayo, Rubén. *Gabriel García Márquez: A Critical Companion*. Westport, CT: Greenwood Press, 2001.

Rodríguez Monegal, Emir. *Jorge Luis Borges: A Literary Biography*. New York: Dutton, 1978.

Stabb, Martin S. *Borges Revisited*. Boston: Twayne, 1991.

Standish, Peter. *Understanding Julio Cortázar*. Columbia: University of South Carolina Press, 2001.

Stavans, Ilan. *Julio Cortázar: A Study of the Short Fiction*. New York: Twayne, 1996.

Williams, Raymond. *Gabriel García Márquez*. Boston: Twayne, 1984.

———. *Mario Vargas Llosa*. New York: Ungar, 1986.

———. *The Writings of Carlos Fuentes*. Austin: University of Texas Press, 1996.

Chapter 4
Women Writers: New Perspectives on Latin America

MEXICO

Mexican women writers are today among the strongest literary voices from Latin America. As a group, their writings are important for English-speaking readers for various reasons. First, their literature appears in English translations more often and closer in time to the publication of the Spanish text than does the work of any other group of Latin American women. The interest in Mexican women's literature is two-fold. First, readers welcome the gender perspective—particularly, the feminist point of view of women writers. Second, their aesthetic experimentation is of a quality comparable to that of their counterpart male writers.

Their commercial success is evident in best-selling novels (such as Laura Esquivel's *Like Water for Chocolate*) and in the publication of short story collections (*A Necklace of Words: Stories by Mexican Women*). Because Mexican women writers have developed theoretical approaches to issues in feminist writing, they are welcome guest speakers in U.S. academic and political settings, addressing the subject of writing as a woman in Mexico. Two subjects are at the heart of their writing: living under the oppression against women from political, social, and religious institutions and their role as leaders of a budding feminist movement.

Mexican women are also significant because they were among the first Latin American writers to produce feminist literature with national recognition and international exposure. They can be described as pioneers of an emerging feminist literature, both in terms of the development of characters and subjects of interest to women and with regard to their incorporation into the national political arena. Because many of these writers are also university professors or are associated with the Mexican publishing world, they are also well-known literary critics and spokespersons of various feminist trends.

Rosario Castellanos (1925–1974), an admired novelist, poet, and feminist critic, was among the first Mexican women writers to address social issues with a special interest in the Mexican indigenous peoples in Chiapas. Because of her commitment to the Mayan groups of southern Mexico, she created theater workshops in an effort to improve their limited education. Her novel *Balún Canán* (1957; *The Nine Guardians,* 1958) was inspired by her experiences while working with the Tzotzil nation in the highlands of Chiapas. Although not an accurate anthropological novel (Castellanos was not of indigenous descent), it is an important text in that it presents native women characters.

Mexican women writers were also part of the innovative Boom movement. Elena Garro (1920–1998) wrote her novel *Los recuerdos del porvenir* (1963; *Recollections of Things to Come,* 1969) within the experimental trend of magical realism. In this novel, Garro displayed an interest in historic movements in Mexico, but her approach, like that of male experimental writers, is not realistic. She wrote about the Cristero war, guerrilla warfare associated with events that followed the Mexican Revolution. Garro placed a special emphasis on the war and on its consequences on the indigenous population, however. A testimony to her special contribution to contemporary Latin American literature is the fact that the Argentine short story writer Jorge Luis Borges considered Garro a principal writer in the development of fantastic literature. She also wrote scripts for the Mexican cinematic production.

Elena Poniatowska

Elena Poniatowska (1932–) is today Mexico's premier woman writer, emerging from her country's journalism community to become one of its best-known reporters. Her journalism career can best be described in terms of activism dedicated to open denunciation of such problems as homeless children (*El niño: niños de la calle,* 1999). In 1979, she was the first woman to receive Mexico's highest award in journalism.

The influence of her initial career as a newspaper reporter is evident in her literary production, which is divided into fiction and testimonial writings. Of those trends, two works are outstanding. The first is *La noche de Tlatelolco* (1971; *Massacre in Mexico,* 1975). It is Poniatowska's collection of chilling testimonies about a 1969 student demonstration that led government police officers to attack thousands of young people. The number of deaths is still a matter of controversy between activists and officers of the Partido Revolucionario Institucional (PRI), Mexico's principal political party and the head of the government at the time of these events. Poniatowska's book is a journalistic masterpiece. The well-known Mexican poet Octavio Paz described it as a "historical chronicle" that "shows us history before it has congealed and before the spoken word has become a written text" (vii). As a gesture of political solidarity, she refused to accept a national prize for *Massacre* from Mexican President Luis Echevarría . The second of her most notable works is the novel *Querido Diego, te abraza Quiela* (1978; *Dear Diego,* 1986), which explores muralist Diego Rivera's 10-year relationship with Russian painter Angelina Beloff. This short novel is of particular interest because Poniatowska interviewed Diego shortly before his death in 1957. Poniatowska's interest in art is also evident in her essay "Diego, I Am Not Alone: Frida Kahlo," about Rivera's wife, celebrated Mexican painter Frida Kahlo; the essay was published in *Frida Kahlo: The Camera Seduced* (1992). More recently, she has written about the uprisings of the Zapatistas, who protest the unjust conditions the native peoples of Chiapas face ("Voices").

Another of Poniatowska's important contributions is her translation into Spanish of the best-seller, *The House on Mango Street* (1994) by Chicana novelist Sandra Cisneros. Beyond the fact that an established and awarded writer served as translator, Poniatowska's translation led to the introduction of Chicano literature into the Mexican literary market. Chicanos, people of Mexican descent born in the United States, are the central characters of Cisneros's novel. She addresses the issues that Chicanos often encounter in their acculturation in the United States. Traditionally, Mexican critics, and, to a certain extent, Mexican writers in general, have ignored the booming Chicano literary production. In an interesting historical parallel, Chicano women have created a strong feminist movement with prosperous U.S. Latino literature.

Julieta Campos

Mexican women writers often are quoted as critics of their own literary production, as well as theoreticians of an emerging feminist movement in Latin America. Julieta Campos (1932–), born in Cuba but living in Mexico since 1955, exemplifies the multifaceted woman intellectual. She has served as a translator, as director of the P.E.N. Club of Mexico, and as chief director of a prestigious literary journal. Married to a governor of the state of Tabasco, Campos worked closely with local indigenous communities. Her collection of stories *La herencia obstinada* (1982), which remains without an English translation, gathers the oral tradition of the Nahuatl along with her own critical interpretation.

Brianda Domecq

Brianda Domecq (1942–) is an exceptional case in that she came to learn Spanish as a child after her family moved to Mexico for business; English is her native language. The child of a Spanish father and an American mother, Domecq was born in New York, where she spent her childhood. She spent part of her teenage years attending high school and a year in college in the United States. Upon her return to Mexico, she decided to make Spanish the language of her writing. Her second novel, *La insólita historia de la Santa de Cabora* (1990; *The Astonishing Story of the Saint of Cabora*, 1998), offers a recreation of a historical, unusual, female character, Teresa Urrea, a healer in the northern state of Sinaloa whose public cult became involved with incidents preceding the Mexican Revolution of 1910.

Trends in Women's Literature

Among the youngest generation of Mexican women writers are Angeles Mastretta (1949) and Carmen Boullosa (1954–), writers who display an interest in historical events narrated from a modern vantage point. Mastretta's novel *Arráncame la vida* (1985; *Mexican Bolero*, 1989) has a female protagonist, the wife of a powerful Mexican governor in the early part of the twentieth century. Like Esquivel in *Like Water for Chocolate*, Mastretta explores social and political themes stemming from the triumph of the Mexican Revolution, especially the figure of the strongman and his role in perpetuating chauvinist attitudes.

In her novel *Treinta años* (1999; *Leaving Tabasco*, 2001), Boullosa, who received literary training from Juan Rulfo, also approaches issues pertaining to Mexican women and the social limits that political and religious institutions impose on them. Critics have praised the novel for its ingenious use of magical realism, particularly in its handling of unusual religious events. Boullosa is also an active playwright.

Mexican women writers often speak about issues pertaining to so-called women's literature. Their critical statements refer to their own writing and also to specific problems encountered by women writers in Mexico in mainstream criticism. Their comments also reflect the ongoing critical conversations in Latin America about the role and purpose of literature by women writers. As expected, their opinions on this subject are varied and often contradictory.

Despite their differences, Mexican women writers display points of connection with regard to the ideological purpose of literature produced by women writers. Elena Poniatowska speaks about her strong interest in documentation of social and political ills in regard to "so much suffering and so much injustice" (*Broken Bars* 23). The political connotations present in literature by women writers are, for Brianda Domecq, an expected result of the "woman's view of the world, because of her historically marginalized position, because of her historically confined position" (*Contemporary Mexican Women Writers* 137).

The female characters, who are central in explaining the present and historic chauvinistic status quo, are diverse. Angeles Mastretta has said that her female characters are important because they are "ordinary women, conservative and traditional, who suddenly had something unusual happen to them and they responded in an unusual way" (*Broken Bars* 83). In contrast, Julieta Campos rejects the importance of gender in these characters: "I think that writing is androgynous. Creativity frees very archaic images and themes of humanity and in those depths the feminine and masculine are interwoven and blurred" (*Women Voices from Latin America* 95–96).

Laura Esquivel's *Like Water for Chocolate* addresses key preoccupations from a feminist point of view. Although not a realist novel, it presents a view of Mexican women toward the end of the Mexican Revolution of 1910. In an interesting approach, the novel follows closely the lives of women characters who struggle and challenge chauvinistic social restrictions. One of its strongest contributions is the characterization of various girls and women who openly challenge the status quo. The fight, which is both ideological and personal, takes on an interesting edge by drawing from a variety of sources, ranging from events inspired in magical realism to the influence of children's literature and the cooking of recipes.

Laura Esquivel (1950–)

The commercial success of Laura Esquivel's first novel *Como agua para chocolate* (1989; *Like Water for Chocolate*, 1992) placed her at the top of the list of Mexico's best-selling novelists. This novel is important for two reasons. First, it is the script for *Like Water for Chocolate* (1991), a production that is considered the first of a series of original films that brought Mexican cinema international acclaim. Second, *Like Water for Chocolate* led to a new literary trend: cooking recipes as an integral part of the narrative structure. Like the Chilean novelist Isabel Allende, Esquivel's work is representative of magical realism and features an interesting narrative that centers on women characters facing unusual circumstances.

Esquivel was born in Mexico City into a working-class family. She studied children's pedagogy and became a kindergarten teacher. Her first literary pieces were plays for children and scripts for children's television programs. Her Taller de Teatro y Literature Infantil, a workshop for the writing and performance of a theatre for children, was an important contribution to Mexican children's literature.

Writing children's literature was an important part of Esquivel's literary training, and literary themes that are often associated with children's literature are present in her writing. Because of Mexico's early dependence on Spanish and Argentine works, it did not have its own national tradition of children's literature. Esquivel was therefore a pioneer in this field. Today Mexican children's literature, including television programming for children, is widely available in Latin America and, most recently, in the U.S. Latino market.

Interested in writing for a booming Mexican film industry, Esquivel studied screenwriting with the Mexican director and actor Alfonso Arau. Under his direction, Esquivel wrote the script for "El taco de oro," a film that won best screenplay in Mexico in 1985. More recently, Esquivel wrote the script for "Little Ocean Star" (1994), a children's feature.

Arau directed the film version of *Like Water for Chocolate* from a screenplay adapted by Esquivel. The film, released in Mexico in 1992, displays superb cinematography and powerful visual renditions of scenes inspired by magical realism. Successful depiction of magical realism on film is a challenge; past film versions of the genre, such as the works of Colombian novelist Gabriel García Márquez, have failed to capture critical attention. *Like Water for Chocolate* was, however, an immediate international success, winning numerous honors. It inspired a series of films that would use food and cooking as metaphors for human passion and relationships. *Like Water for Chocolate* broke records among U.S. moviegoers. It was the longest-running foreign film in U.S. history, as well as the highest grossing. Despite the film's commercial success in the United States, however, it did not receive an Oscar nomination.

Like Water for Chocolate's English translation, which appeared in 1992, became a best-seller in the United States after the film's release. The novel was on the *New York Times* best-seller list for more than a year, an outstanding achievement. In 1994, it won the American Bestsellers Book of the Year (ABBY), the first time a foreign book received this prestigious award. The novel has been translated into thirty languages and has broken sales records around the world. As a result of its commercial success, Esquivel published *Intimas suculencias* (1998; *Between Two Fires,* 2000), a collection of stories and critical articles that expand on the aesthetic of "food literature."

Esquivel's novels continue to receive critical praise in Mexico and the United States. Her second novel, *La ley del amor* (1995; *The Law of Love,* 1996) caught the attention of critics because of its unique incorporation of a compact disc, with music for the reader to play while reading specific passages. Like her previous novel, it incorporates materials from contemporary popular culture, such as cartoons. Her third novel, *Tan veloz como el deseo* (2001; *Swift as Desire,* 2001) returns to the theme of unrequited love, which inspired *Like Water for Chocolate*. Her interest in children's literature is evident in *Estrellita marinera* (1999), a short novel not available in English translation. It traces the adventures of two children after they inherit a circus inhabited by most unusual characters.

The positive worldwide reception of *Like Water for Chocolate* provided exposure to women writers that went beyond mere curiosity among readers interested in the latest generation of Latin American authors. The novel is important because of its experimental approach to a conventional story, which focuses on the plight of three daughters facing the impositions of an aging mother at the beginning of the twentieth century in rural Mexico. In a refreshing departure from the traditional structural elements of the novel, Esquivel incorporates popular elements associated with women. The novel's subtitle: *A Novel in Monthly Installments, with Recipes, Romances and Home Remedies* introduces the reader to other elements of feminine popular culture, which are integral to the plot.

Echoes of Mexican short story writer Juan Rulfo and Colombian novelist Gabriel García Márquez are evident in the work. The rural background of Esquivel's novel reminds the reader of Rulfo's barren and isolated settings, where impossible things are bound to happen. As in García Márquez's *One Hundred Years of Solitude*, the events in *Like Water for Chocolate* center around life in a household. It is also significant that Esquivel's first novel, like Chilean Isabel Allende's *The House of the Spirits*, sets out to test the limits of magical realism as a mode of literary expression. *Like Water for Chocolate* can be viewed as experimentation with the aesthetics of magical realism from a feminine perspective.

The novel presents the history of the De la Garza, an upper-level Mexican family, living close to the Mexican-U.S. border at the time of the Mexican Revolution. An unusual element of the story is that Mama Elena, the head of the family, differs from the traditional literary matriarch. She is not a nourishing and loving mother; on the contrary, she is oppressive and tyrannical. Her insistence on obedience to chauvinistic customs, particularly those that kept women away from activities associated with men, forces the characters to take unusual actions.

The novel opens with the birth of Tita, the novel's protagonist. Tita was born in the kitchen. Mama Elena's delivery of her baby is described in a passage reminiscent of religious accounts: "Tita was literally washed into this world on a great tide of tears that spilled over the edge of the table and flooded across the kitchen floor" (6). After her birth, Nacha, the family's cook, collects the dried tears, which had turned into salt, filling a ten-pound sack for use in the house's cooking. An omniscient narrator points out that Tita's future has been predetermined by fate and tradition. Mama Elena restricts her youngest daughter to the kitchen, and consequently, Tita becomes a masterful cook.

Immediately after Tita's birth, her father, Juan de la Garza, dies under suspicious circumstances. The news comes as a terrible shock, having dire effects on Mama Elena's health; she is even unable to continue nursing Tita.

Thanks to Nacha's intricate knowledge of cooking, Tita survives on nourishment from popular rural foods. From this point on, Tita spends her childhood in the kitchen, where, under Nacha's tutelage, she becomes an accomplished cook. Her cooking knowledge appears to be primal, characterized as a "sixth sense" (7).

After the death of her husband, Mama Elena decides that Tita, as her youngest daughter, will be in charge of her care until her death. This meant, to Tita's dismay, that she would not be allowed to marry until after Mama Elena dies. Tita seems to be a submissive daughter, seeking refuge in the kitchen. She becomes an excellent cook, to the delight of her mother and her two sisters. Her life, described as "the joy of living . . . wrapped up in the delights of food" (7), seems complete until the moment she falls in love with Pedro.

Mama Elena remains firm in her decision not to allow Tita to marry. She bases her argument on ancient cultural and familial traditions. When Pedro comes to ask for Tita's hand in marriage, Mama Elena rejects his petition. To his surprise, Mama Elena offers Rosaura, her eldest daughter, instead. Pedro accepts, telling Tita later that he did so only to ensure that he and Tita could be together.

Mama Elena, a wicked woman with a terrible character and an inclination for enforcing unusual punishments, puts Tita in charge of the wedding feast. She hopes that these tasks will make Tita understand her fate. Tita's reputation as a gifted cook is well known in the area, and Mama Elena demands a lavish wedding reception, worthy of their high social position.

Tita prepares a fabulously decorated wedding cake. Its preparation takes a great deal of time and the dexterity of an accomplished cook. An interesting narrative element is the reproduction of the cake's recipe, which stands beside the narration of Tita's reaction while she makes it. Creating the cake brings Tita into a nervous outburst. She starts crying over the batter before Nacha, who is helping her, can stop her. After tasting it, Nacha decides that Tita's tears have not affected the cake, and they continue. The cake has been affected, however, as the narrator's foreshadowing comment implies: "No, the flavor did not seem to have been affected; yet without knowing why, Nacha was suddenly overcome with an intense longing" (35).

The following day, Nacha is bed-ridden and unable to manage the reception, for which Mama Elena now holds Tita fully responsible. Depressed by her mother's cruel treatment, Tita nonetheless complies with her wishes and presents her best face. At the reception, Tita first learns from Pedro about his plans to seek her sexually while being married to her sister. Mama Elena interrupts the conversation and forbids them ever to speak privately again. Tita, as usual, agrees.

The reception comes to a sudden halt after the wedding cake is served. As Nacha had experienced the night before, the guests are overcome with "a great wave of longing" (39) after eating the cake, followed by uncontrollable crying. The scene ends with all guests becoming ill and covering the bride's gown with their vomit. Although Mama Elena brutally punishes Tita, this unusual incident marks the beginning of Tita's struggle in her confrontation with traditional culture (her mother's insistence on keeping her single) and her sexual liberation (Tita's bold agreement to become Pedro's lover).

A series of strange events, all associated with Tita's elaborate dishes, increase the level of interest in the novel. The reader is treated to twelve recipes, each of which is an integral component of a particular scene's action. These recipes represent a different narrative style, at one time being the only kind of writing that women were allowed to write and publish. Cooking recipes have a special language and a special way to involve the reader in the preparation of food. They are not taken lightly. As Tita demonstrates, they have special power "to evoke the past, bringing back sounds and even other smells that have no match in the present" (9).

The characters of *Like Water for Chocolate* illustrate the social groups they represent, and particularly, their opinions about women and their role in postrevolutionary Mexican society. For example, Mama Elena's strong characterization as the reigning matron of the de la Garza family, is Esquivel's analysis of the misuse of culture to oppress women. Mama Elena's actions make her a caricature of prevailing inflexible, oppressive attitudes toward women. She is, however, an outdated character. In the end, she dies by her own hand, still under Tita's care, not because Tita was forced to attend to her, but because it was her duty as a loving daughter.

Mama Elena echoes the stepmother of "Cinderella," but this mature woman who brutally imposes her will on her young, defenseless daughter, unlike Cinderella's stepmother, has a political connotation. The stepmother's hatred for Cinderella is mere jealousy of the girl's beauty and charm, qualities her own daughters lack; the stepmother, therefore, keeps her Cinderella out of public view, presumably so that her own two unmarried daughters may find suitors. Although Mama Elena's restrictions on Tita have similar intentions, her actions also result from her insistence on maintaining the status quo, which dictates that women must be submissive to their families. Mama Elena exploits chauvinist social traditions to ensure for herself a devoted maid.

Another important element in *Like Water for Chocolate* is Esquivel's approach to events of the Mexican Revolution, a social movement presented in opposition to Mama Elena's strong conservative values. One of the novel's contributions is Esquivel's analysis of changes in contemporary Mexican society brought about by this key historic movement, and especially the opportunities that it provided to women. The passages about guerrilla action are also interesting because the narration is from the point of view of female characters.

The scenes about revolutionary guerrilla fights during the Mexican Revolution are presented in a realistic manner. Esquivel uses historical accounts of the abuses on the civilian population by guerrilla fighters and by federal armed forces. True to eyewitness accounts by previous writers, such as Mariano Azuela, Esquivel also focuses on the battles. Her perspective is a feminist one, however, pointing out that women were often trapped by both sides of the revolution.

Mama Elena faces the wrath of a local fighter in his attempt to confiscate her ranch. In line with her characterization, Mama Elena challenges the revolutionary leader by threatening his life if he attempts to come into her house. Mama Elena ultimately saves her ranch, and the reader recognizes that this is the same violent, enraged woman with whom Tita must contend. This part of the plot helps to explain why Tita complies with her mother's wishes.

There is one scene, however, that uses magical realism to present an event associated with the revolutionary army. After eating a special dish that Tita had prepared, Gertrudis, Mama Elena's second daughter, races out of the house, overcome by a heat that forces her to jump into an outdoor shower. As she cools down, a guerrilla troop passes by, and, to Mama Elena's horror, they kidnap Gertrudis. Much later, Gertrudis returns to the house. She has become a notorious revolutionary fighter and a liberated woman living out of wedlock with one of the revolutionaries. The comment here is both political and social: in the revolutionary ideology, Gertrudis finds a way out of her subservient role as an unmarried woman waiting to find a suitable husband. At the same time, she openly challenges conservative sexual practices by joining the revolutionary troops, much as Tita has by agreeing to become Pedro's lover.

Like Water for Chocolate's female characters offer a strong message about the consequences of suppression of women. Especially important is the fact that they resist in various ways the limits imposed on them, as in Gertrudis's incredible escape from an ultraconservative mother. Tita also escapes social restrictions. In the end, Tita joins Pedro, her true love, after Mama Elena's death. It was, however, a bold decision, because Pedro is still married to Rosaura. The three of them reach an agreement that allows them to live together, provided Tita and Pedro ensure that no one finds out about their relationship. This arrangement is unconventional for the time; it seems to predict the more radical sexual reforms of the twentieth century.

Esquivel's *Like Water for Chocolate* is a complex novel that shows the influence of her previous work as a screenwriter and playwright. The novel's initial theme (sexual repression at the beginning of the twentieth century in revolutionary Mexico) could well have been conceived as a screenplay or script, rather than a novel, and its episodes offer a view of Mexican culture, particularly of women's traditional role as household managers, cooking and tending to childrearing. The novel is also one of action, however, one that translates well to film. The ingenious combination of these two elements— a highly original plot and a strong ideological message—makes *Like Water for Chocolate* a fascinating reading—and moviegoing—experience.

Among the novel's contributions is its innovative use of magical realism, by which Esquivel explores historical subjects of interest to women in a form that is both amusing and politically charged. The presence of uncommon characters that find themselves in unusual situations, such as Gertrudis's adventures with the militia or Tita's magical experiences in the kitchen, become symbols of the women's ingenious ability to face sexual and political oppression.

PUERTO RICO

Puerto Rico increased in importance as the United States became a political power in the Atlantic at the end of the nineteenth century. An island located in the central Caribbean, Puerto Rico became a U.S. possession after the Spanish-American War of 1898. Both Puerto Rico and Cuba were former colonies of an aging and economically depleted Spain, and both came under U.S. control following the war. Unlike Cuba, however, Puerto Rico did not receive its independence, and in 1917, the U.S. Congress gave American citizenship to Puerto Ricans. In its political management, the island did not have the right to elect its governors. At the beginning of the twentieth century, its leaders were military appointees; later, it fell to the U.S. president to appoint them. These governors were Americans, often people unfamiliar with Puerto Rico and its customs.

In 1946, with the appointment of Puerto Rican politician Jesús T. Pineiro, Puerto Rico had its first native governor. Two years later, Luis Muñoz Marín, a popular politician, was elected governor of Puerto Rico in national elections. A figure of both immense popularity and controversy, Muñoz Marín created the so-called Estado Libre Asociado, a "Commonwealth" formula that is the island's current political status.

The history of Puerto Rico after the Spanish-American War reflects Puerto Rican resistance to a variety of U.S.-controlled governmental impositions. These included the directive to teach only in English in Puerto Rican public schools, beginning in the early years of the 1910s. This practice continued until the late 1940s. In a move to Americanize Puerto Ricans, U.S. teachers were sent to the island, among them members of Catholic religious orders.

The issue of bilingual education is today a highly controversial subject in Puerto Rico. The earliest American-run schools, such as those that religious orders had operated since the earliest part of the twentieth century, brought change to the Puerto Rican educational and social systems. For example, the Redemptorists established educational compounds in marginal neighborhoods. This is the case of the Colegio San Agustín, founded in 1913 in the poor barrio of Puerta de Tierra on the outskirts of San Juan. The school provided primary and secondary education to children, as well as manual training to women of the area. Some private schools were intended for the upper classes as well. Yet while wealthier Puerto Ricans took English as their second language and assimilated American culture into their own, the lower classes remained faithful to the Puerto Rican hybrid African and Hispanic culture. This constant clash of Puerto Rican versus American culture is today an important literary subject for women writers on the island.

Another subject of debate in Puerto Rican literature is the evaluation of the American expansionist practices in the Caribbean. This is a polemical topic that goes to the core of U.S. military strength and control over the major Caribbean islands of Haiti/Dominican Republic and Cuba since the earliest part of the twentieth century. Like Puerto Rico, those islands experienced the socioeconomic consequences of U.S. military campaigns. Haiti experienced an American occupation from 1915 to 1934 and the Dominican Republic endured it four times (1903–1904, 1914, 1916–1924, 1965–1966). This military aggression has created issues that remain important today, such as the countries' ineffective governments, their abject poverty, and the disproportionate number of emigrants from those islands who attempt to reach the United States, often by desperate means.

Puerto Rican writers Rosario Ferré and Ana Lydia Vega have distinctive points of view about the colonialist relationship between Puerto Rico and the United States. Ferré's novel *La casa en la laguna* (1996; *The House on the Lagoon*), set in the early twentieth century, traces the development of modern Puerto Rico after the island's residents became U.S. citizens in 1917. Vega's short story "Cloud over the Caribbean" analyzes the racism and sexism that is prevalent in Caribbean societies. She also examines complex issues of Caribbean immigration into the United States, which Puerto Ricans have experienced since the latter part of the nineteenth century. The two writers are on opposite poles of the political spectrum regarding U.S. influence on Caribbean cultures and national identities.

Rosario Ferré (1938–)

A poet, short story writer, novelist, essayist, and professor of Puerto Rican and Latin American literature, Ferré is among the most vocal commentators on Puerto Rican social and economic structures. As a daughter of a former governor of Puerto Rico, she offers an in-depth analysis of the complex Puerto Rican political scene. Her literature depicts female characters' struggles within gender-based social patterns. Ferré is well known in Latin America because of her strong female characters, which often provide an increasingly important feminist viewpoint.

Ferré's family, established in Ponce, the second largest city of Puerto Rico, was important to the island's history throughout the twentieth century. Her father, Luis A. Ferré, was a prominent political figure. In 1968, he was the first candidate for governor to be elected through the support of a political party that actively sought statehood for the island. His election was a pivotal moment in Puerto Rican politics because his triumph seemed to imply that the U.S. federal government would consider the possibility of statehood for Puerto Rico.

For Rosario Ferré, the issue of statehood is at the ideological core of her analysis of Puerto Rican politics. In the late 1990s, she was quoted as a spokesperson in favor of Puerto Rican statehood. This was a controversial stand because earlier Ferré had voiced her strong support for independence. Many Puerto Rican writers, including Ana Lydia Vega, publicly opposed Ferré's surprising statements.

The political and economic reputation of Ferré's family reflects the radical changes in Puerto Rican society after the U.S. arrival in the late nineteenth century. Her mother's family had a strong connection with the booming sugarcane industry that, until the arrival of Americans, had been the island's largest agricultural export. The development of other agrarian products, such as coffee, brought an end to the power of the so-called sugar barons. The legacy of the sugarcane plantations to the Puerto Rican social fabric was important, particularly in coastal areas. Ferré's work explores this history, characterized by multiple contrasting elements, specifically with regard to race.

With the arrival of the American government, Puerto Rico had to adapt to foreign laws and technology and to new imports introduced by U.S. businesses. The Ferré family made a fortune in the cement industry. With technological advances came radical change in traditional Puerto Rican social patterns. This transformation took place first at the upper levels of society, reflected in their interest in incorporating American ways of life, such as the English language and U.S. pedagogy. The true clash came after lower classes rejected some of the national projects intended to Americanize the island.

Ferré's upbringing reflects the efforts of Puerto Rico's upper classes to incorporate themselves into an American educational system, as well as into a U.S. lifestyle. She, like the children of an increasing number of upper- and middle-class families, attended a Roman Catholic private school. She learned English there and became fully bilingual.

Despite her family's declared pro-U.S. sympathies, particularly evident after her father's election as governor, Ferré publicly announced her preference for Puerto Rican independence. She was a bold proponent, even during her father's term (1968–1972), during which she served as his social assistant after her mother's death. Ferré's sometimes outlandish comments and carefree behavior shocked the fairly traditional political arena of Puerto Rico.

Ferré emerged onto the Puerto Rican literary scene in the 1970s with her cofounding of *Zona de carga y descarga* (*Loading Zone*), a magazine geared mainly to a young readership that was intended to publish the work of up-and-coming young writers. It also had a social agenda, providing space for articles focusing on the Puerto Rican political debates of the time. In particular, *Zona de carga y descarga* addressed the ongoing pro-statehood platform that Ferré's father was championing. This was a pivotal moment for the pro-statehood movement, because he was the first governor to be elected as a candidate of the New Progressive Party, which sought the immediate and unconditional incorporation of Puerto Rico as the fifty-first U.S. state.

It is hard to ascertain whether Ferré's liberal views in *Zona de carga y descarga* affected her father's campaign as a candidate with a pro-statehood platform. It is telling, however, that Mr. Ferré lost a reelection race to a young, charismatic politician who was running for the Popular Party, which was the pro-Commonwealth political party. Puerto Ricans continue to display an ambivalent relationship with the United States. The pro-state movement remains strong, but support for the current status quo of the commonwealth is greater. Literature has traditionally presented a negative view of the influence of U.S. culture and economics on traditional Puerto Rican social values.

Ferré's *Zona de carga y descarga* gave impetus to a growing literary scene. Ferré published in the magazine a number of her own short stories, later published in the collection *Papeles de Pandora* (*Pandora's Papers,* 1976), which she translated in 1991 as *The Youngest Doll.* These stories gave her an international reputation among new female writers from Latin America. She also wrote literary criticism, and in 1980 her collection *Sitio a Eros* (*Eros under Siege*) became one of the first feminist collections by a Latin American woman.

Her interest in Puerto Rican folklore, particularly in stories with motifs of interest to children, is evident in her collection *Los cuentos de Juan Bobo* (1980). This collection, not available in translation, has as its protagonist Juan Bobo, a street-smart peasant boy. Although innocent in appearance, these stories often present a critical view of the economic and social injustices present in Puerto Rican society. They are, however, easy to read and are linguistically at the level of a superior student of Spanish.

Ferré has established a strong international reputation with novels based on historic Puerto Rican events. *Maldito amor* (1986), which she translated into English as *Sweet Diamond Dust* (1988), is a novella that plays with the boundaries between novel and short story. She wrote *The House on the Lagoon* in English, and it became a finalist for the National Book Award. In this novel, Ferré presents the history of modern Puerto Rico from the dual perspectives of a merchant and his wife; the wife lived marginalized as a mere object of sexual and social importance to her powerful husband. Available in English translation is *Eccentric Neighborhoods* (1998), a collection of short stories that first appeared in Spanish in a Puerto Rican newspaper. Her most recent novel, *Flight of Swan* (2001), which Ferré translated into English, also has a strong historical background. It is different from her previous novels. The protagonist is an aging Russian ballerina who finds herself in Puerto Rico at the peak of the Bolshevik revolution. Unable to return to her homeland, she stays on the island, where she encounters characters representative of the various Puerto Rican social classes. Of special historical interest is her involvement with the underground nationalist groups that promote armed rebellion against the U.S. government.

Ferré is a key literary figure in the emerging literary movement of women writers in Puerto Rico and Latin America. She holds a doctorate in Latin American literature from the University of Maryland. She has taught Latin American literature at the University of Puerto Rico and at other prestigious U.S. institutions, such as the University of California at Berkeley, Rutgers, Harvard, and Johns Hopkins. A reputable literary critic, Ferré published a book on the Argentine writer Julio Cortázar, an author whose literary impact is evident in her short stories. Above all, in her historical approach to the development of modern Puerto Rican society, Ferré has become one of the island's strongest advocates of social change, particularly with regard to gender and racial discrimination.

The House on the Lagoon is Ferré's best example of her interest in documenting Puerto Rican history of the beginning of the twentieth century, an important period in the development of today's modern island. It was written from the viewpoint of Isabel, a woman from an upper-class background who decides to write her family history. Although she is writing in San Juan, she is a native of Ponce. There has been a rivalry between these two cities. San Juan, an important import center located on a bay of the Atlantic northeastern coast, became the island's capital in 1521. Ponce, also a commercial center, had a lesser role in the island's political life because of its southern location. It did develop a strong merchant society, however, mainly from its sugarcane plantations, which provided the island's southern coast with a flourishing economy. That wealth produced a rich cultural life in Ponce with strong European undertones, one that rivaled that of San Juan. It also developed a more ornate colonial architecture than San Juan's sober and solid constructions as a fortress capital city.

Isabel's accounts are unusual for several reasons. She writes as a self-made historian. Traditionally women had been excluded from this role, and there was less recognition of their contributions. In Puerto Rico, male writers controlled both the field of history and the genre of the historical novel. Isabel's writing goes beyond the historical novel. In addition to its account of history, she also discloses information about Quintín, her husband, whose family fortune she traces to the efforts and opportunism of a poor Spanish merchant. It is in the inherent tension stemming from historical and personal accounts that the novel finds its strength. As a feminist revision of modern Puerto Rico, the story of Isabel's current state as an oppressed wife and, more specifically, her dislike of her husband's chauvinist control over her and their family, appeals to a wide readership.

Ferré's characters represent several social levels; their personal history is closely woven into the development of modern Puerto Rico. *The House on the Lagoon* opens with the arrival in Puerto Rico of Buenaventura Mendizabal, a poor Spaniard who, like thousands of other Spanish immigrants, was attracted to the island's commercial potential. He arrives on March 2, 1917, the same day that the United States granted U.S. citizenship to Puerto Ricans. To the barely literate immigrant Buenaventura, this action does not seem extraordinary; he simply becomes interested in finding ways to take advantage of the island's new condition. In the meantime, as a recent arrival he takes great care in describing the booming city of Old San Juan. Readers are treated to detailed descriptions of construction after the arrival of the Americans. Of particular historical importance are his comments about the capitol building, a copy of Thomas Jefferson's Monticello. These buildings are in contrast to other impressive structures, mainly military fortifications built in Old San Juan during the Spanish period.

Through hard work, Buenaventura builds a successful commerce of import of Spanish wines and other products, favorite gourmet items of San Juan's upper-class society, who are still in touch with their Spanish roots. He becomes a fairly wealthy man, able to buy real-estate that eventually develops into a plush neighborhood on the outskirts of San Juan. The house on the lagoon is built on this site, a mansion that subsequent generations of Mendizabals would turn into a symbol of their power over the national political arena. The house is an important symbol, like San Juan and the island of Puerto Rico itself; it suffers structural changes as the Mendizabal generations make it adjust to their changing needs.

During this period in which the Mendizabals's progress takes place, Puerto Rico was also experiencing rapid economic change, evolving from an agrarian into an industrial society. The changes in traditional social values were significant, many possible only after U.S. industries allowed women to work. In the process, however, U.S. companies openly abused workers' rights. The increasing number of industries under U.S. control, such as the telephone and the electric companies, caused popular discontent and led to political activism. Of particular historical importance is Ferré's careful documentation of the island's growing textile industry, in which violations of workers' rights, particularly of women workers, produced social discontent. This led to the beginning of Puerto Rican women's participation in national politics.

The House on the Lagoon is, in short, a political history of Puerto Rico and its relationship with the United States. The novel provides detailed historical accounts of this small territory's occupation following a military intervention and its subsequent incorporation as a U.S. territory, an action taken without the Puerto Rican people's approval. The island's political incorporation into U.S. political and economic structures produced a flourishing society, but it also produced tension and rupture in traditional cultural values.

The novel's primary message is not, however, a mere recording of the island's key historical moments. Isabel's narration is remarkable for its highly critical approach to these events. The novel unfolds in the form of her memoirs as the wife of a wealthy businessman and as the daughter of a family influential in Puerto Rican politics. An interesting turn of events occurs, in a complex narrative of numerous characters, when her husband, Quintín, discovers his wife's hidden manuscripts. As the novel continues, Quintín, who initially does not disclose to Isabel that he is reading her papers, begins to write notes in the margins, clarifying or denying his wife's opinion of certain events. His bold, negative remarks about certain of Isabel's strongest feminist passages are equivalent to those of the male view of feminist literature: "Another fault he found was Isabel's tendency to use her female characters as shadow players for her own personality. She had to be careful here; it was a pitfall for mediocre writers" (189).

The House on the Lagoon's most interesting experimental component is Isabel's approach to her husband's arrogant efforts to keep her silent and submissive. Throughout the novel, Isabel addresses her husband's criticism from her newly found point of view as a historian: "History doesn't deal with the truth any more than literature does. From the moment a historian selects one theme over another in order to write about it, he is manipulating the facts. The historian, like the novelist, observes the world through his own tinted glass, and describes it as if it were the truth. But it's only one side of the truth, because imagination—what you call lies—is also part of the truth" (312).

The novel's most interesting critical contribution is Isabel's feminist perspective as she offers her version of the history of modern Puerto Rico after the Spanish-American War. Isabel writes about Puerto Rican history as both a woman and a Puerto Rican nationalist. Her ideological point of view opposes the earliest U.S. regulations of not allowing Puerto Rican history to be taught in public schools: "Can history be so dangerous as to be revolutionary?" (91).

Ferré's writings contributed to the Latin American feminist movement of the 1980s. Her essay "The Writer's Kitchen," from the collection *Sitio a Eros,* helped set the ideological parameters for the increasingly popular feminist literature in Latin America. The article is important in several ways. She analyzes the influence of two major feminist intellectuals, Virginia Woolf and Simone de Beauvoir, on her own works, noting that these writers are much read and appreciated by Latin America's feminists. Ferré's article also stresses her own voice as both a writer and a feminist theoretician. Of particular interest to a student of Latin American societies is Ferré's statement about reasons for writing: "I write because I am poorly adjusted to reality; because the deep disillusionment within me has given rise to a need to re-create life, to replace it with a more compassionate, tolerable reality. I carry within me a utopian person, a utopian world" (214–215). Ferré's commitment to social causes produces strong female characters, who reflect a feminist view of Puerto Rican history. Her readers see challenges to the traditional gender-based social structures prevailing in Puerto Rican and in other Latin American societies. Ultimately, Ferré states in her article, women's literature can often be more radical than men's because "it delves into forbidden zones . . . zones that our rational and utilitarian society makes it dangerous to recognize" (227).

Ana Lydia Vega (1946–)

Ana Lydia Vega is today among the best-known fiction writers from Puerto Rico. A professor of French and Caribbean literature at the University of Puerto Rico, Vega produces literature outstanding for its in-depth exploration of sociopolitical issues pertaining to modern Caribbean countries. In her characterization of the Caribbean, Vega, unlike other Puerto Rican or Spanish-speaking Caribbean writers, goes beyond folkloric interest. She approaches the island nations of Cuba, the Dominican Republic, and Haiti as an area that has historically experienced similar key political and economic developments. A well-known commentator of the Puerto Rican political world, Vega often also addresses local controversies, particularly in her defense of independence for the island.

Vega comes from a middle-class family background; her father owned a neighborhood store, and her mother was a teacher. Her close contact with blue-collar neighborhoods brings to her writings an exploration of Puerto Rican popular lore. She is also a gifted linguist, faithfully reproducing linguistic patterns and the rich expressions of the lower and working classes. She is interested in depicting characters from these classes as literary protagonists, and this is perhaps one of her most important contribution to Puerto Rican literature, which has traditionally focused on characters of the middle and upper classes.

As a spokesperson against social ills, Vega dwells on issues present in contemporary Puerto Rican society. Her writings deal primarily with three subjects: machismo, racism, and Puerto Rico's political and economic dependency on the United States. She is well known for her exploration of risqué sexual concerns and for the use of profane or vulgar language.

She is also interested in the Caribbean's African roots, which although common to all the islands, has developed distinctive characteristics. One aspect of this Caribbean culture is the religious belief systems known as **Voodoo** (from Haiti) and **Santería** (from Cuba). Because these religions came to the region with the slaves, Vega characterizes them in her stories as a concrete example of Caribbean cultures' strong will to survive. Vega's proud view of Puerto Rico's African roots includes her analysis of how these religions overcame foreign imposition. This is a political reading of Caribbean colonialist history, including her opinion that just as these religions survived attempts at conversion by mainstream Christian thought, Puerto Rico will also resist U.S. imposition of its cultural and political values.

Vega's short story collection *Encancaranublado y otros cuentos* (*Overcast and Other Stories*) received in 1982 the prestigious Cuban Casa de las Américas literary award. In 1984, she was awarded the distinguished international Juan Rulfo Short Story Award. She was the recipient of a Guggenheim Fellowship in 1989. *True and False Romances: Macho Latin Meets His Match,* a short story collection in English translation, appeared in 1994.

She has also attempted to develop film production in Puerto Rico. In 1986, she cowrote with Marcos Zurinaga the script for the film *La gran fiesta* (*The Big Party*), which was released in the United States to positive reviews. Vega has also published literary criticism and newspaper articles, writing in particular for *Claridad,* Puerto Rico's pro-independence newspaper. A well-known advocate of independence, Vega was among Rosario Ferré's most vocal opponents when that distinguished novelist made a public announcement in 1998 about her unconditional support for Puerto Rico's incorporation with full statehood into the United States. The options of independence versus statehood, including the third option of continued commonwealth status, have created the most divisive issue in contemporary Puerto Rican political and intellectual circles.

Whereas Ferré's protagonists come from upper-level society, Vega gives voice to popular characters. They are often black or of mixed race, and their experiences, radically different from those of the privileged, offer a radical view of Caribbean society. "Cloud Cover Caribbean" is a story that brings together three male characters, a Cuban, a Haitian, and a Dominican, in an unusual conversation. As the action begins, they are floating aimlessly in choppy waters on a makeshift vessel. They are **balseros,** boat people trying to reach the Florida coast as illegal aliens. Despite the great danger involved, this is a common way for desperate islanders to reach U.S. soil. Unfortunately, the costs are high, with many deaths reported annually.

"Cloud Cover Caribbean" is a brief story that takes place in September at the peak of the hurricane season, "September, agent provocateur of hurricanes, signals for war, filling the seas with urchins and rays" (202). As the story begins, Antenor, a black Haitian, is heading toward Miami, gladly leaving behind his impoverished island: "The putrid mangos, emblems of diarrhea and famine, the war cries of the macoutes, the fear, the drought" (202). Like thousands of boat people from Haiti, he is forced to leave because of the island's dire poverty. His need to leave the island on a makeshift vessel is apparent in the piece of a shirt that functions as a sail. This is a commentary about Antenor's desperation to leave Haiti because he knows that should a tropical storm arrive, his life will be in great danger.

Antenor is also a political exile, as the direct reference to the **macoutes** points out. The macoutes were former security guards of "president for life"

François Duvalier and a private army well known in Haiti for torturing and killing the dictator's opponents. Even after Duvalier's death and the overthrow in 1986 of his successor, his son Jean-Claude, known as Baby Doc, the macoutes continued to exist as a guerrilla group. In short, this is the political history of Haiti, a country heavily subjected to U.S. foreign policy, beginning with a long military intervention between 1915 and 1934. Political commentators have pointed out that the U.S. government was partially responsible for the Duvaliers' illegal regimes. Antenor is eager to leave behind impoverished and politically convoluted Haiti. His brush with the macoutes explains the main reason that Haitian boat people often seek political asylum in the United States. This image is quite different from that presented by the popular media, which portray them as mere economic refugees.

Antenor's sailing is suddenly interrupted not by a storm, but by the appearance of a sinking, makeshift boat. A Dominican man occupies the vessel, and like Antenor he is desperate to reach the Florida coast. Diogenes is a young black man, a fact that seems to link the two characters, despite their differences in terms of national customs and language. They are members of a destitute and marginal ethnic group, ironically described by an omniscient narrator as "the royal pain of being black, Caribbean and poor" (203). It seems that their shared colonial past and extreme poverty may compensate for their national differences and the historical dislike between their two countries.

The men's cordiality comes to a sudden halt when they pick up a Cuban, Carmelo, whose makeshift sail has collapsed. He, too, has abandoned his country. Carmelo's story is not, however, about lack of work in Cuba or about political persecution. Quite the contrary, Carmelo expresses discontent about his obligation to work in sugarcane fields. Diogenes, mindful of the high unemployment rate in his native Dominican Republic, expresses surprise, claiming that there are no jobs available in his homeland, particularly in the sugarcane industry. He adds that the manual workers there are Haitians, whom he then describes in a negative light as *madamos.* The three men begin a series of comments that go to the core of the sociopolitical structures of the three islands.

Antenor, unable to join fully in the conversation because his native language is French Creole, cannot present the other reality for Haitian migrant workers in the Dominican Republic. Indeed, as Diogenes points out, there are a substantial number of Haitians working there during the *zafra,* or the cutting season of the sugarcane, but they are not protected by Dominican laws, so their workers' rights are seldom recognized, and powerful landowners often abuse them.

Carmelo is the most vocal of the three men. He comments fully about his problems with the current Cuban sociopolitical situation. His reasons for setting out on a dangerous voyage are preposterous, however; he has failed in his plan to open in Cuba an agency of "dating services." Cuban laws against prostitution, unfair in his opinion, have prevented him from opening his business. He is hopeful that in Miami his dream will come true. Carmelo's animosity against the revolutionary government extends to Cuban women's strong feminism: "in Cuba the women think they are equal to the men and, you know, they don't want to get out and work the streets" (205). In response to this restriction, Diogenes's comment is equally demeaning to women. According to his social analysis, opportunities to engage in prostitution are widely available in the Dominican Republic; the business is so prosperous that it is now being exported. This is not a joke, although Diogenes intends it as such. It is his chauvinistic view of the fact that Dominican women often leave their homeland, recruited by unscrupulous agencies to work as prostitutes in foreign countries.

A brawl soon starts. When Diogenes and Carmelo get hungry, they discover Antenor's well-hidden food supply and attempt to take it. A struggle follows, and the three men fall into the ocean. They are rescued by an American captain, who has harsh words for them that they do not understand because he has spoken in English: " 'Get those niggers down there and let the spikes take care of 'em' " (206). Finally, a black Puerto Rican addresses the arrivals in a strong statement that ends the story: " 'If you want to feed your belly here, you're going to have to work and I mean work hard. A gringo don't give anything away. Not to his own mother' " (206–207). Their dreams of finding jobs, at least for two of the men, are abruptly, if unpleasantly, fulfilled.

"Cloud Cover Caribbean" is a fierce satire of contemporary Caribbean societies. Vega deals with controversial subjects such as the inherent political tensions among Caribbean islands. The lack of strong, long-lasting relationships among these nations is apparent in the simple image of the three men stuck together in a makeshift boat. It is symbolic that because of their inability to communicate among themselves, they end up in the water. The Atlantic Ocean, like the landscape of the criollista writers, is triumphant not because of its mighty powers but because of the men's inability to put an end to their personal disagreements.

Another controversial point of view in Vega's story is her analysis of ethnic marginality and sexual practices in the Caribbean. The characters who represent the Caribbean nations are black men who display varying degrees of racism toward their fellow travelers. These men are also chauvinists whose words reduce women to sexual objects. Their opinions of women are low and demeaning, revealed in comments that resemble previous racist statements about each other.

One lasting contribution of Vega as a writer committed to social change is her open discussion of racism and of the ill treatment of women in contemporary Caribbean societies. Ideologically, she considers these two social ills to be equally important; society must approach them simultaneously.

Her frank references to sexual practices, particularly prostitution, make her both a daring writer and an ideologue for feminist thought in the Caribbean.

CHILE

Chile is tremendously important to Latin American politics. One of the few Latin American countries with a long tradition of democratic elections, in 1973 Chile suffered a brutal coup that deposed President-elect Salvador Allende. The first socialist president democratically elected in the Americas, Allende had become a center of political controversy—national and international. A strong platform of socialist-oriented projects found political and economic opposition from mainstream Chilean institutions, while U.S. intervention, including direct CIA involvement in events that led to the coup, marked the beginning of a new era of U.S. military involvement in Latin America, particularly in sustained relationships with military governments.

On September 4, 1970, Allende ran on the ticket of the Popular Unity Party (a coalition of socialist and leftist parties) and won the national elections to the surprise of Chileans—and the world. Allende, a seasoned politician who had run in several unsuccessful presidential campaigns, had a well-defined Marxist platform for radical changes. Using the slogan of "The People's Government," Allende immediately began a comprehensive social and economic program that sought changes at the core of traditional Chilean society. Three underdog sectors had particular preference in his plans for social changes: workers, peasants, and indigenous populations.

Among Allende's most impressive plans was a comprehensive agrarian reform. This movement intended to reduce the amount of land that could be privately owned. Allende hoped to redistribute nationalized land to peasants, who had been working for powerful landowners, usually absent from the lands they owned. These landowners often required their workers to buy in their employers' shops, paying with certificates that could be redeemed only at those stores. Farm workers were often left without proper medical care or education for their children. Most of their workers' rights were often denied, and they had to work in inhumane conditions.

Other controversial political moves affected the Chilean economy. Banking centers were controlled by foreign companies, and a large number of private institutions operated Chile's public and private services. Nationalization of foreign companies, particularly of the rich copper mines owned by U.S. investors, led U.S. President Richard Nixon to impose severe financial restrictions. This was the beginning of systematic opposition to President Allende's administration and of the U.S. involvement in a bloody military coup that ended Allende's administration.

Right-wing political parties openly displayed their animosity against the newly elected president. During Allende's first year in political power, however, the government enjoyed a boom. The social platform, particularly the changes that benefited workers and peasants, earned popular approval for Allende. For instance, special educational and vocational programs were created for indigenous populations. He raised minimum wages and, in many cases, nationalized privately owned industries, making the workers their own administrators.

Allende's popularity was short-lived. An increasing financial crisis and highly organized propaganda (mainly from newspapers) against his social reforms provoked numerous protests and strikes. According to U.S. governmental records, the Nixon administration had an active role in a CIA-sponsored campaign intended to damage Allende's popular image and accelerate the country's mounting inflation. With Nixon's approval, large amounts of money went into a program to destabilize the Chilean economy; the program funded demonstrations and strikes, held back basic products of daily consumption in order to provoke national shortages, and, in short, created perfect conditions for a military coup.

Despite his popular national projects, Allende failed to gain the political opposition's support for his platform of social change. A military coup became the means to end his presidency. Ultimately it resulted in Allende's demise. The coup marked the end of the Chilean democratic process, which had lasted some 150 years, and the beginning of a military dictatorship.

The influence of the military in the Chilean government, as in other Latin American countries, indicates its relevance to socioeconomic structures. The Chilean military can be viewed as another example of a strongman, one Allende openly challenged by imposing legal restrictions on its power. Allende failed to curtail the power of the military, however, which allied itself with traditional right-wing political factions.

The military coup, led by Augusto Pinochet, commander-in-chief of the Chilean army, took place on September 11, 1973. It has become infamous around the world for its brutality, Allende's assassination, and the aggressive campaigns against Allende's supporters that would follow. The destruction of the Palacio de la Moneda, the Chilean presidential palace, by heavy bombardment and artillery would be a horrific omen of events that were to take place. A hunt for pro-Allende political activists began immediately on the day of the coup. Illegally imprisoned, they were tortured and brutally killed. Men and women, city dwellers, peasants, and indigenous people suffered tremendous physical punishment. After their deaths, their bodies were crudely disposed of, often in public areas, a lesson for anyone who dared to participate in subversive activities.

Americans knew about Pinochet's totalitarian regime and torture practices in 1982 after the release of *Missing*, a motion picture that won several prestigious international awards. Even earlier, the violence had affected the

United States, however. In 1976 a car bomb went off in Washington, D.C., killing Orlando Letelier, a former Chilean diplomat and a principal political opponent of the Pinochet regime.

Today Pinochet continues to be at the center of controversy. Although international pressure caused him to allow democratic elections in 1990, leading to the election of Patricio Aylwin as president, Pinochet remained active in Chilean politics. In 1998, as allowed by the Chilean constitution, he became a senator-for-life. That year, during a trip to London, he was arrested on charges of violation of international laws for human rights. His case did not proceed, however, and he returned to Chile in 2000.

The importance of Pinochet's legal case as a defendant responsible for crimes against humanity is obvious. Yet international opinion about Pinochet's regime was divided. Former British Prime Minister Margaret Thatcher, for example, publicly defended Pinochet during his house arrest in London.

Writer Isabel Allende, niece of the assassinated president, dwells on the complex Chilean historical incidents that led to the unexpected political rise of Salvador Allende and to his tragic fall at the hands of the military. She is a gifted storyteller who looks at history from the perspective of unusual women characters. Allende's first novel, *The House of the Spirits,* is grounded in the literary genre of the ***testimonio,*** a political tool that seeks to document political incidents in a first-person narrative. She used an innovative device, however; although an eyewitness to the terror of Pinochet's coup, Allende chose fiction as her literary medium.

Isabel Allende (1942–)

Isabel Allende is the woman writer from Latin America with the greatest international readership, and she has a significant influence on an increasingly popular, worldwide literature written by women. Her extensive literary production, which includes novels, short stories, and essays, has been translated into dozens of languages. In the United States, her novels are often on best-seller lists, in both the original Spanish and their English translations. Her work has been discussed across the nation in the popular reading group televised by the television personality Oprah Winfrey. Allende's literature addresses issues that pertain to the sociopolitical condition of Latin American women, with a particular emphasis on Chilean history. Above all, her fiction, with its strong historical perspective, attempts to give testimony of the contributions of women to Chilean society, an intention that finds international appeal among feminist groups undertaking similar projects.

Born in Peru to a Chilean diplomat father, Allende comes from a family of political prestige in her native Chile. Salvador Allende, the first president elected from a socialist political party in Latin America, was her uncle and godfather. Like her biological father, her stepfather, whom she considers her father, also had a prominent diplomatic career, including, among other posts, working at the prestigious Chilean embassy in Argentina during the administration of President Allende. This close contact with the Chilean political scene contributed to Isabel Allende's development of a strong sense of social activism, particularly after a military coup deposed President Allende. She also developed a profound interest in Chilean history; her books often explore the complexities of modern Chile by means of an examination of key historical events.

Besides Allende's interest in Chilean society, she has also focused on her own family history. Unlike most other Latin American writers of her stature and literary importance, she has documented her own life. *Paula* (1994) is an autobiography that she began writing as a letter to Paula, her daughter who had been in an irreversible coma since 1991. Hoping to keep her daughter aware of the events that she was missing, Allende began to write about her own life and that of their grandparents. The result is a fascinating account of Allende's diverse roles as a mother, as a woman in a chauvinist society, as a political activist during the Chilean military regime, and as the most recognized woman writer from Latin America.

The importance of Allende's mother and of her stepfather during her childhood, and also the presence of her grandparents, make the reading of *Paula* a means for understanding her literary production. Like other Latin American writers, she drew on the lives of her grandparents, especially of her grandmother, whose influence she characterizes as magical. She describes her grandmother, Memé, and her ability to predict the future, to read people's minds, to talk to animals, and to move objects with the power of her sight. Memé was an ethereal being, in contrast to her husband, Tata, whom Allende presents as a man with a strong character, as tough as the rocky Chilean coast. Of her childhood in the grandparents' house, Allende has said, "I was a sad and solitary child, but my childhood was full of magical things, strong emotions, changes and upsets, ghosts that roamed through the rooms and escaped through the mirrors (*Conversations* 40). The dichotomy in her grandparents' characters became a literary model for her first novel *La casa de los espíritus* (1982; *The House of the Spirits,* 1985).

Allende's father abandoned his family shortly after the birth of his third child. They were living in Lima, where the father served as part of the Chilean diplomatic delegation. He would never see his family again. Allende's mother survived the social stigma of being abandoned by her husband. Eventually, she remarried, another Chilean diplomat, whom Allende today considers her spiritual father. With him the family spent considerable periods of time abroad. Among the cities that left an impression on Allende is La Paz, the Bolivian capital, where she suffered animosity because of wars fought by Chile, Bolivia, and Peru over border disputes.

Allende also remembered her life in Beirut, Lebanon, during her early teenage years. There she attended a Quaker school and learned French and

English. She also read the Bible extensively and came into contact with philosophical and religious thoughts other than her native Roman Catholic beliefs.

After her return to Chile, Allende attended a private English school. She was at ease with the English language, and classical British writers had a strong influence on her writing. In fact, she has stated that she read the classic English writers, such as Shakespeare, more than she read Spanish and Chilean classics. Of particular interest in her childhood was her discovery of *A Thousand and One Nights,* which she read in its uncensored version. She remembers reading other writers during her formative years, including Emilio Salgari, Bernard Shaw, Jules Verne, Mark Twain, Oscar Wilde, and Jack London. She also enjoyed historical novels about the Roman Empire and "anything that had violence in it" (*Conversations* 125).

Allende presents in *Paula* a portrait of herself as a young woman. For instance, she makes no mention of her reasons for not going to college, a decision that must have caused concern in her career-oriented family. She started working as a secretary, without training, for the Food and Agriculture Organization of the United Nations. Working for the Department of Information, she was charged with writing information pieces for the agency. Her training during this period was pivotal to her future professional endeavors, particularly because she was writing in Spanish for the first time after years of education in other languages. She also translated into Spanish romantic novels written in English for a time. This job was short-lived, however; according to Allende, she was fired when she insisted on making substantive changes to the plot to present the female protagonist in a more realistic and less stereotypical fashion.

Her entrance onto the Chilean literary scene came in 1967, when she started writing for *Paula,* the first magazine for women in Chile. According to Allende, she had not sought the job. The journal's editor became interested in her writing after reading a letter that Allende had sent to her mother. In Chile, the feminist magazine caused a considerable stir because it presented articles, often on controversial subjects, that explored issues of interest to women. Allende wrote several columns, among them comic articles under the sarcastic title "Civilize Your Troglodyte." Her work in a journal for women put her into contact with international feminist literature, particularly the works of the renowned French activist Simone de Beauvoir. She also wrote a romance section, called "Love Mail," and answered letters from readers under the pseudonym of Francisca Román. Allende wrote serious articles as well, pieces about "marginal" figures, such as assassins. In her autobiography, Allende remembers with particular pride her interview with a professional businesswoman who talked to her freely, although under an assumed name, about her reasons for being unfaithful to her husband. This article in particular, Allende proudly remembers, created controversies about the prevalent view of women among the rather traditional and chauvinistic Chilean society.

Allende has commented on the effects that writing as a journalist had on her skill as a writer. She speaks of the lessons she learned by writing in a synthetic, objective, and precise style. She says that journalism was a "fundamental" element in her future literary production: "Journalism taught me to know and love words, the tools of my trade, the material of my craft. Journalism taught me to search for truth and to try to be objective, how to capture the reader and to hold him firmly and not let him escape" (*Conversations* 42). She also became a gifted researcher, immersed in her deep interest in history and, in particular, in anecdotes from the life experiences of common citizens.

Between 1970 and 1975, Allende was involved in theatrical and television productions. Her play *The Ambassador* was well received in Chile. She became a well-known media personality through her journalistic work and through her involvement in comedy shows for national television. She also worked on several short films.

The conservative character of Chilean society ended with the 1973 military coup that deposed President Salvador Allende. Isabel Allende offers in her autobiography a graphic and chilling description of the events that shook Chile and the world. Her depiction of President Allende's courageous decision not to accept exile in a foreign country and of his suicide at the moment the military invaded the Palacio de la Moneda made him a political icon of international fame. (Whether Allende killed himself or died in Pinochet's bombardment of Palacio de la Moneda, the Presidential Palace, is still today in question.) With the president's death, as Isabel Allende proudly points out in her autobiography, opponents of the new regime became an international symbol for those seeking political and social justice.

After the coup, Isabel Allende became actively involved in a complex system that secretly sought to send individuals in danger of retaliation by the new, illegal military government out of Chile. Her family's strong diplomatic connections provided a safe means of escape, despite the severe penalties imposed on civilians. This was the beginning of a shameful period in modern Chilean history; the number of political activists subjected to illegal imprisonment and torture reached well into the thousands.

Allende's autobiography brings to life the horrors of censorship endured in Chile after the coup. Allende writes that the restrictions went beyond the abolition of democratic institutions, such as the dissolution of Congress, and intruded into the intimacy of daily life. For example, she remembers the military's chauvinistic attitudes. Its members often stopped women in the streets to cut off the legs of their trousers because, according to the military's view, only men should wear pants. Men wearing long hair had to cut it short, because long hair was considered effeminate. Men soon stopped wearing beards because they might be suspected of being communists; bearded men were traditionally associated with Cuban revolutionaries.

In her personal life, Allende suffered from strict military censorship. Her post at *Paula* magazine ended when it became more of a vanity than a political publication. She was also fired as the director of a magazine for children, *Mampato*. According to her version, a week after the coup, an issue that highlighted gorillas, including a cover with pictures of four of the animals, was considered a critical depiction of the recent military events. This was the beginning of strict censorship that lasted for most of the fifteen years of the military regime under the leadership of General Augusto Pinochet. Initially, the sale of *The House of the Spirits* was banned in Chile, and the novel was known in Chile only through foreign visitors who smuggled copies into the country.

By 1975, fifteen months after the coup, Allende had to leave the country abruptly after receiving anonymous threats to her life. Her cover as a non-political activist had begun to wear thin, and she began to attract the attention of the military police. She was lucky; unlike many activists, she was never imprisoned, a common maneuver used by the military government to extract confessions from individuals suspected of involvement in underground political activities. Kidnapped at night, these activists, known as the *desaparecidos,* "the disappeared ones," suffered torture that often led to deaths. This tragic chapter of Chilean history is documented in graphic episodes of Allende's *The House of the Spirits*.

Exiled in Caracas, Venezuela, a country that welcomed a number of the Chilean political refugees, Allende worked as a newspaper reporter for a Venezuelan newspaper. She was struggling to make ends meet, however, so she took a second job as an office administrator for a private school. She also wrote scripts for television programs.

With the publication of *The House of the Spirits,* Allende became an immediate success in Spain and in Latin America. The rapid development of her reputation both in Spanish-speaking countries and in most international literary markets, such as the United States, France, and Great Britain, was nothing less than a dream come true for an unknown Chilean newspaper reporter in political exile in Venezuela. She became an international celebrity with the release in 1993 of the film version of *The House of the Spirits*.

Allende's novels are translated into some 35 languages. They continue to be best-sellers throughout the world. *De amor y de sombra* (1984; *Of Love and Shadows,* 1987), a fictional historical recreation of the 1978 discovery in Chile of the illegal graves of fifteen Chilean peasants murdered during the Pinochet regime, was made into a film in 1994. Her novel *Eva Luna* (1987; *Eva Luna,* 1988) and the short story collection *Cuentos de Eva Luna* (1989; *The Stories of Eva Luna,* 1991) display her interest in transmitting the voices of Latin American indigenous women as protagonists of unusual stories. Most recently, her novel *Retrato en sepia* (2000; *Portrait in Sepia,* 2001) explores the California gold rush of the middle nineteenth century and its connection with Chilean explorers. She has a personal view of U.S. history, having moved to California in 1987. Plays based on *The House of the Spirits* and *Eva Luna* have been performed in theaters in the United States, in London, and in Iceland.

A busy guest lecturer and visiting professor, Allende appears worldwide at universities and with writers' groups. In the United States, she has taught at the University of Virginia, Montclair College, Barnard College, and at the University of California at Berkeley, among other academic institutions. She has received many awards, among them the French Chevalier dans l'Ordre des Arts et des Lettres, and recognition as the Feminist of the Year (1994) by the Feminist Majority Foundation. With special personal pride, she accepted the Gabriela Mistral Award in 1994, Chile's most prestigious literary prize, from the recently elected president Patricio Aylwin.

Isabel Allende's interest in exploring Chilean history is evident in *The House of the Spirits*. The novel's genesis is located, however, within the personal documentation of her family history. She has commented on the reasons for writing the novel. While in exile in Caracas in 1981, she received the news that her grandfather was dying. Unable to travel to Chile because of political restrictions, she decided to send a letter to her dear grandfather, which she started writing on January 8. She now believes this date to be her lucky day, so she claims to start any major literary project on January 8. That letter became a novel, published by a Spanish publishing house the following year.

Allende's initial project, the writing of a letter as a documentation of her family's history, is important at various levels. Letters, journals, and diaries have traditionally been the only written vehicles to document women's daily experiences, particularly activities or roles associated with their social functions, such as their work at home or the raising of children. These chores are usually deemed unimportant or menial, and are considered unworthy as literary subjects. Diary entries and letters are a perfect medium for the expression of one's private feelings and emotions. Women's writing, whether that of professional writers or the private work of individuals, is often restricted to these media or to genres such as romantic or sentimental novels. In the early 1980s, Allende experienced difficulty while trying to have her novel published by a reputable Spanish-language publisher. In fact, she tried several companies in various Latin American countries before a female Spanish agent took an interest in her novel. Allende has often noted that women's literature is still viewed as marginal from the mainstream production by male writers, a commentary on today's climate for women writers in Latin America.

The writing of intimate, confessional pieces may be seen as training for formal, mainstream literary production, and this seems to have been the case for Allende, who, like her mother and her grandmother, is an avid writer of letters and diaries. Allende has been a prolific writer of letters to her mother since the age of fifteen. She writes daily to her mother, and her mother responds at a similar rate. They carefully preserve these letters, presumably for other generations to read. Of particular interest to the historical background of *The House of the Spirits* is Allende's use of some of the testimonial material documented in her letters, mostly of her experiences working with underground groups after the coup.

For Allende, writing became a practical endeavor that was not linked to gender restrictions. As she states in *Paula,* "the record of our lives is safeguarded against poor memory" (88). Thus, in her subject matter, her dying grandfather becomes the intended reader of her novel, in a process in which he is not only the author's inspiration but also one of her narrators. Allende documents the influence of her grandfather in *Paula.* His literary character is that of a wealthy landowner who gains power in the Chilean political system. In short, he represents the old social system, including a traditional view of social structures, with a particular antifeminist slant.

Despite their political disagreements, Allende remained close to her grandfather until she was forced to leave Chile. He was her literary inspiration, according to her autobiography, "Tata provided me with enough material for all the books I have written, possibly for all I will ever write. He was a virtuoso storyteller, gifted with perfidious humor, able to recount the most hair-raising stories while bellowing with laughter. He held back none of the anecdotes accumulated through his many years of living: the principal historical events of the century, the excesses of our family, and the infinite knowledge acquired in his reading" (*Paula* 119). Further proof of his influence on her life was Allende's promise to him that she would be willing to help him to die. This was a promise she could not keep. Instead, she wrote *The House of the Spirits.* What makes Allende's novel different from other historical approaches to family histories is her appropriation of her grandfather's memoirs. In a fascinating style, he appears as both a protagonist and a critic of his own story.

Allende writes her novel within a linear plot in which multiple narrators trace the history of a fictional family, the Truebas, from the beginning of the twentieth century to their involvement in the events leading to a military coup in the 1970s. It is not, however, a historical novel in the traditional sense. For example, although the protagonists are placed within specific social structures, the country remains unnamed, as are the political leaders involved in the coup that deposes a socialist president. This anonymity has more than one literary function. It can be viewed as Allende's comment on her native Chile's military censorship of political materials critical of the regime at the time that she wrote the novel. More important, her sociopolitical reading of Chilean history becomes a lesson about all Latin America.

The reader nonetheless is aware that this unidentified country is Chile. It is Esteban Trueba, the novel's patriarch, who provides this information.

Trueba, a strong-willed man who built a fortune by exploiting his peasant workers, displays a strong attachment to the land, an attitude that resembles the attraction felt by the early Spanish explorers. Having worked in various areas of the country, he is proud of his country's geography, which is identical to that of Chile: "Through the window of the train he watched the passing landscape of the central valley. Vast fields stretched from the foot of the mountain range, a fertile countryside filled with vineyards, wheatfields, alfalfa, and marigolds. He compared it with the sterile plateaus of the North, where he had spent two years stuck in a hole in the midst of a rough and lunar horizon whose terrifying beauty never ceased to interest him. He had been fascinated by the colors of the desert, the blues, the purples, the yellows of the minerals lying on the surface of the earth" (41–42). His clinging to the land is on one hand symbolic of his claim of control over the workers whom he exploited as he built a considerable fortune. It is also a metaphoric characterization of the Chilean personality, which, as Allende has repeatedly pointed out, is closely related to Chile's irregular and isolated geography: "Chile is a country where nature, the weather, and race determine the character of the people. We live practically on an island. We are separated from the rest of the world by the Andes, the Pacific Ocean, and a great desert to the North. Then the country ends to the South in Antarctica" (*Conversations* 451).

The House of the Spirits has a strong appeal because it can be read as a historical novel but also because it dwells on sociopolitical events presented from the perspective of women protagonists. They are gifted storytellers whose diaries and letters narrate their family history. The novel opens with the writings of Clara, who, married to wealthy Esteban Trueba, remembers the peculiarities of her family origins. Born into a wealthy, upper-class family, Clara has unusual psychic powers, such as clairvoyance and the ability to move objects without touching them. She predicts her own family's future. At the beginning of the novel, she predicts the death by mistaken identity of an unnamed relative. Rosa, her sister, had been engaged to Trueba, but, as Clara had predicted, she died by a mistake; she drank poisoned whiskey that was intended for her father, Severo del Valle, who was a political candidate.

After the death of her sister, Clara decided to stop speaking. Nine years later, she would speak again to accept Esteban Trueba's marriage proposal, which, moments before, she had predicted. Trueba, heartbroken after the untimely death of his beloved Rosa, had transformed Tres Marías, the abandoned and ruined family plantation, into a wealthy enterprise. Clara, the pristine spirit of light, as her name suggests, went to live in the countryside, where she would experience the rage of Trueba, the inhuman landowner.

Esteban Trueba, although also of an upper-class background, was, at the beginning of the novel, a mere adventurer. His father had lost his fortune and left the family without the resources to maintain a luxurious life. Upon meeting Rosa del Valle, an enigmatic woman "with green hair and yellow eyes—the most beautiful creature to be born since the days of the original sin" (6), he used his illustrious name to convince the del Valle family to allow him to marry their daughter. Only one problem remained: his lack of money to set up a household. He then decided to try his luck searching for gold in the northern mines, and he succeeded. Unfortunately, Rosa died before his return, a fact that prompted his decision to take refuge in his ruined family estate. Once it became a reputable ranch, he returned to the city to marry Clara Trueba.

Clara's ethereal personality, surrounded by family spirits, is in contrast to the exploitative nature of her husband. The novel's multiple plotlines follow clashes between two powerful personalities, gentle Clara and brutal Esteban. Clara follows the pattern of the life of a typical lady of her class, and Esteban is an oppressive landowner.

Unlike many city women of her class, Clara displays beliefs related to the primitive culture in which she lives. Clara's alleged supernatural powers are normal in a rural area where *curanderos,* the local spiritual healers, claim such psychic phenomena. In an interesting turn of events, Clara becomes a social ally of the local peasant women, whom she attempts to educate both in literacy and in ideology. The peasants also learn about religion and social ideas from the local priest, who provides political training to the abused peasants. These characters have an influence on the social underdogs because of their religious authority, a comment on the importance of the spiritual world among members of an agrarian community.

Esteban Trueba is a highly realistic character. His traits are within the traditional characterization of the powerful and often invincible landowner. He is also a narrator of his male-oriented tasks as Tres Marías's patrón. His self-generated passages, written in the first person, can be classified within the criollista style. He is the strongman located in a wild setting that he came to dominate by means of his violent personality. As Tres Marías's strongman, he exerts control over his peasants. He cheats them out of payment for their work and denies them workers' rights. In addition, some of his actions, such as the abandonment of his children born out of wedlock, go unpunished by the local legal authorities.

The international appeal of Allende's *The House of the Spirits* may lie in its complex narrative lines. Some of the characters, such as Clara, are fascinating figures because of their immersion in events within the symbolism of magical realism. Others, such as Uncle Marcos, are depicted as adventurers, involved in events that are strange not because they are impossible, but because they are illogical. The crossing of the Andes in a handmade flying device becomes, therefore, an attempt to state that incredible events can take place and, indeed, do take place.

Allende carefully reconstructs Chilean sociopolitical history through the technique of magical realism. She uses a realistic approach, however, for events that, although incredible, are true, as when she depicts the rise of socialism and the triumph of the first socialist president of Chile. A chain of events begins with Esteban Trueba's cruel treatment of his peasant laborers and political leaders' violation of basic civil rights. For such reasons the workers' power overcomes the conservative politicians in a national election. The unreal element is not the triumph of a socialist candidate but the violent reaction that the military initiates afterward.

At the end of *The House of the Spirits,* the military deposes the president and begins an illegal rule. What follows, particularly the violence against political activists opposed to the regime, crosses the line from history into fiction. This section of the novel is not only the most real but also the most incredible. The incredible is not based on impossible events but on the fact that these horrific incidents actually take place. Alba, Clara's granddaughter, is involved with underground political groups, and like thousands of other activists, she is kidnapped and tortured.

Allende links Alba masterfully to two previous, obscure characters. The first is Esteban García, a product of her grandfather's violation of a peasant woman. He becomes an officer in the military forces. He is Alba's torturer in graphic scenes that, as presented in the film version of the novel, address the boundaries of human versus animalistic behavior. The second character is Esteban Trueba's friend Tránsito, a woman who owns a hotel intended for illicit sexual encounters. Because of her intimate acquaintance with military leaders and as a favor to Esteban, she is able to obtain freedom for the otherwise doomed Alba. This incident comments on the social restrictions imposed on women and the means they use to evade them.

More than a political commentator, Isabel Allende considers herself a storyteller: "Storytelling is a way of preserving the memory of the past and keeping alive legends, myths, superstitions, and history that are not in the textbooks—the real stories of people and countries" (*Conversations* 102). Her work presents these stories through unusual characters, whom she has labeled as marginal and defined as "people who stand unsheltered by the system, who somehow defy authority, defy the stereotypes" (*Conversations* 229). These characters, many of them women, are Allende's most important contribution to a contemporary Latin American literature based strongly on male protagonists.

ARGENTINA

The history of the Argentine military has sociological elements of interest to students of Latin American cultures. First, the long presence of the military in the civil government, including several coups and forced military regimes, places Argentina among the Latin American countries most influenced and threatened by its well-organized and trained armed forces. Thus, the figure of the military as a strongman is a constant reminder of their political power and of their ability to interrupt civil government at will. The civilians' divided opinions about the military's right to intervene in national political affairs is either unconditional approval or passionate hatred.

Second, the strong Argentine military tradition has created a popular culture of its own with icons of international fame. One of them, Eva Perón, the wife of President Juan Domingo Perón, acquired great celebrity because of the musical *Evita* (1979) by composer Andrew Lloyd Weber. Evita, like her controversial husband, is an important factor in understanding life under a totalitarian regime. Like a dictator or a military-man-turned-president, she is surrounded by heated debates about her political and social platforms.

Juan Domingo Perón was an important personage in his own right. An army officer, he supported a 1943 coup and became part of the military junta that ruled Argentina for the next three years. He became a political candidate with the support of a party of his own creation. In 1946, he was elected president in a democratic election. This was the beginning of a political movement known as *peronismo,* fostered by Perón's Peronista Party.

Perón's political platform calling for redistribution of Argentina's wealth had strong popular appeal, particularly among the working classes and the workers' unions. It is arguable, however, that his charismatic wife, affectionately known as Evita, was a major support in his presidency. A well-known actress and radio personality, Evita was a beautiful woman whose humble, rural past became Perón's connection with the working and peasant classes that elected him president in a surprising victory. Evita became then a symbol of Perón's populist Argentina. The glamorized image of Evita is at the core of Weber's musical, which simply characterizes her as a woman whose social programs were geared to support Perón's tainted government.

Evita was, however, a figure with a political career of her own. Restricted by the gender boundaries of her duties as the Argentine first lady, she started institutions of social charities that further advanced her image as protector of the dispossessed, the *descamisados,* or "shirtless," in opposition to the well-dressed upper class. Seemingly bottomless funds for her many projects, schools, hospitals, and orphanages came from the workers' unions. Other sources were national businesses that were often pressured to donate money to Evita's foundations. This was the generous Evita, who became well known outside Argentine politics in a glamorous 1947 visit to Europe. In Argentina that year, she was a key figure in the passage of a law granting the vote to women.

Evita's untimely death of cancer in 1952 occurred at the peak of what appeared to be a promising political career, unusual for a Latin American woman of that time. She had become the most popular female icon in contemporary Latin American history. Her death was also the beginning of incredible events, which started with a national cult of Evita, reflected in the public display of her perfectly embalmed corpse during her grandiose funeral services. Events surrounding the whereabouts of Evita's corpse after a coup deposed Perón, three years after her death, fall within the realm of the fantastic. This subject appears in the novel *Santa Evita* (1995) by Argentine Tomás Eloy Martínez (1934–). Perón and Evita continue to be a focus of national attention, in books, films, and critical articles about their influence on Argentine politics, society, and popular culture.

After Evita's death, Perón lost popularity among various underclass social groups and faced growing opposition from the military and from organized political parties. The absence of his glamorous wife focused more attention on the totalitarian practices of his government. In 1955 a military coup put an end to Perón's government and opened the way for a series of military governments that extended into 1973. This long period of military control had a dramatic influence on the country's political and social life. It also affected literary production, particularly the work of short story writer Jorge Luis Borges, who often clashed with the totalitarian rule by the military.

In an interesting turn of events, the military government allowed democratic elections in 1973. Perón was allowed to return to Argentina, and after an absence of eighteen years he won the elections. He died the next year, and Isabel, his wife and the vice president, became Argentina's president. Her totalitarian government, which sent into exile writers such as Tomás Eloy Martínez, and the military's intense dislike of her produced a coup in 1976. This would be the beginning of Argentina's cruelest military regimes.

Known as the **Dirty War,** Argentine military governments between 1976 and 1983 used sustained, violent, repressive measures to restrict public opinion, especially that of activists who opposed the regime: intellectuals, writers, teachers, professors, and religious people who were systematically arrested without legal grounds and taken to military facilities. They were the Argentine *desaparecidos,* whose numbers are still a subject of controversy, with estimates ranging from ten to thirty thousand. As in Chile, the dark events around the horrific abuse of the desaparecidos would provide concrete proof of the military's power.

Drastic censorship by the totalitarian military regime limited news coverage about the fate of the *desaparecidos.* In 1976, creation of the Asociación Madres de la Plaza de Mayo became a national movement that was among the first groups to denounce publicly the crimes against the desaparecidos. It was only after the fall of the military government in 1983, however, that Argentines and the rest of the world would know the truth about the horrible abuses of human rights perpetrated against the activists. One type of event in particular would become a center of heated national controversies: the illegal adoption of hundreds of babies born to women who disappeared during illegal incarceration.

Two years after the end of the military government, the Argentine film *The Official Story* (1985) addressed the issue of the *desaparecidos,* particularly of the whereabouts of children born during their mothers' imprisonment. A superb screenplay traces events in Argentine military history, beginning in the nineteenth century. The film allows the viewer to see Argentine society in 1983, just before the collapse of the military government, which had experienced political defeat by Great Britain in 1982 during the brief Malvinas-Falkland Islands War, and the country was in the midst of an economic crisis as a result. The film offers a historical analysis that seeks to explain the complex conditions that allowed the military to take over the civil government and, in particular, to succeed in its bloody campaigns against the *desaparecidos*.

The accounts of human rights violations by the military have appeared in testimonies of both military personnel and the former political prisoners. Three texts are mandatory reading. The first is *The Flight: Confessions of an Argentine Dirty Warrior* (1996), by a former captain of the Argentine navy Adolfo Scilingo. This book offers chilling accounts of his participation in disposal of tortured victims, thrown from airplanes into the ocean. The second is *Prisoner without a Name, Cell without Number* (1981), by the Argentine journalist Jacobo Timerman, which details his imprisonment and torture for being a political activist and a Jew. The third is *The Little School: Tales of Disappearance and Survival in Argentina* (1986) by Alicia Partnoy, which presents the testimony of her illegal incarceration and torture. Legal cases against the Argentine military have been brought to the attention of international legal forums. Since the early 1990s, European countries, such as France in 1990, have placed on trial and found guilty in absentia military personnel involved in the disappearance, torture, and killing of their own nationals or of Argentines with dual citizenship.

Argentine fiction writers have approached the incredible events that allowed the military regime to sustain a complex system of repression, resulting in the disappearance of thousands of activists. In *Un secreto para Julia* (2000; *A Secret for Julia,* 2001) by the Argentine novelist Patricia Sagastizábal (1953–), Julia is a first-generation British-Argentine born in London. Her mother, Mercedes, is in Great Britain as an exile from the Dirty War. She has never revealed to Julia the identity of her daughter's father. After sixteen years, unusual circumstances force Mercedes to begin telling her story as a victim of torture in a single, simple statement: "what I am about to recount is part of quite a convoluted tale" (13). The story dwells, however, more on the exploration of Mercedes's psychological reaction to her horrific experiences than on descriptions of the actual torture. Like many real women, she was imprisoned, tortured, and raped by her jailers. As implied in the title, Julia's father was a jailer who raped Mercedes. The psychological implications go beyond such a traumatic experience. Mercedes must face the fact that Julia, her beloved daughter, is the product of a terrible past that Mercedes is unable to forget.

Novelist and short story writer Luisa Valenzuela, in her story "The Censors," presents an analysis of the psychological effects of life under the censorship of a totalitarian regime. Valenzuela carefully describes the negative results of such an experience, including unexpected behaviors and mental states. In today's highly militarized world, Argentina's history may serve as a warning of the tragic consequences of uncontrolled military power.

Luisa Valenzuela (1938–)

Short story writer and novelist, Luisa Valenzuela stands out among the internationally famous women writers from Argentina. Her works are complex explorations of the dark side of the human psyche. Learned in Argentine history, Valenzuela offers a sound view of national cultural patterns, particularly of issues that pertain to national politics. Of special literary interest is her exploration of Argentina's military background, including the dynamics behind the practice of torture and the country's massive censorship under military dictatorships. She writes from a feminist perspective; her approach to Argentine history includes a detailed analysis of gender-bound obstacles, often stemming from the strongly chauvinistic military past.

Born in Buenos Aires into a professional family, Valenzuela's background allowed her superb academic opportunities. Her mother was Luisa Mercedes Levinson (1909–1988), a well-known figure in Argentine literature and other arts. A novelist, short story writer, playwright, and screen writer, Levinson immersed her daughter in the vibrant Argentine literary world. As a child Valenzuela displayed an early interest in writing. At age six, she produced a poem, which she dictated to her mother, because she did not yet know how to write. Through her mother, Valenzuela would meet famous writers such as Jorge Luis Borges, with whom her mother had a close working relationship, and the novelist and short story writer Julio Cortázar, an outstanding Latin American writer and a distinguished member of the Boom movement. Valenzuela has expressed her great admiration for Cortázar's warm personality and for his work.

Other writers who had a strong influence on Valenzuela's writing were those associated with *Sur,* a literary journal with an international reputation. As a group, they became Valenzuela's literary mentors. From their discussions, Valenzuela would learn about the world's most innovative writers, such as, Franz Kafka, William Faulkner, Albert Camus, Virginia Woolf, and Samuel Beckett. Her works display her knowledge of diverse academic interests. She has a particular interest in anthropology and ethnography, with special emphasis on masks used in religious rituals. World religions have been a favorite subject since her childhood.

At the age of eighteen, she published her first story in *Ficción,* a local literary publication under the direction of Juan Goytisolo, a famous Spanish novelist in exile. Goytisolo recommended that Valenzuela start writing novels, but, enrolled at the University of Buenos Aires, she had other plans. She became involved with avant-garde student groups, performing street the-atrical performances. She also wrote for several popular magazines on a vari-ety of subjects, from sports to subjects of special interest to women. In short, she was well connected with contemporary Argentine popular cul-ture, and this would be an important element in her future fiction.

After she married, Valenzuela moved to Paris, where she wrote her first novel, *Hay que sonreír* (1966; *Clara: Thirteen Short Stories and a Novel,* 1976), partially inspired by her experiences in Paris. Writing that novel became her way to deal with feelings of isolation, of being a foreigner in a large city. The novel was a success in Argentina. In 1973 it became a film, *Clara,* based on a script that Valenzuela wrote. While in France, Valenzuela worked for Radio Difusion Française, where she wrote special programs cre-ated for Latin American audiences. Like other Latin American writers before her, her experiences in France would be pivotal in her future literary pro-duction. She has pointed out that she met almost all the writers of the avant-garde movements of the **New Novel** (a new phase in French narrative) and the journal *Tel Quel,* which published experimental writings.

After her return to Buenos Aires in 1961, Valenzuela continued working with local newspapers of national and international reputation. She worked for Argentina's largest and most reputable newspaper, *La Nación.* A prolific contributor of feature articles, for two years she wrote short essays for "Images from Inside Argentina." For this popular column, she traveled extensively throughout Argentina, receiving national exposure of great value to an up-and-coming writer. Valenzuela has commented on her lessons learned as a newspaper writer, especially her training in the precision of writ-ing dense and concise stories (García Pinto 196).

Her discovery of the diverse Argentine geography, so different from the cosmopolitan city of Buenos Aires where she grew up, made her seek explo-ration of all the countries of the South American Southern Cone. In 1967 Valenzuela embarked on a trip on the Amazon, following the river into the neighboring countries of Bolivia, Peru, and Brazil. On another trip she vis-ited Mexico, where she felt the attraction of that country's indigenous cul-tures: "there is its indigenous world, buried, quite crushed, but at the same time very alive, and you can feel that" (García Pinto 198). Culture-based subjects on native Latin American groups, including a prominent interest in religious belief systems, are evident in Valenzuela's work.

In 1969, Valenzuela received a Fulbright grant to join the University of Iowa's International Writers Program. There she shared experiences with other young Latin American writers, such as Carmen Naranjo, Fernando del Paso, and Néstor Sánchez. She produced then her first novel *El gato eficaz,* published in 1972. Other extended trips abroad to Mexico and throughout Europe allowed her time to write. A year of living in Barcelona in 1972 put her into contact with Spanish intellectuals and with other Latin American writers living in the lively culture of that city. She remembers with particular interest her exploration of the city's Roman ruins, a visual testimony of the importance of Spain in the Roman Empire.

Valenzuela was back in Argentina in 1974, at a time of high political uncertainty. General Juan Perón, elected president in 1973, seemed to have lost his support among powerful military circles, which had allowed general elections after their dictatorship. Perón's death in office left a shaky government in the hands of his wife and vice president, Isabel de Perón, who was deposed in a military coup in 1976. Valenzuela experienced this period, which became the inspiration for her short story collection *Aquí pasan cosas raras* (1976; *Strange Things Happen Here*, 1979).

Valenzuela's stand against military dictatorship at the time is evident. She edited *Crisis,* a magazine with a strong political outlook, a national voice of political discontent. Valenzuela's *Strange Things Happen Here* gives testimony to the earliest of the military's abuses. She testified that in 1976 she nearly fell victim to military wrath; shortly after she had left for a trip to the United States, the police came to her home with an arrest warrant.

She left Argentina in voluntary exile in 1979. Shortly before her departure, Valenzuela had become part of a complex network of activists who were successful in smuggling out of Argentina official documentation on the military campaign, the Dirty War, which had led to the disappearance and deaths of political activists. These *desaparecidos,* or "disappeared ones," and the convoluted, repressive military infrastructure became important subjects in Valenzuela's best-known novel, *Cola de lagartija* (1983; *The Lizard's Tail,* 1983). This novel dwells on the cult of "The Dead Woman," a cryptic allusion to Eva Perón, Juan Perón's first lady during his first presidency (1946–1955).

Valenzuela lived in New York City from 1979 to 1989, where she taught Latin American literature and offered seminars for writers at Columbia University and at New York University. She was a Guggenheim fellow in 1983. While in New York, she continued writing for newspapers, such as the *New York Times.*

Valenzuela has lived in her native Argentina since 1989. She continues to have an active role in the literary documentation of the Dirty War and often comments on her experiences of living under a military regime and the psychological trauma to the national psyche:

There was no freedom left; you couldn't do anything. We couldn't collaborate. It was impossible because the repression was furious and penetrated everything. And you never knew where the next blow was coming from. At first it was open, and you could always see it coming. But then came the paramilitary groups, the parapolice, the gangs hired to incite violence, and I didn't think I'd be able to write anymore if I stayed. I felt asphyxiated. Besides, something very strange happened. People began to acknowledge and justify the situation, saying it was a dirty war. You couldn't talk to anyone. If you said someone had disappeared, they'd tell you the person must have done something. (García Pinto 208)

Her novel *Realidad nacional desde la cama* (1990; *Bedside Manners,* 1995) offers a surrealist approach to the experiences of a Latin American woman who is visiting her native country, which remains nameless, after living in exile for many years. The traumatic experiences of military persecution are greater than just the physical damage.

Like Julio Cortázar, another Argentine writer and her literary mentor, Valenzuela sets out to explore the psychological mechanisms behind the dictatorship in Argentina following the military coup of 1976. Human rights violations of thousands of *desaparecidos,* their torture and, in many cases, deaths while in concentration camps or inside military facilities, are still matters of controversy in Argentine political circles. Valenzuela's short story "The Censors" is not an eyewitness account of these crimes. Instead, in a simple and straightforward story, she explores the military censorship that allowed cover-up of illegal activities by their own staff.

Valenzuela's short story describes how military censorship went beyond the power of official censors. It had a negative psychological effect on civilians, who often became their own most severe censors. The censorship that had been initiated for printed publications, such as newspapers and books, extended even to regular conversation with friends in the privacy of one's home. How an institution can have such an overwhelming control over the people is Valenzuela's concern in "The Censors."

"The Censors" is extremely concise. There is only one protagonist, a colorless character named Juan. As the story begins, Juan finds the address of Mariana, a friend who has just moved to Paris. Such a mundane event leads to a series of unusual situations. An omniscient narrator informs the reader that the knowledge of Mariana's address came from unstated and mysterious circumstances that must be kept anonymous because highly confidential sources are involved. Juan believes that Mariana's address is her message to him that she loves him, so he immediately writes her a letter.

The narrator also serves as the eyewitness to changes in Juan's behavior after he writes the letter. According to the narrator, the letter marks the beginning of Juan's downfall. This is a dark comment about a presumed love letter to an absent love.

After mailing the letter, Juan experiences changes in his personality. He cannot concentrate at work and spends countless sleepless nights. He obsesses over "the letter," which is described as "irreproachable, harmless" (25). Soon the reader realizes that Juan is not worried about a negative reaction from Mariana (presumably to his romantic letter), but about a complex process of censorship by professional censors at the post office.

In her exploration of the psychological mechanisms behind censorship, Valenzuela chooses to write in the genre of the absurd. This is evident in the narrator's exaggerated description of the process of censorship as Juan imagines it: "He knows that they examine, sniff, feel, and read between the lines of each and every letter, and check its tiniest comma and accidental stain"

(25). Juan makes a sudden decision: he will become a censor in order to intercept his own letter.

Juan's becoming a postal censor is central to Valenzuela's study of the psychological effects of living under a totalitarian censorship. His tasks as a devoted and efficient censor are described within the aesthetics of the absurd. Techniques related to the absurd present incredible events that appear innocuous to a disturbed character. Juan becomes a man with an obsession: he has to intercept his letter before another censor does. The task itself is presented as an impossible deed.

The process of the censors' reading correspondence is, indeed, absurd. For example, after a letter is mailed, the censoring can take months and, in complex cases, years. In those extreme cases, as the sender and the receiver patiently wait, their lives are at stake because the authorities view all letters as potential subversive texts. From the censors' absurd points of view, statements such as "the weather's unsettled" or "prices continue to soar" (31) are a message in code to overthrow the government. What type of government and what country Valenzuela leaves unsaid. This is part of her own censorship, for she seems to be reproducing in her story the censorship that she has experienced.

The government in "The Censors" appears to be operated by the military, as indicated in departmentalized sections of the Post Office's Censorship Division. In a highly bureaucratic system, Juan starts working in Section K, an area where envelopes are screened for explosives. The job is dangerous, as he soon realizes when an envelope explodes and a fellow worker loses his right hand. In another section, other censors inspect the envelopes for poisonous dust. These sections reveal the military's obsession with obstructing the guerrilla activities of subversive groups.

Soon Juan is transferred to another division, after having warned the postal administration that disgruntled workers were planning a strike. This event explains why Juan, surprisingly, begins to agree with his superiors. His reasons for betraying his fellow workers remain unexplored. Was Juan aiming for a fast-track promotion so that he might gain access to other sections where his letter might be? Or was Juan purposely helping to identify enemies of the system? These are questions that remain unanswered, and they are at the core of the story's message.

At the end of the story, Juan has become the best of the censors. He has forgotten the real reason behind working as a censor, as the narrator critically points out: "Soon his work became so absorbing that his noble mission blurred in his mind" (29). He finds his letter to Mariana, which he coldly censors "without regret" (31), despite knowing that he will be executed, "one more victim of his devotion to his work" (31).

The story has a specific political message. Juan's zealous behavior, reflected in his voluntary confession of subversive activity, is a direct product of the totalitarian regime of this unnamed country. One can argue that the absurdity in Juan's behavior is not his ultimate sacrifice as the best censor of the hated Post Office's Censorship Division but the process that leads him to become a censor in the first place. The narrator points out that, like Juan, many others had become censors in order to find personal letters. They were allowed to become censors because the authorities doubted that they would be able to find them. At any rate, these individuals were the best censors because they had a dual quest: to find their letters and to prove to their superiors that there was no motive in their impeccable performance other than a desire to serve the system well.

As the story ends, the reader realizes that the narrator's comments are part of an official report on Juan's performance as a censor. The narrator becomes identified with "they," whom the reader must assume are Juan's supervisors—the ultimate censors. Symbolically, their power over the civilian population includes their ability to know the people's concealed motives and their intimate thoughts. Juan is not punished because he attempted to rescue his letter, but because he dared to break down the system: "Well, you've got to beat them to the punch, do what every one tries to do: sabotage the machinery, throw sand in its gears, that is to say get to the bottom of the problem to try to stop it" (27). Although this appears to be a direct quote from Juan, the reader may interpret it as the censors' transcription of information on Juan provided by an acquaintance of his. The power of the censors is, therefore, reinforced as almost endless.

It can be argued that in "The Censors" Valenzuela wrote a story from the perspective of a writer fearing censorship. Juan's absurd task, reading letters with a keen eye, becomes a metaphor for the restrictions imposed on writers. Juan is also a character who experiences a significant existential crisis. This is visible in his sudden transformation from an activist against a totalitarian regime into the most conscientious of the censors. The comment is political and goes to the core of complex psychological reactions to life under a dictatorial government.

BIBLIOGRAPHY

Allende, Isabel. *Conversations with Isabel Allende.* Ed. John Rodden. Austin: University of Texas Press, 1999.
———. *Eva Luna.* Trans. Margaret Sayers Peden. New York: Knopf, 1998.
———. *The House of the Spirits.* Trans. Magda Bogin. New York: Knopf, 1993.
———. *Of Love and Shadows.* Trans. Margaret Sayers Peden. New York: Knopf, 1987.
———. *Paula.* Trans. Margaret Sayers Peden. New York: HarperCollins, 1995.
———. *Portrait in Sepia.* Trans. Margaret Sayers Peden. New York: HarperCollins, 2001.
———. *The Stories of Eva Luna.* Trans. Margaret Sayers Peden. New York: Atheneum, 1991.

Campos, Julieta. *La herencia obstinada: análisis de cuentos náhuas.* México: Fondo de Cultura de México, 1982.

Castellanos, Rosario. *The Nine Guardians.* Trans. Irene Nicholson. New York: Vanguard Press, 1960.

de Beer, Gabriella. *Contemporary Mexican Women Writers: Five Voices.* Austin: University of Texas Press, 1996.

Domecq, Brianda. *The Astonishing Story of the Saint of Cabora.* Tempe, AZ: Bilingual Press/Edición Bilingüe, 1998.

Esquivel, Laura. *Between Two Fires: Intimate Writings on Life, Love, Food and Flavor.* Trans. Stephen Lytle. New York: Crown, 2000.

———. *Estrellita marinera.* Barcelona: Planeta, 1999.

———. *The Law of Love.* Trans. Margaret Sayers Peden. New York: Crown Publishers, 1996.

———. *Like Water for Chocolate: A Novel in Monthly Installments, with Recipes, Romances, and Home Remedies.* Trans. Carol Christensen and Thomas Christensen. New York: Doubleday, 1992.

———. *Swift as Desire.* Trans. Stephen Lytle. New York: Crown, 2001.

Ferré, Rosario. *Eccentric Neighborhoods.* New York: Farrar, Strauss & Giroux, 1998.

———. *Flight of the Swan.* New York: Farrar, Strauss & Giroux, 2001.

———. *The House on the Lagoon.* New York: Farrar, Straus & Giroux, 1995.

———. "The Writer's Kitchen." Trans. Diana L. Vélez. *Lives on the Line: The Testimony of Contemporary Latin American Authors.* Ed. Doris Meyer. Berkeley: University of California Press, 1988: 212–227.

———. *The Youngest Doll.* Lincoln: University of Nebraska Press, 1991.

García, Kay S. *Broken Bars: New Perspectives from Mexican Women Writers.* Albuquerque: University of New Mexico Press, 1994.

Garro, Elena. *Recollections of Things to Come.* Trans. Austin: University of Texas Press, 1969.

Martínez, Tomás Eloy. *Santa Evita.* Trans. Helen Lane. New York: Knopf, 1996.

A Necklace of Words: Stories by Mexican Women. Ed. Marjorie Agosín and Nancy Abraham Hall. Fredonia, New York: White Pine Press, 1997.

Partnoy, Alicia. *The Little School: Tales of Disappearance and Survival in Argentina.* Trans. Alicia Partnoy, Lois Athey, and Sandra Braunstein. Pittsburgh: Cleis Press, 1986.

Poniatowska, Elena. *Dear Diego.* Trans. Katherine Silver. New York: Pantheon Books, 1986.

———. "Diego, I Am Not Alone: Frida Kahlo." *Frida Kahlo: The Camera Seduced.* San Francisco: Chronicle Books, 1992.

———. *Massacre in Mexico.* Trans. Helen R. Lane. Columbia: University of Missouri Press, 1991.

———. *El niño: Niños de la calle, Ciudad México.* Syracuse, NY: Syracuse University Press, 1999.

———. "Voices from the Jungle: Subcomandante Marcos and Culture." *The Zapatista Reader.* Ed. Tom Hayden. New York: Thunder's Mouth Press, 2002: 373–381.

Sagastizábal, Patricia. *A Secret for Julia.* Trans. Asa Zatz. New York: Norton, 2001.

Scilingo, Francisco, & Horacio Verbitsky. *The Flight: Confessions of an Argentine Dirty Warrior.* Trans. Esther Allen. New York: New Press, 1996.

Timerman, Jacobo. *Prisoner without a Name, Cell without a Number.* Trans. Toby
     Talbot. New York: Knopf, 1981.
Valenzuela, Luisa. *Bedside Manners.* Trans. Margaret Jull Costa. London: High Risk
     Books, 1995.
———. *Clara: Thirteen Short Stories and a Novel.* Trans. Hortense Carpentier &
     Jorge Castello. New York: Hartcourt Brace Jovanovich, 1976.
———. *The Lizard's Tail.* Trans. Gregory Rabassa. New York: Farrar, Straus &
     Giroux, 1983.
———. *Strange Things Happen Here.* Trans. Helen Lane. New York: Hartcourt
     Brace Jovanovich, 1979.
Vega, Ana Lydia. "Cloud Cover Caribbean." Trans. Mark McCaffrey. *Short Stories by
     Latin American Women: The Magic and the Real.* Ed. Celia Correa de
     Zapata. Texas: Arte Público Press, 1990: 202–207.
———. *True and False Romances: Macho Latin Meets His Match.* Trans. Andrew
     Hurley. London: Serpent's Tail, 1994.

SUGGESTED READINGS ON LATIN AMERICAN WOMEN WRITERS

Bergmann, Emile L. *Women Culture and Politics in Latin America.* Berkeley:
     University of California Press, 1990.
Castillo, Debra. *Talking Back: Toward a Latin American Feminist Literary Criticism.*
     Ithaca: Cornell University Press, 1992.
Correas de Zapata, Celia, and Margaret Sayers Peden. *Isabel Allende: Life and Spirits.*
     Houston, TX: Arte Público Press, 2002.
Erro-Peralta, Nora, and Caridad Silva. *Beyond the Border: A New Age in Latin
     American Women's Fiction.* Gainesville: University Press of Florida, 2000.
Fishburn, Evelyn. *Short Fiction by Spanish-American Women.* New York: Manchester
     University Press, 1998.
Hintz, Suzanne. *Rosario Ferré: A Search for Identity.* New York: Peter Lang, 1995.
Jehenson, Myriam Yvonne. *Latin American Women Writers: Class, Race and Gender.*
     Albany: State University of New York Press, 1995.
Jörgensen, Beth E. *The Writing of Elena Poniatowska: Engaging Dialogues.* Austin:
     University of Texas Press, 1994.
Lashgari, Deirdre. *Violence, Silence and Anger: Women's Writing as Transgression.*
     Charlottesville: University Press of Virginia, 1995.
Levine, Linda Gould. *Isabel Allende.* New York: Twayne, 2002.
O'Connell, Joanna. *Prospero's Daughter: The Prose of Rosario Castellanos.* Austin:
     University of Texas Press, 1995.
Partnoy, Alicia. *You Can't Drown the Fire: Latin American Women Writing in Exile.*
     Pittsburgh: Cleis Press, 1988.
Stoll, Anita. *A Different Reality: Studies on the Work of Elena Garro.* Lewisburg, PA:
     Bucknell University Press, 1990.

Chapter 5

Writing about Cultural, Ethnic, and Religious Identities

THE CULTURAL AND POLITICAL STRUGGLES OF THE LATIN AMERICAN POPULAR AND INDIGENOUS COMMUNITIES

An important interest in contemporary Latin American literature, particularly since the 1960s, is the struggle among the popular and indigenous communities to maintain their cultural, ethnic, and religious identities. During the Conquest and even today, the surviving indigenous communities throughout Latin America have experienced open marginalization from national social and political institutions. They are often pressed to abandon their ancient native customs as a condition for their incorporation into mainstream societies. Their adherence to their native languages, religious beliefs, and social traditions has been, however, their tool for expressing political discontent.

Other popular groups with close links to regional cultures, such as campesinos, as farm and field workers are known in Latin America, have experienced similar racist attitudes from society at large. Of mixed ethnic backgrounds, the campesinos, unlike the native groups, have incorporated into their rural culture a number of the elements of "learned" culture, or the concepts that presumably make up a "civilized" society. Unlike indigenous peoples (with whom they often live side by side), the campesinos speak Spanish, dress in nonnative garb, and observe Western cultural and religious traditions. They have failed, however, to gain social and political recognition. As their experience indicates, insensitive governments see the campesino merely as a disposable manual laborer, to be exploited by absentee landowners and oppressive governments.

As native communities, campesinos have maintained local traditions despite mainstream society's rejection and pressure to abandon them. Theirs is an agrarian culture with customs borrowed from several religious sources, often merging the rituals of the Roman Catholic Church with indigenous faith. Other cultural manifestations are reflected in the kind of task performed in a particular area. In cattle-raising zones, for example, a particular cultural type emerged, such as the *charro,* or the Mexican cowboy. These different and colorful rural traditions appear commonly in literary texts as representative of true national values.

Because of the terrible life conditions experienced by indigenous and campesino groups, it is not surprising that they have taken part in major political struggles. Their quest to attain better working conditions, for example, has been the subject of international debates. They have organized themselves into workers' unions and into other political groups to make the violations of their human rights known and to fight for better social conditions. Incorporation into guerrilla groups was the most radical expression of their political dissatisfaction. Both the indigenous groups and the campesinos have suffered terrible consequences, with exorbitant numbers of deaths at the hands of military commandos, and many are forced into exile.

The history of oppression against ethnic groups and their hope for a better future as seen through preservation of their culture are important subjects in modern Latin American literature. The **historical novel** is an important literary trend in the documentation of cultural and political differences in Latin American societies. The genre underwent significant ideological changes during the 1960s with the inclusion of underprivileged social groups as characters of literary importance. As in the testimony genre, the historical novel focuses on historical events, fully documented by means of detailed research. The sources of information come both from written histories recorded in books and in other written documentation and from oral versions available within marginal communities.

Latin American writers are particularly interested in depicting events rarely documented in official national histories. They are also political activists; writing about cultural traditions leads them to document organized governmental repression. Cultural differences and the willingness of groups to associate native traditions with political discontent are at the core of the historical novel. For the campesinos, rural culture is also an important theme, because it is a symbol of the common people's resistance to compromise their traditions in order to become assimilated into mainstream society.

Indigenous groups' own documentation of abuses to their communities has created striking and powerful testimonies, reports that recount their incorporation into organized political movements. Native activists write from the ideological perspective of a modern chronicler, speaking frankly about their lives and about their people's confrontations with mainstream culture and political structures. Many indigenous communities still do not speak Spanish, and these writers must overcome the linguistic barriers. With their testimonies, they have started to put an end to self-imposed separation from mainstream society. In their documentation of native cultural values, they speak about an ethnic "consciousness," a new way to view the various social components that make up national identity.

Written as a traditional autobiography, the **testimony** has become an important literary genre and a political tool for marginal groups in Latin American societies. The testimonial account of a Native American writer reveals truthful, firsthand anthropological information. The reader of these testimonies is an outsider to the indigenous communities and becomes, therefore, a student in a series of lessons about the indigenous communities. The information provided is varied, including social and religious traditions, within the account of the writer's personal experiences as a member of that native group. Discussion of these cultural elements is intended as a way to explain the indigenous psyche or their understanding of national identity within their position as a member of a marginal social class.

The testimony also has a strong political intention: it is a vehicle for documentation of the abuses and crimes committed against these indigenous Americans. Writers are witnesses to terrible events and, within the legal tradition of a testimony, they provide an account of those events, with details previously ignored in official historical accounts. Their confrontations with highly organized military governments are true lessons in humanity's will to survive and in the communities' strength to face and overcome adversity. These accounts, like their more cheerful cultural lessons, have a didactic purpose and a more personal meaning. They are strong messages of love for one's community and of hope for a better world; they work for a society of the future in which divisive cultural, political, or religious differences can be overcome.

This chapter focuses on the strong presence of cultures of indigenous and campesino groups of the Central American countries of El Salvador, Guatemala, and Nicaragua. The choice of this area is both geographic and ideological. These cultures have played an important role in the development of traits associated with today's Central American national identities. Although these groups represent a considerable percentage of these countries' populations, they have been kept marginal to mainstream social institutions. Struggles for the recognition of their human rights have been chaotic, reflected in their involvement in strikes and in guerrilla groups.

Manlio Argueta, a committed writer activist from El Salvador, speaks on behalf of the oppressed Salvadoran indigenous and campesino communities. Argueta's historical novel *Cuzcatlán, Where the Southern Sea Beats* traces development of political activism through organized guerrilla warfare in El Salvador, with particular emphasis on the important role of peasants in the armed conflicts against military governments. Argueta also writes about the complex rural cultural patterns of the Salvadoran campesino. His novel is a striking tribute to the campesinos' will to remain together and to celebrate native traditions in the face of extreme poverty and mainstream society's pressure that they be incorporated into modern ways of life.

Rigoberta Menchú, Nobel Peace Prize winner and international spokesperson for the defense of indigenous groups around the world, offers a poignant testimonial account of the political persecution of the Maya-Quiché in her native Guatemala. Her autobiographical account, *I, Rigoberta Menchú, An Indian Woman in Guatemala,* reveals a rare view of the Maya-Quiché culture, depicted as a strong way of life that has survived terrible oppression, beginning in colonial times. Today they resist through clashes with military governments. Although at odds with current images of modern life, Menchú's positive characterization of native traditions presents them as possible models for a fair society. Along with her political denunciations of present and past oppressions of all indigenous communities, she also communicates a hopeful message that the native and the Western-oriented cultures in Latin American can live together peacefully.

The testimonial writing of Ernesto Cardenal, a Nicaraguan priest and a poet, examines the merge of political activism and organized religious thinking that is so common in Latin American societies. Like Argueta and Menchú, Cardenal took part in organized political groups opposed to the dictatorial governments of the Somoza family, from 1936 until the triumph of the Sandinista Revolution in 1979. A prolific writer of political and religious poetry, he is internationally known for his social work in a commune of peasants located on a remote archipelago on Lake Nicaragua. There a group of peasants commented on the Gospel from a political point of view. Cardenal transcribed their oral analyses and published them as *The Gospel of Solentiname.* Today this collection is important because it reflects the peasants' development of a political consciousness and their understanding of their role in national politics.

Beyond a passion for their countries' ancient folklore, these writers have in common a commitment to undergo a serious exploration of culture, away from biased analytical points of view. They are not mere folklorists; instead, their writing speaks about how the underprivileged can voice opinions about social and political issues through their practice of cultural traditions. The lessons for readers outside these cultures are profound and personal, because these groups' experiences are at the core of life values shared by others around the world.

Manlio Argueta (1935–)

Poet and novelist Manlio Argueta is among the best Central American writers. He is a political activist in his native El Salvador, and his work has been used in campaigns on behalf of destitute peasant and indigenous populations. He is a gifted narrator, who combines in-depth research of historical sources with his personal experiences and others' testimonial accounts of political events in El Salvador. Because of his open opposition to the oppressive Salvadoran military governments, Argueta lived in exile for several years. He then became an international spokesperson in opposition to the killings of dissidents, using his powerful novels and poetry, which have been translated into a dozen foreign languages. In addition to his commitment to social change, he writes poetry that sings praises to popular themes, such as Salvadoran nature, and traditional romantic themes, such as his love for women.

A member of a literary group of young writers known as the Committed Generation, Argueta started writing in the mid-1950s amid a convoluted and highly restrictive national political scene. A group of university students and young writers in the capital city of San Salvador became directly involved in politics and made their poetry a platform for social change: "our slogan was 'the poet has to be an example.' That meant that we had to denounce injustices and also to put forward a definition of the role of the writer in a society like ours" (Varela 2). This group, which included fellow student writer Roque Dalton (1935–1975), became popular, and they took their public readings to the streets of San Salvador, as well as to political rallies and student events. Dalton's committed writing, along with the extensive production of Argueta and of poet and novelist Claribel Alegría (1924–), are today mandatory reading for those interested in understanding El Salvador's complex political history. The three of them documented key events leading to a violent, bloody civil war, beginning in 1980.

The writers of the Committed Generation were unable to publish their activist poetry in national publishing houses, because it contained strong political elements calling for equal rights for all citizens, particularly for the peasant and indigenous populations. Instead, they published their own journal, a makeshift publication, *La Pájara Pinta,* which they distributed, often free of charge, throughout the country. With this publication, they developed a national reputation that extended to other Latin American countries.

Argueta's literature is intimately related to the complex political history of his native El Salvador. Historians point to the years between 1931 and 1979 as crucial in the development of an underground guerrilla movement that opposed a series of dictatorial military governments. In 1932, a confrontation between indigenous activists, headed by José Feliciano Ama of the Izalco nation, and the armed forces of the National Guard provoked a massacre. The activists were claiming the right to own land and demanding social reforms in social and political systems in an attempt to gain more political representation. During the next few years, severe censorship took place and an estimated 30,000 natives perished in armed conflicts.

Consequently, all native traditions were officially banned, including specific restrictions against wearing traditional clothing in public, performing religious or community rituals, and using native languages.

As Argueta has pointed out, two purposes led to the restriction of both the observance of native customs and research in Salvadoran national indigenous cultures. First, the government hoped to curtail investigation of the mass killings it had committed against the indigenous peoples. Second, the native populations preferred to keep their popular cultures and traditions hidden from the public at large. According to Argueta, these groups, the Izalcos in particular, "hid their language, their music, their dance, their dress and other customs" (Hernández 3). The official restrictions against folkloric research came to an end in 1975, when El Salvador hosted the Miss Universe pageant. Although Argueta has a negative opinion of this international show of "talking dolls," he believes that it led to exploration of indigenous cultures (Hernández 3). That display of indigenous culture at the Miss Universe pageant had an ideological purpose, however. By showcasing colorful indigenous garb, for example, the show attempted to present modern El Salvador's "civilized face," in opposition to the primitive side of its indigenous cultures (Hernández 3).

Violence on the political scene intensified throughout the 1970s. Popular dissent was evident after the founding of the Fuerzas Populares de la Liberación Farabundo Martí in 1970, a leftist front that a decade later became the Farabundo Martí National Liberation Front (FMNL), a conglomerate of four guerrilla groups. The world became a witness to the horrors of the war in 1980 with the assassination of Archbishop Oscar Romero, whose criticism against the Salvadoran government had made him a popular figure among national leftist groups. The film *Romero* (1989) depicts his murder, which took place while he was conducting mass in a church full of people. In 1981, the FMNL officially declared an armed confrontation against the military government. Accusations of human rights violations against combatants on both sides were frequent. In particular, the FMNL's assassination of a number of mayors elected between 1985 and 1988 severely tarnished the movement's political image.

It was a long, cruel confrontation. From 1980 to 1992, an estimated 75,000 people died as a result of the Salvadoran civil war. The United States became directly involved, providing financial and military support to the Salvadoran government, despite the fact that international organizations had named El Salvador as a country that committed serious human rights violations, including the tortures and murders of innocent people. In 1992, under a United Nations peace treaty, the civil war came to an end; social and economic reforms began, including recognition of the FMNL as a legal political party. Argueta, spoke in psychological terms when he commented on the importance of this peace treaty, saying that it marked the beginning of El Salvador's analysis and the resolution of a series of traumas (Hernández 2).

International recognition of Argueta came with the 1970 publication of his first novel, *El valle de las hamacas,* which is unavailable in English translation. In it he sets out to explore Salvadoran indigenous roots: "I gather legends based on indigenous mythology, although mixed with modern elements, since many of our myths are no longer just indigenous, but have elements from the Colonial period and of the era of the independence in the nineteenth century" (Hernández 2). This was a calculated political move on his part, because such a pro-indigenous stand could mark him as a communist (Hernández 3). A second novel, *Caperucita en la zona roja* (1977; *Little Red Riding Hood in the Red Light District,* 1998), which won a prestigious international prize in Cuba that same year, cemented Argueta's literary reputation as an emerging, socially committed writer. This novel depicts the military oppression that existed in El Salvador throughout the 1970s. He uses Little Red Riding Hood in a symbolic approach to discuss issues associated with warfare that often remain unexplored, such as the sexual exploitation of women. The novel continues to be one of Argueta's most appreciated among his El Salvadoran readership.

Further international attention came after the publication of *Un día en la vida* (1980; *One Day of Life,* 1983), a novel that follows the vicissitudes in the life of an indigenous woman in El Salvador. One notable aspect of the text is that the characters are not fictional, but are actual people with whom Argueta had recorded extensive conversations—common citizens who had experienced the civil war in Salvador in difficult and profound ways. This technique of documenting real-life events is known as a ***testimonio,*** or literature of testimony, and it holds great importance for Argueta: "I began to see the people no longer as an abstract being or theoretical, as we sometimes see them, the people as a socio-political concept, but the people in concrete form, that is to say, as a person that I know, who suffers" (Varela 10). His testimonial literature explores two trends: military confrontation and Salvadoran native customs.

Argueta went into exile in Costa Rica after the publication of *One Day of Life.* The Salvadoran authorities confiscated copies of the novel and banned the sale or the possession of it. He did not return to El Salvador until 1992, after the Salvadoran government and the FMNL had signed a peace agreement. He is today the director of El Salvador's National Library and continues to have an important role as a distinguished commentator on national politics.

Argueta has spoken about his decision to produce novels, setting aside his enthusiasm for poetry. He has described his novels as a collective "historical saga" of El Salvador that includes the wider perspective of events seen from the point of view of common characters. Argueta also considers it his duty to present historic events accurately, especially those that military censorship had previously tried to keep secret. Finally, he incorporates elements of popular tradition as materials worthy of literary treatment, including life in the countryside and details about the cultures of Salvadoran indigenous groups. Above all, he is mindful of his ideological responsibility to portray a well-balanced view of the various social structures in modern El Salvador.

Argueta writes from a contemporary political perspective. He has stressed "the need to express our tradition and to express in my works the national indigenous elements, as well as to bear witness of transculturation and to examine urban problems in depth, within a modern subculture of the novel" (Hernández 4). Argueta's historical novels can be viewed as a product of his interest in documenting local cultures, just as the Spanish chroniclers did during and after the Conquest. He is different from them, however, in that his reproduction of native indigenous cultures of Salvador supports a strong ideological message that calls for social change, including financial reparation for thousands of dispossessed campesinos and native groups. Unlike the Spanish chroniclers, Argueta is closer to the native chroniclers who wrote about Latin American indigenous groups with a political intention. Argueta's view of Salvadoran history stresses the ongoing need to secure social justice, initiated the moment Spanish conquistadors began colonizing the New World. As Argueta graphically depicts in his novels, the political forces at play in El Salvador are complex, just as they were in colonial times, but they can be understood when examined against significant historic events.

Argueta's novel *Cuzcatlán, donde bate la Mar del Sur* (1986; *Cuzcatlán, Where the Southern Sea Beats,* 1987) merges the political activism of organized guerrilla warfare in El Salvador into significant historic accounts that shaped the country's political and social scene in the twentieth century. As the novel opens, a twenty-four-year-old woman of indigenous and peasant background is riding a bus toward San Salvador, Salvador's capital city. The narration is striking because it appears almost in the form of a military report or as the recorded testimony of a witness in court. The reader soon realizes that the woman had been a member of a leftist guerrilla group. She is describing her reasons for joining the group, which she did shortly after arriving in San Salvador. She has two children and, because of her activism, she worries about their safety. She is also fearful for her life and the lives of her immediate family, who are living in the countryside. As a safety precaution, she uses an alias, Beatriz, and remains anonymous. In short, her character is a symbol for all the many women who took part in underground guerrilla warfare activities.

Despite her anonymity, Beatriz provides considerable information about her personal background. She is of peasant stock, a mestiza with close ties to local indigenous groups, reflected in her description of native traditions. This information appears amply throughout the text in passages that interrupt her vivid recollections of political activism. This is an effective narrative technique, which maintains a balance between Beatriz's memories of her life in the countryside and of her underground activities. In addition, Beatriz serves as a chronicler of historic events witnessed by past generations. She is not a historian in the academic sense but simply remembers a number of anecdotes that came to her through oral histories.

Beatriz's accounts of her military activities and the documentation of her family's life in the countryside are representative of the *testimonio*. There are three characteristics inherent in the genre. First, the *testimonio* draws from oral techniques of confession of facts about an important event, which an eyewitness, usually one who is affected by the event, narrates in the first person. Second, the eyewitness addresses an implied reader directly, one who is reading about these events as an outsider. Third, the eyewitness-narrator emphasizes the lessons learned from the events in a didactic process from which the reader receives instruction.

Argueta's novel *Cuzcatlán* is not a pure example of the *testimonio*, however, because Beatriz is fictional. This technique allows the writer more flexibility in telling the stories of previous generations. In contrast to the traditional *testimonio*, Beatriz tells these anecdotes as she had heard them from relatives, who had heard them from past generations. In this interesting technique, Argueta's meticulous knowledge of the history of El Salvador is obvious, as is his gifted ability to sustain the reader's attention to a detailed historical text.

Cuzcatlán's strong interest in Salvadoran history is evident in a quotation from Pedro de Alvarado, San Salvador's conquistador. It serves as the novel's opening dedication. Alvarado, writing to Hernán Cortés, conquistador of Mexico and his immediate supervisor, describes the fierceness of the natives of the city of Cuxcatlán, today San Salvador. The passage reports in a puzzled tone that although the town is in rebellion, all men suddenly left the city for the nearby mountains. A second quotation, from a Commander Jonás, presumably a guerrilla soldier, to a foreign journalist comments on those same mountains. Jonás's comments go to the core of war strategy: the mountains are "nothing but a theater for this shitty war" (1). Five hundred years after the Conquest, the war from the mountains continues. Historic accounts recorded that the Cuxcatlán warriors came back from the mountains and faced Spanish aggression.

A mountains served a second purpose, however: they provided native groups safety and the opportunity to preserve cultural practices away from the imposition of foreign traditions. Argueta sees himself as a folklorist. According to his own design, he sets out to reproduce the "Salvadoran rich culture" in *Cuzcatlán*, as reflected in the traditions of the "simple people" of El Salvador (Varela 12). Argueta's choice of depicting primarily peasant traditions goes against the traditional literary approach, which sets the city as an example of national identity or as representative of acceptable cultural values. It is also unusual that a female character takes on the role of spokesperson at two important levels: the political (as a guerrilla fighter) and the social (as a peasant). The development of a strong female protagonist is among Argueta's most important contributions to contemporary Latin American literature.

Beatriz is proud of her native background. She communicates this to the reader by means of informed descriptions of the agrarian culture. She relates so much to nature that her descriptions of herself are contained in statements that speak about the influence of the natural surroundings on her psyche:

Element of nature which is special to me: metate. It's a precious stone, made from the lava of volcanoes; my parents, grandparents, and great-grandparents all made a living from it. They made grinding stone. For grinding corn. We peasants grind corn using the strength of our arms. On a metate base shape like a small washtub, using a pestle, also made of metate, we mash corn that has been cooked in water and ashes. The ashes help to soften it. After a few pounds of the pestle, which is also called the handstone, the corn becomes a spongy white dough, which has a pleasant feel and a very agreeable taste. That's what we peasants live on. We form a dough into a tortilla by kneading it with our fingers and palms, then we put it over the fire on a comal, or clay griddle. The tortilla is our bread. It is life. (3)

The association of corn, a basic staple in the campesino diet, is also religious. According to legend, man is made out of corn, created by a powerful god, Gucumatz, using the grinding process of making tortillas. Beatriz's belief in immortality is attached to the indigenous opinion of nature: "We are corn and water. The species will not perish. That is how it is told from generation to generation" (73).

Beatriz does not present an idyllic picture of life in the countryside, however. It is a hard life, where nature as a giving mother can also be cruel. The constant threats of floods, dry spells, and land erosion have forced a considerable number of peasants to seek jobs outside the fields where past generations worked. Many other campesinos were slaves on indigo plantations, working with a highly toxic plant that was used for manufacturing dye tablets. The working conditions there were miserable, and the death rate was high; women and children, too, worked these plantations, often in the worst circumstances.

A descendent of hardworking peasants, Beatriz is a strong fighter both physically and spiritually. Her story about joining in guerrilla warfare provides the reader a well-rounded introduction to her understanding of complex Salvadoran politics. Unlike the usual portrait of the campesina woman as ignorant of the country's historic past, Beatriz is well aware of a long series of injustices toward peasants at the hands of powerful landowners, foreign companies, and the local government. They are lessons that she learned as a child or stories she has heard about abuses of power and crimes against campesino activists (such as details about the 1932 indigenous massacre) that came down to her via oral tradition.

Another of Beatriz's interesting traits is that she represents a new generation of campesina activists trained in organized political associations. Her story, like that of many other young women, started with her decision to leave the countryside for the city, seeking a better life as a factory worker. Her economic condition did not improve, however; thus, she became involved with work unions and eventually found her way into warfare groups. She is a political activist who narrates both her personal story and El Salvador's through her memories of the painful stories about family members marginalized because of their campesino background.

Argueta's literary contribution in *Cuzcatlán* can be illustrated in one important characteristic. He is a self-made historian and folklorist of Salvadoran customs, in particular of those traditions that are associated with national identity. He has pointed out that the exploration of popular folklore in El Salvador during the guerrilla years was not well received. Identified with leftist political points of view, indigenous traditions became associated with a history prior to the arrival of the Europeans. The activist message is loud and clear: the censored traditions will survive again, just as they survived the brutal processes of the Conquest.

As Argueta illustrates through the story of Beatriz, El Salvador has experienced trauma and a convoluted and violent past. Despite the violence, or perhaps because of it, El Salvador has shaped a unique system of family relationships—families related by blood or by the bond of shared ideologies.

Rigoberta Menchú (1959–)

Rigoberta Menchú is today among the best-known women activists in the world. Exceptional circumstances forced her to enter the political arena in her native Guatemala. The daughter of indigenous peasants from the Guatemalan highlands, Menchú's cultural heritage is Maya-Quiché, an ancient tradition that is often at odds with modern life. She dramatically traced changes in her life in her autobiography *Me llamo Rigoberta Menchú y así me nació la conciencia* (1983; *I, Rigoberta Menchú, An Indian in Guatemala,* 1984). Like thousands of other Maya-Quiché, she grew up poor and marginalized from mainstream social institutions, such as schools and health care centers. It was not until after her childhood that Menchú learned to speak and read Spanish. That decision was the beginning of her involvement in political associations seeking radical improvements in the dire conditions of Guatemala's indigenous communities.

Against all odds, the former illiterate Indian woman became an international spokesperson for indigenous communities. In tribute to her devoted labor as a pacifist, she received the Nobel Peace Prize in 1992, the first time that this prestigious award was given to a person of indigenous background. Although she denounces present and past oppression of all indigenous communities, she also communicates a hopeful message. She stressed in her Nobel Prize acceptance speech that the indigenous past must be an example to follow in a complex world that faces experiences similar to those of the native peoples: "Our history is a living history, that has throbbed, withstood and survived many centuries of sacrifice. Now it comes forward again with strength. The seeds, dormant for such a long time, break out today with some uncertainty, although they germinate in a world that is at present characterized by confusion and uncertainty" (Acceptance 10).

As a firm believer in the Mayan culture as part of universal "body of thought" (*Crossing Borders* 171), she has dedicated part of her efforts to diffusion of her native culture's ancient knowledge at all levels—social, political, religious, and philosophical. Her image as a proud indigenous woman, always wearing a colorful *huipil,* the native Maya-Quiché garb for women, is well known throughout the world. Today, the Rigoberta Menchú Foundation, which she created in Guatemala in 1995, continues her work for the betterment of indigenous communities in Guatemala and around the world.

Menchú's international reputation is related to her opposition to strong military aggression against the national indigenous villages in Guatemala beginning in 1981. Under a military dictatorship, the Guatemalan army had started campaigns against guerrilla groups, some of them associated with native political associations. In *I, Rigoberta Mechú,* her graphic accounts of the torture and killing of her relatives gave impetus to an international campaign against the cruel Guatemalan civil war.

The Guatemalan guerrilla warfare began in 1954 with a military coup against President Jacobo Arbenz. This event has relevance to U.S. foreign policy in Central America because of alleged CIA support of the Guatemalan military. Direct U.S. involvement took place after the election of President Ronald Reagan in 1980. Against U.S. public opinion, the Reagan administration supported the Guatemalan military regime in its campaign of aggression against subversive groups. At the end of the war in 1996, there was an estimated death toll of 70,000 to 120,000 people, including a large number of indigenous peoples. The country was financially devastated, and its infrastructure lay in shambles. Thousands of refugees fled to Mexico and the United States; some 200,000 were displaced and homeless throughout Guatemala.

In 1998 the Recuperation of the Historical Memory Project reported on the human rights violations in Guatemala during this violent war. The findings showed that the army was overwhelmingly responsible for the 150,000 dead and 150,000 missing as a result of the war, as well as for up to 1 million refugees (Galeano 100). This report included the testimonial accounts of thousands of war victims, just as Menchú had done in her *I, Rigoberta Menchú.* That same year, Menchú published *Crossing Borders,* a biographical testimony that expands on *I, Rigoberta Menchú.*

Because of her work with indigenous political groups, in 1981 Menchú was forced to go into exile in Mexico. She started working closely with the

United Nations to promote international legislation for the protection of ethnic and cultural minorities worldwide. She also promoted agreements in Guatemala toward resolution of the civil war. In 1982, she was among the founding members of the United Representation of the Guatemalan Opposition, an organization that exiled Guatemalan activists created to denounce the ongoing civil war in Guatemala. The next year, she published *I, Rigoberta Menchú* at the peak of the war. The book became an immediate best-seller, and Menchú became an active speaker in worldwide political and academic circles.

Further denunciations on behalf of the Guatemalan indigenous community came with her participation in the documentary *When the Mountains Tremble* (1983). The film, which includes interviews with Menchú, along with military and governmental officials, traces her previous work in Guatemala as an indigenous activist opposing the historical causes of the civil war. It is a visually striking documentary with actual footage of fighting in the city and mountains.

Menchú comes from a peasant and indigenous background. She was born in the rural village of Laj Chimel near the town of San Miguel de Uspantán in the northeastern Guatemalan highlands of the Cuchumantes Mountains. The inhabitants of Laj (Little) Chimel are direct descendents of the Maya-Quiché, one of twenty-two ethnic groups. Each one, Menchú states in her autobiography, speaks a different language that the others do not understand and has distinctive cultural traditions. Menchú grew up in a tight community in the loving care of activist parents.

It was not an idyllic childhood, however. Life in the village was difficult because of its mountainous terrain. There were no streets; people or horses carried the goods necessary for survival. Houses were made of natural materials. The mountains provided breathtaking beauty, however, which she would later leave to work on coastal farms and in factories in Guatemala City.

Both of her parents had respected positions as community leaders in Laj Chimel. Menchú characterizes them in *I, Rigoberta Menchú* as founding members of the small village, which remained monolingual and free of foreign cultural traditions. They were also the village's "representatives," a position that Menchú describes as "someone whom the community looks up to like a father" (7). Her mother was also an experienced midwife, an important role in a isolated area far removed from conventional medical facilities. She was also knowledgeable about herbal medicine, an ancient art of the Quiché that has been transmitted through the generations. This close connection with nature, portrayed as mankind's main provider, is fully evident in Menchú's autobiographies.

The indigenous people of the mountains, or the Altiplano, were forced to find work in *fincas,* large plantations located on the fertile, warm Guatemalan coast. Menchú describes them as "vast extensions of land," owned by "very few" families (5). These absentee landowners also had tremendous political clout. The workers stayed at the *fincas* for extended periods, up to eight months at a time. They then returned to the remote villages in the mountains to plant corn and beans, the only crops that would survive in the less fertile ground of the Altiplano. As conditions worsened, they unwillingly returned to work on a *finca*, in a vicious cycle of exploitation. As Menchú states, "From what my parents said, they lived this harsh life for many years and they were always poor" (6).

Work on a *finca* was incredibly hard on the body and taxing to the family structure. As the sixth sibling of nine children, Menchú started to work on a coffee plantation as an eight-year-old child. There she first witnessed physical abuse against the workers—primarily illiterate and monolingual Quiché who came down to the southern Guatemalan coast to work in sugar and cotton plantations. The two-day trip to the coast was made in a covered truck that carried the workers, together with their families, farm animals, and provisions. Because the trip was so long, Menchú remembers, animals and small children inevitably soiled the trucks. The smell was "unbearable" (21), a preamble to the life that awaited these eager workers.

The working conditions in the coastal farms were horrendous. For the people of the Altiplano, the low elevation and hot weather produced pulmonary illnesses. The workers lived in **galeras,** large shacks with roofs made of palm or banana leaves. According to Menchú, some four to five hundred people crowded into these makeshift facilities, with their animals and possessions. The primitive toilet facilities were another problem. In the direct, incisive style that is characteristic of her autobiography, Menchú takes on this indelicate subject: "In the mornings we'd take turns to go off into the scrub and do our business. There are no toilets in the *finca*" (35). She continues her description in a succinct manner: four hundred people, divided into groups, would go to "the hills," a disgusting place with "lots of flies on all that filth up there" (35). To make things worse, Menchú notes, there was only one water tap in her *galera*, not "even enough for us to wash our hands" (35).

Another example of abuse of Guatemala's indigenous peoples is found in Menchú's description of the poor treatment of children who worked in the *fincas*. It is on this topic that Menchú offers one of her most direct denunciations, and her tone is not without rage. She writes about her own childhood experiences while working in the *fincas,* and these horrible memories are placed in sharp contrast to her recollections of life in the remote mountains of northern Guatemala. Menchú tells how two of her brothers died while working in the *fincas,* one after planes sprayed pesticides over the field where he was working and the other from malnutrition. Such recollections speak to the lack of medical care, as well as to the general lack of concern for the indigenous population among Guatemalan authorities.

Menchú's love for children is also part of her Mayan background. Throughout *I, Rigoberta Menchú* she emphasizes her love and strong connection with children, noting that Mayan culture places a strong importance on raising children, a task that the elders and the adult community at large consider a shared responsibility.

Although she was only twenty-three years old at the time her renowned autobiography was published, Menchú was writing as an elder. This is an important point because, as she begins her testimony in *I, Rigoberta Menchú,* she is speaking from various points of view: "This is my testimony. I didn't learn it from a book and I didn't learn it alone. I'd like to stress that it's not only my life, it's also the testimony of my people. . . . The important thing is that what has happened to me has happened to many other people too: My story is the story of all poor Guatemalans. My personal experience is the reality of a whole people" (1). She transmits, like her elders, "wisdom, hope and culture" (*Crossing Borders* 212). Although the narration of terrible anecdotes make up a significant part of both her autobiographies, Menchú also emphasizes the resilient character of indigenous cultures, which have survived colonialist attempts ever since the arrival of the Spanish conquistadors.

Menchú traces her development as a political activist to having worked as a child on the coastal *fincas.* She includes detailed accounts and realistic descriptions of the many tasks that children performed. At age ten, she was picking some forty pounds of coffee beans a day, much like an adult worker. The process of picking the beans was not arduous, just tedious, but overzealous overseers often harassed the pickers, warning them that they would be responsible for payment of any damaged plant. Menchú also reveals the ways in which the workers were tricked during the process of weighing their loads so that they were underpaid. These scenes echo previous literary descriptions by criollista writers who wrote about crimes committed against rural workers throughout Latin America.

Because the indigenous workers did not speak Spanish and because they came from various backgrounds without a common language, they were easily marginalized. They were also kept ignorant of their rights as workers. In an amusing anecdote, Menchú provides an example of the cultural ignorance of the rural indigenous workers. Menchú was seven years old when she first saw cars during her first visit to Guatemala City: "I thought they were animals just going along" (31). At the time, she, like most of her fellow Maya-Quiché, was monolingual and ignorant of the basic cultural foundations of Spanish-speaking Guatemalan society. It was as if they were living an invisible life.

In the early years of her youth, Menchú went to Guatemala City to work as a maid for an upper-class family. She moved to the capital, away from the *fincas* where all of her family members were still working, to escape the low pay and the terrible working conditions. She was hopeful that a more stable job in the city would provide additional funds for her needy family. Instead, she found herself at the mercy of an abusive mistress, who often underpaid her and denied her workers' rights.

Like many other young indigenous women, Menchú experienced social rejection because of her humble status and because of her inability to speak Spanish. Her employers exerted almost complete control on inexperienced Rigoberta, who was living in the capital city alone. Menchú was fortunate compared to some other young women, however. She avoided a life of prostitution, often the only choice of desperate, unskilled, indigenous young women in the large city.

From her father's campaigns on behalf of the destitute and abused indigenous workers, Menchú soon learned the tools of political activism. A substantial portion of *I, Rigoberta Mechú* addresses the violence of the Guatemalan army against indigenous political and guerrilla fighters. Two cases stand out: the kidnappings, tortures, and murders of her activist brother and of her mother. Some passages offer detailed accounts of various torture techniques, including beatings, pulling out nails, cutting off body parts, and, the ultimate insult in indigenous culture, the mistreatment and destruction of the corpses.

This book should be mandatory reading for those interested in the development of grassroots indigenous political associations in Guatemala. It is also an important source of information about the incorporation of women into guerrilla groups, including their active participation in armed confrontations.

Key testimonial accounts in Menchú's 1983 autobiography have been contested. In his book, *Menchú and the Story of All Poor Guatemalans* (1999), anthropologist David Stoll argues that Menchú's examples of her own family's conflicts with the Guatemalan government may have been taken from other known cases, not particularly from those of her immediate relatives. As expected, Stoll's book has generated controversy in Guatemala and abroad, particularly in the United States, Mexico, and Spain, countries in which Menchú has a considerable number of both admirers and detractors. The reader interested in following details of this controversy, including comments by Menchú and by Stoll, should consult Arturo Arias's collection of documents *The Rigoberta Menchú Controversy* (2001).

In addition to the political value of Menchú's testimony in *I, Rigoberta Menchú* and *Crossing Borders,* the autobiographies are important sources of information about the Maya-Quiché culture. Passages provide outstanding examples of the Maya-Quiché's rich skills in oral communication. It is also evident, however, that Menchú was very selective about the type of information she was willing to reveal. In *I, Rigoberta Menchú,* she warns that she finds it offensive that people who are not of indigenous cultures often wear these cultures' attire. A stronger objection in *Crossing Borders* offers one reason that the Maya-Quiché have decided not to disclose details of their religious beliefs: "Famous brains" have plagiarized indigenous thoughts without crediting the original cultural sources (170). Menchú equates culture with indigenous identity: "Our identity is based on tradition, on ancient culture and history" (*Crossing Borders* 222). Menchú makes it clear that violations or mocking of the Maya-Quiché cultural belief systems are not taken lightly.

Among Menchú's major topics in both of her autobiographies is the Maya-Quiché religious ceremonies and her people's strong belief in the power of Mother Earth. The Maya-Quiché nation displays a strong attachment to the earth, which they revere in complex ceremonies focused on the various cycles of planting and harvest. The traditions and customs about agricultural tasks are communicated generation after generation via a rich oral tradition: "my father told us all about the marvelous things there were in our land (and thinking of our ancestors of course), and the closeness of the peasant to nature" (191). Menchú reproduces short excerpts of prayers for Mother Earth. They are striking illustrations of the peaceful approach of the Maya-Quiché to human existence: "Mother Earth, you who gives us food, whose children we are and on whom we depend, please make this produce you give us flourish and make our children and our animals grow" (57).

Readers of Menchú's autobiographies should find in her revelations about the Maya-Quiché culture both anthropological data and statements of the ways in which native customs can become means of protest. One example of the latter is her emotional description in *I, Rigoberta Menchú* of a massive protest organized by the Maya-Quiché people at the Guatemalan Congress building. The march was large, with numerous indigenous protesters, along with students, peasants, and union members. The police attempted to intimidate the speakers, among them Menchú's brother, who was about to address the crowd when an agent raised a rifle at him. He did not fire, however, because suddenly a young girl, Menchú's sister, prevented the shooting by standing between the two men with a white flower. The flower, particularly a white flower, is a symbol of peace in Western culture. Menchú teaches her reader that it has a strong connotation for the Maya-Quiché as well. A flower is cut, Menchú states, only when it really is needed or when it represents something important. As she ends her anecdote, she emphasizes the people's reaction to her little sister's gesture: "Well, all the people on the demonstration held bunches of flowers to mean that they appealed for respect for human life and also for the solution to their plight" (197). The reader learns about the Maya-Quiché's strong connection with Mother Earth as well as their pacifist stance in facing the armed aggression of an unjust government.

Menchú goes beyond traditional depictions of indigenous life. Among her outstanding contributions is her explanation that elements of native cultures can become the means for protest. She is, in her own words, an "Indianist, not just an Indian, I'm an Indianist to my fingertips and I defend everything to do with my ancestors" (*I, Rigoberta Menchú* 166). As an Indianist she is a powerful spokesperson on behalf of indigenous communities in Guatemala and, by extension, of all struggling ethnic communities. Her lessons apply to all of us, however, not only indigenous peoples, because, as she states in *Crossing Borders,* all humans came from the earth: "Not only were indigenous peoples born of the earth. All humanity came from the earth. We are her children. As the human race is gradually enslaved by its own progress, it attacks the holistic nature of the earth, ignoring the safety of generations to come" (155). Her message addresses ethical, religious, and ecological responsibility for the earth and its inhabitants.

RELIGION AS A POLITICAL WEAPON

Ernesto Cardenal (1925–)

Ernesto Cardenal, as a priest, poet, political thinker, and visual artist, is an exponent of a multifaceted, socially committed component within the Roman Catholic Church in Latin America. His critical writings about the role of Catholicism in the political structures of Latin American societies are an integral part of **liberation theology,** an activist movement calling for social equality. Cardenal's close association with the Nicaraguan Sandinista Revolution made him a popular international figure after his forced exile from Nicaragua in 1977. With his political and religious poetry he became among the most effective spokespersons for the Frente Sandinista de Liberación Nacional party, the Sandinista guerrilla group. His poetry collections and his volumes of critical essays and religious writings have been translated into a dozen foreign languages.

Cardenal was born in Granada, Nicaragua, the oldest colonial city in Central America. The city's rich historical background exerted an influence on his writing. In describing his family's connection to foreign aggression against Nicaragua, he takes the reader into the history of an American mercenary soldier, William Walker. In 1856, Walker arrived from Texas into this area and proclaimed himself president of the country. According to Cardenal, one of Walker's followers defected from his army and married into Cardenal's family. Cardenal's family has a prestigious background with strong connections in the national literary scene. He is related, for example, to important Nicaraguan poets Pablo Antonio Cuadra and José Coronel Urtrecho.

Poetry attracted Cardenal at an early age. He was seven years old when he wrote his first poem. Because of his privileged social background, he received a private education at a Jesuit school in Granada. In addition to the superior education it provided, the school encouraged its students to write literature, which was printed in student publications.

After graduation from secondary school, Cardenal traveled to Mexico City, where he attended the famous Autonomous National University. His exposure to life in the Mexican capital city influenced his decision to continue writing poetry. Although he published some poems at the time, this extended period of four years in Mexico was important because he immersed himself into a flourishing cultural life. He became also interested in visual arts, particularly sculpture.

After his graduation in 1947, Cardenal studied American literature at Columbia University. As with his experiences in Mexico City, details of his life in New York City appear in his writing. His interest in American poetry was strong, and it became an inspiration for his own poetic production. The influence of American poets, particularly of Walt Whitman, Ezra Pound, and William Carlos Williams, is notable in his own poetry. It may have been at that time that he started an extensive project of translation into Spanish of representative American poetry in collaboration with fellow Nicaraguan poet José Coronel Urtrecho. This collection was published in 1963 at the peak of the Beat movement. A tireless traveler, Cardenal spent about two years in a tour around Europe. He returned to Nicaragua in 1950 with a strong desire to renovate the fairly traditional poetic production of his native Nicaragua.

In 1952 Cardenal attempted to revive the national literary scene, particularly to encourage the publication of poetry. In a small publishing house, he published local poets, his own poetry, and his translations of the epigrams of Latin poets Catullus and Martial. He was also the host of literary gatherings, some of which were secretive meetings against the Somoza regime. The activities took place in a bookstore with the support of his colleague Coronel Urtrecho.

Cardenal's poetry protesting the dictatorship of Nicaraguan President Anastasio Somoza led him into the national political scene. This critical poetry, which he signed with the pseudonym of Anónimo Nicaragüense (A Nameless Nicaraguan) became known beyond Nicaraguan circles when the distinguished Chilean poet Pablo Neruda published it in Chile. Cardenal would be forced to continue writing his poetry underground, however. *Hora Cero (Zero Hour)*, among his earliest anti-Somoza poems, began circulating underground in 1956. It was part of an increasingly large number of publications, most of political nature, against the repressive Somoza dictatorship. Two years earlier, the April Rebellion, a guerrilla attack on the presidential palace, had failed to depose Somoza. Cardenal had participated in that rebellion. Because of tightened censorship following these events, there was a ban on publication of all revolutionary materials.

In 1956 Cardenal exhibited some of his sculptures in Washington, D.C. It is unclear whether the exhibit came about because of his increasing participation in anti-Somoza activities, but it is evident that Cardenal displayed a strong interest in expressing himself in various artistic media. As in his poetry, his work in the visual arts reflects multiple sources of inspiration. He explores the popular craft in Nicaragua of pottery making, as well as native "primitive" painting. Also inspired by European vanguardism, he has explored the figurative sculpting of the figures of saints and of well-recognized symbols, particularly religious icons such as the fish (a symbol of early Christianity). His carvings of saints are also inspired by Nicaraguan folklore, in terms of both aesthetics and popular devotion.

In a surprising decision, Cardenal decided to enter a religious order and become a Trappist monk in 1956. Members of the Order of the Cistercians of the Strict Observance, the Trappists live in semienclosed monasteries and perform work in agricultural settings, often their only means of financial support. They are known for strict observance of penitence, frugality including in their eating habits, and schedules of intense prayers and spiritual exercises. For his religious training, Cardenal traveled to Kentucky in 1957, where he became a novice in the Monastery of Our Lady of Gethsemani, where Thomas Merton became Cardenal's Novice Master. Merton, an internationally known writer, had published a number of important books on the monastic life and spiritual growth. Merton's teachings about the importance of the Bible as a vehicle for meditation and as a model for community life were key elements in Cardenal's future poetry and political writings.

During his training with Merton, Cardenal stopped writing poetry, but he kept a journal. Those entries later provided material for two important religious-oriented texts: *Gethsemani, KY* (1960), a poetry collection that places emphasis on the role of nature in his religious contemplation, and *Vida en el amor* (1970; *To Live Is to Love*, 1972), a prose diary that explores the reading of biblical texts from a leftist point of view. Merton, who remained Cardenal's mentor, wrote introductions to both volumes.

Because life in the monastery was difficult, including the performance of extremely strenuous physical activities as part of his religious training, Cardenal became seriously ill at Gethsemani. He had to leave for Mexico, where he joined a Benedictine monastery in Cuernavaca. This second choice of religious order was again a calculated move. The Benedictines place emphasis on education and community service in a variety of tasks, manual and intellectual. During this period, he returned to producing political poetry with *Estrecho dudoso* (1966; *The Doubtful Strait*, 1995), a poem in which he traces elements in the political history of Central America from the conquest to modern times. By the mid-1960s Cardenal had become well known throughout Latin America as a political poet, particularly after the publication in Cuba of his poetry collection *Poemas de Ernesto Cardenal* (1967).

After his ordination in 1965, Cardenal decided to start a religious commune in Nicaragua. He had the approval of Merton, who reportedly considered going to Nicaragua to help run the project. In 1966 Cardenal's dream became a reality, with the founding of a village on a small and remote island. His work, both religious and artistic, with the local peasants had international exposure, especially after the publication of the English translations of three of his religious poetry collections: *The Psalms of Struggle and Liberation* (1972), which won that year's Christopher Book Award; *The Gospel in Solentiname* (1976), and *Apocalypse, and Other Poems* (1977). These important books reflect the influence of the popular liberation theology on Cardenal's poetry and on his work with the community of Solentiname. Because of Cardenal's close association with the Sandinista fighters, Somoza's army dismantled the commune in 1977 and Cardenal fled abroad.

During the 1970s, Cardenal spoke on behalf of the Sandinista Revolution that was taking place in Nicaragua. Because of the English translations of most of his abundant poetry, Cardenal's name became closely associated with the ideological platform of the Sandinista. There are strong political themes in his *Zero Hour* (1971), a collection that attempted to rekindle the nationalist spirit by bringing to the forefront the figure of a fallen patriot: César Augusto Sandino. Cardenal became better known, however, for modern themes and popular urban icons, such as those in his collection *Marilyn Monroe and Other Poems* (1975).

After the triumph of the Sandinista Revolution, Cardenal returned to Nicaragua, and he became the minister of culture. His decision to accept a government post caused difficulties with the Vatican. Pope John Paul II suspended his vows as a priest for the duration of his political career. As a politician, he became a Sandinista spokesperson on the role of culture in a revolutionary society: "Culture has to be democratic, so that the great majorities have access to it; and not only access to our national culture, but to universal culture. And so that our people may be not only cultural consumers, which is very important, but also producers of culture" (164). His most famous project was his direction of the National Literacy Commission, which provided the infrastructure for huge campaigns against illiteracy, which took place throughout Nicaragua in 1980. For his efforts during these campaigns, Cardenal was nominated for the Nobel Peace Prize.

Despite his administrative duties, Cardenal continued to write. His poem, *Quetzalcoatl* (1985), is an important contribution to anthropological research in the mythology of that divinity, indigenous to Central American native groups. It appeals both to children and to adult readers. An edition published in 1985 in honor of Cardenal's sixtieth birthday includes drawings that illustrate the story portrayed in the poem. Despite the high cost of its production, it appeared in a hardbound text. The extraordinary beauty of this book and the charming colored sketches of scenes related to Quetzalcoatl reflect the poet's desire to attract the attention of young readers. Although it is not available in English, *Quetzalcoatl* would be an excellent text for children learning Spanish as well as a good lesson on Central American indigenous cultures.

Cardenal's poetry attempts to assimilate elements of two great American indigenous civilizations: the Maya and Nahuatl (Central America) and the Inca (South America). He is an indefatigable researcher, a folklorist who incorporates indigenous cultures into the historical process that produced today's Nicaraguan national identity. His collection *Golden UFOs: The Indian Poems* (1992) contains poems that praise Latin American indigenous cultures, including a positive view of religious practices inherited from them. He is, according to his own statement, a historian but a historian of cultures that are alive: "Much of my poetry is historical. But it is not a matter of an old, dead history. On the contrary, it is a living, present history, and therefore poetic" (Gámez Cersósimo 5).

With the defeat of the Sandinista government in the elections of 1990 came internal divisions among its major leaders, particularly between Commander Daniel Ortega, the former president, and Sergio Ramírez, one of the original founders of the FSLN. Cardenal decided to withdraw from the Sandinista Party. Today he is the vice president of Casa de los Tres Mundos, a literary and cultural institution in Managua that seeks to explore the three major cultural components in Latin American societies: Spanish, native, and African. With this institution, he continues his mission of disseminating Nicaraguan culture and teaching the underprivileged. One program is artistic training of homeless children, who sell their work in the center's gallery.

Cardenal continues to travel abroad, especially to the United States, for well-attended readings of his poetry. His poetry has retained international popularity and is often part of the musical repertoire of famous singers, such as Spanish singer and composer Joan Manuel Serrat. His latest work is his autobiography, *Vida perdida*, not yet available in English translation. He is, above all, a vociferous spokesperson for the underprivileged in Latin American societies, a priest and a poet who has maintained the delicate balance between his two strongest interests: a religious, contemplative approach to human existence and an activism for the creation of a fair and equitable community.

Cardenal had a major role in the development of the **Liberation Theology** in Latin America. Liberation theology is a radical movement that took place within the Catholic Church in Latin America beginning in the mid-1960s; it sought social justice for the underprivileged, especially peasants and indigenous communities openly mistreated by powerful landowners and unjust governments. Also during the 1960s, after changes in the traditional structure of the Church, for instance, the adoption of vernacular languages instead of Latin, the Latin American Catholic Church started to incorporate the devotion of local religious folklore. The movement, usually known as the **Church for the People,** sought to create a setting for worship with a special appeal to multiethnic Latin American communities. Among the many examples of incorporation of diverse customs is the use of local music and instruments and the observance of indigenous rituals as part of the mass or within traditional Catholic rituals.

The appeal of the Church for the People is best exemplified in its numerous projects within poor communities throughout Latin America, designed primarily to improve the lives of the impoverished through vocational training or, in many cases, by providing basic literacy or schooling that is not available to them from government sources. An important learning tool was the teaching of religious texts, especially from the Bible. In line with the Church for the People's emphasis on the common people, the analyses of biblical texts took on an unusual characteristic. Unlike the typical belief that a religious figure, usually a priest, interprets the significance and, more important, the application of the message of a religious text, the members of the Church for the People were responsible for this task.

The Church for the People organized important projects throughout Latin America. These centers did not go unnoticed as they provided tools for the people's empowerment, mainly through their understanding of oppression. Those involved in the Church for the People often clashed with the Vatican's orthodox dogma and its choice to maintain neutrality in local government. Their most challenging encounters were, however, with local governments, some of which were under the control of military powers.

Liberation theology's commitment to the poor and destitute coincided with the highly political 1960s, when Latin American countries were experiencing social and political crises and a number of countries were in political upheaval. Fighting the control of right-wing military governments, the revolutionary Cuban government, beginning in 1959, had a major influence on the spread of socialist and Marxist ideology. The social projects undertaken in Cuba, such as massive literacy campaigns, became an inspiration for both the Church for the People and underground political groups. They had similar goals: radical change in the old government and the improvement of abysmal social and economic conditions in Latin American countries.

The Church for the People undertook a variety of projects throughout Latin America. Perhaps the best known today is Cardenal's Christian commune. Cardenal founded Our Lady of Solentiname on the remote island of Mancarrón in the archipelago of Solentiname in Lake Nicaragua. "Solentiname," or Celentinametl, from the Nahuatl language, means "a place for many guests." Cardenal intended to pursue his self-designed "contemplative retirement" in such a place "fortunately hard to reach, outside the paths of merchants and tourists," as he mentions in his introduction to *The Gospel of Solentiname* (vii). Soon, his community became, in his words, a "lay monastery" and began serving about one thousand people, or ninety families. Because of the geographic isolation of the islands, the illiteracy rate among these poor peasants and fisherman was high. They also lacked training in modern agricultural techniques and were unfamiliar with modern machinery. The community was extremely poor, isolated from technology and medical services, and left to their own means of survival.

Two activities became synonymous with Cardenal's community. One was the local tradition of drawing primitive paintings of the local flora and fauna on household objects, such as water gourds. Cardenal recognized the artistic potential of the people, and after formal training by professional artists, the members of the commune began producing paintings under the auspices of a cooperative known as Pintores Primitivistas de Solentiname (Primitive Painters of Solentiname). The other activity was developing the concept of the cooperative among the community, an important lesson in organization that the inhabitants of Solentiname applied to various businesses. In the case of the Primitive Painters Cooperative, eleven years after its founding and immediately after the destruction of the community by an attack from the Nicaraguan National Guard, Cardenal proudly remembered that their paintings were sold outside Nicaragua—in New York, Washington, Paris, Germany, Venezuela, and beyond.

The community of Solentiname produced other crafts intended for sale in Nicaragua and as souvenirs for the numerous visitors who came to witness the increasingly popular religious and social center. As with the primitive painting, crafts produced by the commune drew from local manual tradition and the use of natural materials. Pottery and woodcarving became popular artistic creations among the artisans, many of whom were instructed by visiting artists. Other interesting manual works included the use of silver, leather, and bronze. In keeping with the community's increasing interest in the arts, a museum exhibited pre-Colombian archeological pieces found in the area. A gallery served as space for formal exhibits and as a teaching space, as well as a store.

Solentiname was a model of community effort and of the type of project that can be possible despite small budgets. According to Cardenal, a dilapidated church was rescued, and several primitive structures, mainly huts, became meeting centers. Toward the end, Solentiname could host a number of national and international guests in a communal guesthouse. The commune also received financial support from abroad. Among the projects that never came to pass was a dairy and cheese factory that a German company was planning to help establish.

Solentiname's reputation was built from a radical change in the traditional outlook of the church as a space devoted solely to religious activities. Although there was a church in Solentiname before his arrival, the locals had abandoned it, and it had fallen into ruins. With the help of the commune members, the church was rebuilt—but with two important changes. First, the church lacked the traditional icons that are so characteristic of Catholic churches throughout Latin America. Instead of being a space used only for masses and other sanctioned functions, it became a communal space for meetings. To the horror of some local opponents, people often smoked and drank there. In keeping with a pro-environment campaign and in recognition of the fabulous setting of the island, mass was often celebrated outdoors. This custom, in the nature-loving hippie era of the late 1960s, would soon be imitated throughout Latin America.

The second change in the Solentiname church went to the very core of the mass, an important Catholic ritual. Those attending Cardenal's services were in charge of analyzing the readings from the Gospel. They were inspired by the liberation theology position that, because the Gospel was written by people much like the poor, marginal, and illiterate community of Solentiname, the destitute would understand the inherent message of social justice. This was a radical position, as a member of the Solentiname group discussions pointed out: "We're all equal. The only teacher is Christ, who is identified with the poor. The only teacher we have is the people" (*The Gospel of Solentiname* 295).

Our Lady of Solentiname's most famous project at the international level was the community's commentaries on Gospel readings. As Cardenal explained it, the process was relatively simple. Either as part of the Sunday service or after it, the community commented on biblical passages. This was a radical departure from the Church's traditional posture, which delegated solely to the priest the task of interpreting religious texts. On the other hand, Cardenal accepted an important tenet of liberation theology that made the practitioner responsible for adapting the message of the readings to his or her own life. The passages, particularly those from the New Scriptures, the "Good News" (to the poor), in Cardenal's words, became associated with liberation theology's message to liberate the underprivileged from social, economic, and, controversially, political boundaries.

As was to be expected, the handling of religious texts with a political intention had international opposition, particularly because the interpretations often made direct references to Communist thinkers such as Mao Tsetung, Fidel Castro, and Che Guevara. In particular, after his death in Bolivia in 1967, Guevara appeared as an ideal leader for the struggle to build a just society. The Solentiname community also commented on issues of national and international politics. Their references to oppression by the military governments of Nicaragua's Somoza and by Chile's Augusto Pinochet regimes were daring under the strong censorship and the threat of physical punishment against those who dared to voice dissenting political views.

In *The Gospel of Solentiname,* Cardenal transcribed a number of the commune's commentaries of the Gospel. The readings cover a variety of subjects, all of them relating to the teachings of Christ. The people's analyses are striking because many are profound observations about texts that are difficult in terms of content and language. The commentaries reflect profound religious experiences, which Cardenal described in the introduction of *The Gospel of Solentiname:* "The true author is the Spirit that has inspired these commentaries (the Solentiname campesinos know very well that it is the

Spirit who makes them speak) and that it was the Spirit who inspired the Gospels" (viii). The lessons learned led to "**the spirit of community unity,**" a term that one of the participants coined. At the end, that same religious spirit would move them into joining in armed confrontations against the Somoza regime.

Under the ideological concept of life in the spirit of community unity, the people of Solentiname made the Gospel a symbol of their own experiences of living in a commune. That life, modeled after that of the first Christians, also had similarities with pre-Columbian indigenous communities, particularly in their embrace of nature, which stopped being an obstacle to civilization and became a generous provider.

Today, one of Solentiname's contributions to alternative ways of life in Latin America may lie in the peasants' interpretations of religious belief systems—in this case, Jesus Christ's teachings—as a vehicle for political change. Their comments were concise and at times rather unusual analyses of complex and obscure biblical texts. A reading of *The Gospel of Solentiname* documents the development of the commune's ideas as they took Christ's teachings as the basis for life in a fair society.

The primitive paintings inspired by the Gospels indicate that the message of liberation was central to the commune. In those reproduced in *The Gospel in Art by the Peasants of Solentiname,* the artists painted scenes using the modern setting of Solentiname and themselves as the protagonists of the stories. The most visually striking paintings are those of violence, such as Herod's massacre of the newborn babies, in which the soldiers in charge of the killings appear in military fatigues.

Despite the violence that raged throughout Nicaragua at that time, the Solentiname commune sought to build a movement seeking social justice by means of strength the community found in existing religious doctrines. When compared with Rigoberta Menchú and the Maya-Quiché of Guatemala, the sociopolitical parallels between these two marginal communities are similar: high rates of illiteracy and mortality, and abuses of power from government and private sectors, among other social ills. It is significant that the indigenous communities in Guatemala and the Solentiname commune found an ally for their political struggle in religious association.

Cardenal is one of a long list of Latin American priests who took upon themselves the defense of poor and marginal communities. He followed in the footsteps of priests during the colonial period who courageously wrote against the inhuman treatment of indigenous populations at the hands of unmerciful landowners. Beyond the significance of his message calling for a new definition of religious life in a time of terrible political strife, his project in Solentiname stands out for its incorporation of rural life into positive literary images. His fresh approach to nature as an essential part of a religious experience makes him a forerunner in a pro-peace, ecologically oriented movement with a strong indigenous background. He is, above all, a committed writer, with a gift for merging Latin American political activism and aesthetics into literature of international appreciation.

BIBLIOGRAPHY

Argueta, Manlio. *Cuzcatlán. Where the Southern Sea Beats*. Trans. Clark Hansen. New York: Random House, 1986.
———. *Little Red Riding Hood in the Red District*. Trans. Edward Hood. Willimantic, CT: Curbstone Press, 1998.
———. *One Day of Life*. Trans. Bill Brow. New York: Vintage Books, 1983.
———. *El valle de las hamacas*. Buenos Aires: Editorial Sudamericana, 1970.
Arias, Arturo. *The Rigoberta Menchú Controversy*. Minneapolis: University of Minnesota Press, 2001.
Cardenal, Ernesto. *Apocalypse, and Other Poems*. Trans. Thomas Merton, Kenneth RexRoth, and Mireya Jaimes-Freyre. New York: New Directions, 1977.
———. *The Doubtful Straight*. Trans. John Lyons. Bloomington: Indiana University Press, 1995.
———. *Golden UPFs: The Indian Poems*. Trans. Carlos Altschul and Monique Altschul. Bloomington: Indiana University Press, 1992.
———. *The Gospel in Art by the Peasants of Solentiname*. Ed. Philip and Sally Scharper. New York: Orbis Books, 1982.
———. *The Gospel in Solentiname*. Vol. 3. Trans. Donald D. Walsh. New York: Orbis Books, 1979.
———. *Marilyn Monroe and Other Poems*. Trans. Robert Pring-Mill. London: Search Press, 1975.
———. *Quetzalcoatl*. Managua: Nueva Nicaragua, 1985.
———. *To Live Is to Love*. Trans. Kurt Reinhardt. New York: Herder and Herder, 1972.
———. *The Psalms of Struggle and Liberation*. Trans. Emile G. McAnany. New York: Herder and Herder, 1971.
———. *Vida perdida*. Barcelona: Seix Barral, 1999.
———. *Zero Hour and Other Documentary Poems*. Trans. Paul W. Borgeson. New York: New Directions, 1980.
Galeano, Eduardo. "Let's Shoot Rigoberta." *The Rigoberta Menchú Controversy*. Ed. Arturo Arias. Minneapolis: University of Minnesota Press, 2001: 99–102.
Gámez Cersósimo, Pablo. "La vida encontrada de Ernesto Cardenal: Entrevista de Ernesto Cardenal." http://www.libreriahispana.com/cardenal/gamez.html.
Hernández, David. "La aldea local se vuelve universal: Diálogo con Manlio Argueta." http://www.librusa.com/entrevista_manlio_argueta.htm.
Menchú, Rigoberta. "Acceptance and Nobel Lecture." http://www.nobel.se/peace/laureates/1992/tum-lecture.html.
———. *Crossing Borders*. Ed. and trans. Ann Wright. London: Verso, 1998.
———. *I, Rigoberta Menchú, An Indian Woman in Guatemala*. Ed. Elisabeth Burgos-Debray. Trans. Ann Wright. London: Verso, 1984.
Stoll, David. *Rigoberta Menchú and the Story of All Poor Guatemalans*. Boulder, CO: Westview Press, 1999.

Varela, Rafael. "Entrevista con Manlio Argueta." http://www.2culturas.com/entre vistas/argueta/argueta.html.

SUGGESTED READINGS ON CENTRAL AMERICAN LITERATURE

Carson, Lori M., and Cynthia L. Ventura. *Where Angels Glide at Dawn: New Stories from Latin America*. New York: HarperTrophy, 1990.
Craft, Linda. *Novels of Testimony and Resistance from Central America*. Gainesville: University Press of Florida, 1997.

SUGGESTED ANTHOLOGIES ON LATIN AMERICAN LITERATURE IN TRANSLATION

Caistor, Nick. *The Faber Book of Contemporary Latin American Short Stories*. London: Faber & Faber, 1989.
———. *Columbus' Egg: New Latin American Stories on the Conquest*. London: Faber & Faber, 1992.
Canfield, Cass. *Masterworks of Latin American Short Fiction. Eight Novellas*. New York: HarperCollins, 1996.
Colchie, Thomas. *A Hammock Beneath the Mangoes: Stories from Latin America*. New York: Dutton Book, 1991.
———. *A Whistler in the Night World: Short Fiction from the Latin Americas*. New York: Plume, 2002.
Correas de Zapata, Celia. *Short Stories by Latin American Women: The Magic and the Real*. Houston: Arte Público Press, 1990.
Fuentes, Carlos, and Julio Ortega. *The Picador Book of Latin American Stories*. London: Picador, 1998.
———. *The Vintage Book of Latin American Stories*. New York: Vintage Books, 2000.
Garfield, Evelyn Picon. *Women's Fiction from Latin America: Selections from Twelve Contemporary Authors*. Detroit: Wayne State University Press, 1988.
Ibieta, Gabriella. *Latin American Writers: Thirty Stories*. New York: St. Martin's Press, 1993.
Jaramillo Levi, Enrique, and Leland H. Chambers. Trans. Leland H. Chambers. *Contemporary Short Stories from Central America*. Austin: University of Texas Press, 1994.
Leonard, Kathy S. *Cruel Fictions, Cruel Realities: Short Stories by Latin American Women Writers*. Pittsburgh: Latin American Literary Review Press, 1997.
MacNees Mancini, Pat. *Contemporary Latin American Short Stories*. New York: Fawcett Premier Book, 1974.
Manguel, Alberto. *Other Fires: Short Fiction by Latin American Women*. New York: Potter, 1986.
Menton, Seymour. *The Spanish American Short Story: A Critical Anthology*. Los Angeles: University of California Latin American Center, 1980.

Poey, Delia. *Out of the Mirrored Garden. New Fiction by Latin American Women.* New York: Doubleday, 1996.

Ramírez, Anthony. *The Best of Latin American Short Stories.* Los Angeles: Bilingual Book Press, 1994.

Ross, Kathleen, and Yvette Miller. *Scents of Wood: Short Stories by Latin American Women Writers.* Pittsburgh: Latin American Literary Review Press, 1991.

Stavans, Ilan. *Prospero's Mirror: A Translators' Portfolio of Latin American Short Fiction.* New York: Curbstone Press, 1988.

Torres-Rioseco, Arturo. *Short Stories of Latin America.* New York: Las Americas, 1963.

Chronology of Historic Events in Latin American Culture

1521	The first black slave revolts on the island of the Dominican Republic take place
1533	Francisco Pizarro conquers the Inca empire in Cuzco
	Bishop Juan de Zumárraga introduces the printing press to Mexico
1535	Pizarro establishes La Ciudad de los Reyes (modern-day Lima)
	Civil war in Peru is fought between conquistadors Diego de Almagro and Francisco Pizarro
	Pope Paulo III states that the indigenous populations of the Americas are "true men" with rights to personal freedom and to own property
1550	Translation into Spanish of *Popol Vuh,* the Mayan sacred religious text
	The Devastation of the Indies, a historical account of the abuses against indigenous populations, is written by Spanish chronicler Fray Bartolomé de las Casas
1566–1640	Juan Rodríguez Freyle, Colombian short story writer
1609	*Royal Commentaries,* a pro-*indigenista* historical account by Peruvian Inca Garcilaso de la Vega
1645–1700	Carlos de Sigüenza y Góngora, Mexican intellectual
1651–1695	Sor Juana Inés de la Cruz, Mexican poet and playwright
1652?–1697?	Juan del Valle Caviedes, Peruvian poet
1762	British occupation of Havana
1776–1827	José Joaquín Fernández Lizardi, the first Mexican novelist
1776	Independence of the United States is declared
1780	Túpac Amaru leads rebellion against Spanish government in Peru
1781	Revolt against the Spanish government in Colombia
1783–1830	Simón Bolívar, liberator of Venezuela
1789	French Revolution
1793–1804	Haitian revolution: Haiti becomes the first independent country in Latin America
1797	Spain loses the Caribbean islands of Trinidad, Tobago, and St. Lucia to Great Britain
1803	U.S. purchase of Louisiana
1808	Napoleon invades Spain
1810–1821	Mexican War of Independence
1818	Bernardo O'Higgins liberates Chile

1821	Independence of Mexico
	U.S. purchase of Florida
1822	Beginning of the abolition of slavery in the Dominican Republic (1824 in Central America, 1873 in Puerto Rico; 1886 in Cuba; 1888 in Brazil)
	Independence of Gran Colombia, today Colombia, Venezuela, and Ecuador
1823	First wars of independence in Argentina and Perú
1830	Ecuador and Venezuela separate from Colombia
1836	Independence of Texas
1836–39	War among Peru, Bolivia, and Chile
1841	*Sab*, an abolitionist novel by Cuban Getrudis Gómez de Avellaneda
1845	U.S. annexation of Texas
1846–1848	Mexican-American War
1861–1865	U.S. Civil War
1862–1867	France invades Mexico
1864–67	Maximilian I is appointed Emperor of Mexico
1867	*María*, romantic novel by Colombian Jorge Isaacs
1871	*Cumandá*, a pro-indigenous novel by Ecuadorian Juan León Mera
1872	*Martín Fierro*, a gaucho epic poem and best-seller in Argentina
1876–1910	Dictatorship of President Porfirio Díaz of Mexico
1879	War of the Pacific, Chile against Peru and Bolivia
1895–1898	Cuban War for Independence
1898	Spanish American War
1901	*El Zarco, The Bandit*, a novel by José Ignacio Altamirano, about guerrilla warfare leading to the Mexican Revolution
1902	Independence of Cuba under U.S. protection
1903	Independence of Panama
1909–1933	U.S. invasion of Nicaragua
1910–1920	The Mexican Revolution
1912–33	U.S. occupation of Nicaragua
1914–1924	U.S. invasion of the Dominican Republic
1914	Inauguration of the Panama Canal by the United States
	U.S. occupation of Veracruz, Mexico
1915–1934	U.S. occupation of Haiti
1916	*The Underdogs* by Mexican novelist Mariano Azuela
1916–1924	U.S. occupation of the Dominican Republic
1917	Puerto Ricans become American citizens
1924	U.S. invasion of Honduras

1926   *Don Segundo Sombra,* a gaucho novel by the Argentine poet and fiction writer Ricardo Güiraldes
The Exiles and Other Stories, a criollista collection of stories by Uruguayan Horacio Quiroga

1928   Founding of the Revolutionary National Party (PRI) in Mexico

1929   *Doña Barbara* by the Venezuelan novelist Rómulo Gallegos

1930   *Legendas de Guatemala* by the Guatemalan short story writer and novelist Miguel Angel Asturias

1930–1961   Dictatorship of Rafael Trujillo in the Dominican Republic

1931–1944   Dictatorship of Jorge Ubico in Guatemala

1932–1935   War of El Chaco between Bolivia and Paraguay

1939–75   Dictatorship of General Francisco Franco in Spain

1944   *Ficciones* by the Argentine short story writer Jorge Luis Borges

1947   *Men of Maiz,* an *indigenista* novel by Guatemalan Miguel Angel Asturias

1949   *The Kingdom of this World,* a magical-realist novel by Cuban Alejo Carpentier

1954–1989   Dictatorship of Paraguayan Alfredo Stroessner

1955   *Pedro Páramo* by the Mexican short story writer Juan Rulfo

1957–71   Dictatorship of François Duvalier (Papa Doc) in Haiti

1959   Cuban Revolution

1961   U.S. invasion of Cuba (Bay of Pigs)
No One Writes to the Colonel by the Colombian novelist and short-story writer Gabriel García Márquez

1962   *Recollections of Things to Come,* a feminist novel by Mexican Elena Garro

1965   U.S. invasion of the Dominican Republic

1966   *Biography of a Runaway Slave* by Cuban Miguel Barnet

1967   *One Hundred Years of Solitude* by the Colombian novelist Gabriel García Márquez
Death of Ernesto (Che) Guevara in guerrilla warfare in Bolivia

1968   Military coup in Panama
Student massacre in Mexico City

1970–1973   Presidency of Socialist Salvador Allende in Chile

1971–86   Dictatorship of Jean-Claude Duvalier in Haiti

1973   Augusto Pinochet's coup against President Allende

1973–1984	Military junta in Uruguay
1973–1990	Military dictatorship of Augusto Pinochet
1976–1983	Military coup in Argentina
1979	Triumph of the Sandinista Revolution in Nicaragua
1982	Publication of Chilean Isabel Allende's *The House of the Spirits*
	War between Argentina and Great Britain in the Malvinas/Falkland Islands
1983	General Manuel Noriega becomes president of Panama
	Rigoberta Menchú publishes *I, Rigoberta Menchú*
1989	U.S. invasion of Panama and fall of General Noriega
	Democratic elections in Chile
1990	Violeta Chamorro is elected president of Nicaragua, ending the Sandinista government
1992	Rigoberta Menchú wins Nobel Peace Prize
1994	Subcommandant Marcos leads the Zapatista Revolution in Mexico
	The North American Free Trade Agreement (NAFTA) between Mexico and the U.S. goes into effect
1996	Peace treaty ends warfare in Guatemala
1998	Hugo Chávez wins presidency of Venezuela with a socialist platform
2002	Right-wing movement attempts coup against Hugo Chávez

Index

About the Author

RAFAEL OCASIO is Professor of Spanish at Agness Scott College. His areas of expertise encompass Latin American literature as well as Afro-Cuban culture.